The Tactical Knife

Praise for *The Tactical Knife*

"I've really enjoyed *The Tactical Knife*. James Morgan Ayres has gotten down through what seems like miles of words and opinions from those who mostly are not trained. He has defined what really matters. He's the real deal, been there and done that."

—Wayne Goddard, Master Smith of the American Bladesmith Society.

"It has been a unique experience to get to know James Morgan Ayres over these past years. He is well known for his rugged style of testing and fair and realistic evaluations of field tools. James is a true professional and uses his own years of 'real field time' experience in Special Forces to 'hard test' knives and tools.

I have come to realize that each knife that he tests and reviews is a reflection of his ability to use and depend upon the knife's ability to perform under continual stress and in rugged environments. The quality of the reviews and the fine photos add to the enjoyment of the readers of his books.

James has got great empathy for those who read and use his reviews to finalize their own choice for a personal knife, after all it is true that 'your life may depend upon it.' "

—Mike Fuller, President, TOPS Knives

"It's hard to imagine a book on this or any other subject that is more encyclopedic, better illustrated, or more fun to read. Knife lovers will drool over this one."

—Jim Morris, author of the award winning *War Story*, and Special Forces Major (retired)

"I must admit, I was excited at the thought of a definitive book on tactical knives. Why? As a long time special operations soldier and knife maker I was curious as to the definition of a 'Tactical Knife.' I then quickly realized that as a sniper and combat veteran, I should probably be the guy who knows! Therein lies the reason for the writing of this book. Mr. Ayres' definitive, well-illustrated guide to a task-specific genre of knives will be a mainstay of my knife reference material."

—Curtis V. Iovito, SFC, US Army Special Forces (retired), Spartan Knives LLC

The Tactical Knife

A Comprehensive Guide to Designs, Techniques, and Uses

By

James Morgan Ayres

Foreword by Mykel Hawke

SKYHORSE PUBLISHING

Skyhorse Publishing books may be purchased in bulk at special discounts for sales promotion, corporate gifts, fund-raising, or educational purposes. Special editions can also be created to specifications. For details, contact the Special Sales Department, Skyhorse Publishing, 307 West 36th Street, 11th Floor, New York, NY 10018 or info@skyhorsepublishing.com.

Skyhorse® and Skyhorse Publishing® are registered trademarks of Skyhorse Publishing, Inc.®, a Delaware corporation.

Visit our website at www.skyhorsepublishing.com.

10 9 8 7 6 5 4 3 2 1

Library of Congress Cataloging-in-Publication Data is available on file.

ISBN: 978-1-62873-701-1

Printed in China

CONTENTS

FOREWORD BY MYKEL HAWKE

eath comes to us all. Every Warrior knows this. He not only understand this, he embraces it and spends all of his days making ready for it. A Warrior knows that every engagement may be his last. So, he avoids them when he is able. A Warrior never makes the foolish assumption that his opponent will be easily defeated, because to underestimate a foe is an invitation to disaster.

To this end, a Warrior studies all weapons and all ways that can help him be best prepared for battle to prevent that inevitable death for as long as possible. Short of hand-to-hand combat, the knife is the most intimate amongthe pantheon of weapons. The stick and stone may be older, but they are blunt and their death brutal. The knife is lethally swift. This speedy, deadly tool, when wielded well in the hands of a seasoned practitioner of the art of knife fighting, can strike more fear into the heart of an opponent than even the most modern firearms.

Therefore, the knife, as a weapon, as a tool, is a symbol of the Way of the Warrior. It means life or death as well as close combat. It means stealth, and it means skill. These reasons resonate in any Warrior's heart when he sees the knife—that it symbolizes one of the most ancient and sacred tools of mankind. The knife itself has a rich history in medicine, religion, politics, society, and even simple culinary and cultural aspects of humanity's endeavors. But there is nowhere the knife is more powerful than as a symbol of the art of war.

James Morgan Ayres comes from a diverse background, which is vital to addressing such a weighty topic. As simple as it seems on the surface, *The Tactical Knife* is likely one of the most important and influential tools in the development of mankind's fate from the beginning of time until the modern day. As well as being a practiced martial artist, James is a tried and true "Warrior Class" human, a former member of the US Army Special Forces.

Known as the Green Berets, they are considered to be some of the best soldiers in the world among elite military forces today. Ayres comes from an era of serving with the Green Berets when they were at the forefront of modern day guerrilla warfare. The 1960s were a period of change in the world, and the Green Berets, created from the OSS in World War II, were at the forefront of that change as they adapted to the new face of warfare and conflict through guerrilla warfare, deception, and stealth.

From these Warriors comes their nickname the "Quiet Professionals." These soldiers are the world's only dedicated unconventional warfare specialists, and as such, their crest bears the symbol of the dagger, intimating the requirement for one to get close to his foe in order to silence him forever with the fatal stealth of the blade. It is this background Ayres brings to the book, as well as the same exacting and demanding standards of discipline, training, testing, and performance—the hallmark of Special Forces—that Ayres brings to his testing methods for *The Tactical Knife*.

Every blade was put through the same paces, all based on real experience and real use, to evaluate all the properties we value, need, and demand in the performance and purpose of *The Tactical Knife*.

I must confess, that I had some trepidation about my own blade being put to such arduous testing, knowing James Morgan Ayres and the other quality blades he was testing. But I knew he would not falter or favor any one blade over another; as a true warrior and professional soldier he would seek truth above all.Thankfully, the blade held and I was honored to be able to write some of my thoughts regarding how I felt about this book, the history of the tool, and the man doing the testing.

It is a wonderful thing, when one turns to a book for real knowledge, and one finds that the power of the truth was not lost to modern demands for hype and sales. It is this honest and honorable approach to such a classic symbol and powerful tool that makes James Morgan Ayres' book, *The Tactical Knife*, such a worthy and worthwhile read. Whether you're a newbie or an old school aficionado, this book is a great addition to your knowledge base and your reference library.

—Mykel Hawke, author of *Hawke's Green Beret Survival Manual*, star of Discovery Channel's *Man, Woman, Wild* and Travel Channel's *Lost Survivors*, and Special Forces Captain (retired) and combat commander

INTRODUCTION

What is a tactical knife? Anyone who has an interest in knives—collector, hobbyist, aficionado of the blade, knifemaker, or user— knows that there is, and has been for some years, a tactical knife fever gripping the industry. But how do we define a tactical knife to distinguish it from all other knives? Can we define it?

A friend who's not into knives recently asked me, "What is a tactical knife?" I had a hard time answering him. I mumbled a bit and finally said that a tactical knife is a kind of survival knife but not exactly that. He then asked me to define a survival knife. Well, then we were off to the races. The answer to that question would fill another book. Finally, I gave him the classic definition of a survival knife: it is the knife you have with you when you have to survive. I suppose that could also be the definition of a tactical knife: the knife you have with you when you really need one, when things go bump in the night, your car slides off the edge of a cliff, an earthquake hits and your building starts crumbling around you, or they're coming through the wire and you're out of ammo. This, of course, means that a tactical knife could be any knife. So what are the qualities of the ideal survival or tactical knife, and what are the differences between, say, a paring knife and a tactical knife?

I decided to ask people I knew in the knife community, as well as those I knew in what could be referred to as the tactical community. Here are some of the answers I received:

"A tactical knife is a knife that fits a specific role according to its use."

"Anything black and twice the price."

"The knife you have in your hand when some son of a b**** is coming at you."

"A tactical knife is one you can take to war that will survive in the worst possible environment and under the hardest use."

"Put saw teeth on it, spray it black, and it's tactical."

"It's like a survival knife, something you can depend on when something bad happens."

"Tactical is just a marketing name knifemakers came up with to sell knives."

"The strongest knife you can find that still cuts good."

"It's a meaningless term. Any knife can be a tactical knife depending on how you use it."

"My Swiss Army Knife is the best tactical knife there is. I can do anything with it."

▲ A collection of small tactical knives favored by the same people who used the Minox camera and KGB pocket watch in the photo.

▲ A selection of Janbiyas and other tactical knives from the seventeenth century found in the Grand Bazaar of Istanbul.

"Dude. It's the steel you pack when things might go south."

I couldn't find two people in the knife community who agreed with one another. Only a few of my acquaintances in the tactical community—active military, civilian covert operators, and the like—had any idea what I was talking about. It mostly seemed that people in the knife community and those who read knife magazines or spend time on the Internet on knife related forums were familiar with the term tactical knife. Many of us seem to think we know what a tactical knife is, but when pushed to define the term, we can't agree. It's kind of like the famous statement on obscenity: I can't define it, "but I know it when I see it."

Given that the term gets tossed around quite a bit, and that I agreed to write a book with the title *The Tactical Knife,* I wanted to pin down the meaning of the term. I've got a pretty good idea of what constitutes a knife, and I thought I knew the definition of tactical.

But I decided to check a couple of dictionaries to make sure. Here is what I found:

- done or made for the purpose of trying to achieve an immediate or short-term aim
- showing skillful planning in order to accomplish something
- used or made to support limited military operations
- undertaken or for use in support of other military and naval operations
- characterized by adroitness, ingenuity, or skill

So are we talking about knives that are used in support of military operations or those that can be characterized as having the qualities of adroitness, ingenuity,

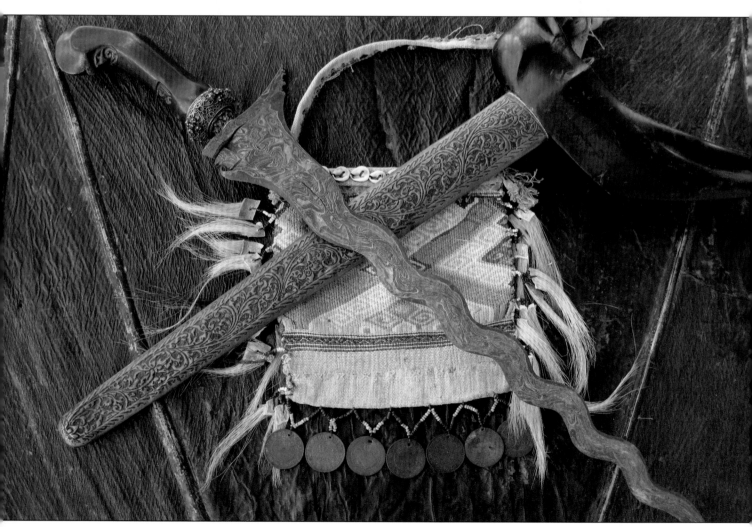

▲ A tactical nineteenth century Kris, sheath, and small pouch taken in trade by the author in Indonesia.

▲ A tactical Kindjal and dagger from the Caucasus, nineteenth century, with sterling silver scabbards.

or at least having features that would support such qualities? Possibly. Sort of. But maybe not exclusively.

Judging by many of today's offerings—from factories, custom makers, magazine articles, and Internet postings—one might think that a tactical knife only had to be black and have serrations or saw teeth—as some said—to be tactical. But there's a good deal more to it than that.

In general, a tactical knife differs from an ordinary knife in that it is designed to be used in extreme situations. Some examples are wilderness or urban survival, to build an emergency shelter, to rip through a locked fire door, to cut your way out of a car sinking in a river, or as a defensive weapon. It is sort of a combination utility and survival tool and emergency weapon. Sometimes I think a tactical knife is any knife used to solve a problem. I'll go out on a limb with my current working definition:

> **A tactical knife is an all-purpose knife useful for everyday tasks according to your needs, but it also will serve as an emergency tool or weapon in extreme situations.**

In my view, a tactical knife is not a special purpose tool—such as a wood worker's carving knife—or a purpose-designed weapon—such as the Fairbairn–Sykes dagger. Nor does a tactical knife have to be black, have saw teeth, or have a tanto point.

I think one of the reasons for our confusion on this topic is that so many functions—as well as knives designed for those functions—overlap. Any knife, after all, is a multiuse tool, and any knife can be used as a weapon. As a wise friend once said, "Any knife is of many uses. You can cut your bread. You can cut your neighbor." It seems to me that within my definition of tactical knives, there are four distinct subcategories: wilderness survival knives, urban survival knives, combat or fighting knives, and knives suitable for war. Even though there is some overlap, each of these categories has its own requirements and special needs. However, each can have a combination of features that will allow it, to a certain extent, to serve the needs of the other categories.

For example, a wilderness survival knife needs to excel at woodcraft, field dress game and foraged food, and be comfortable to work with for extended

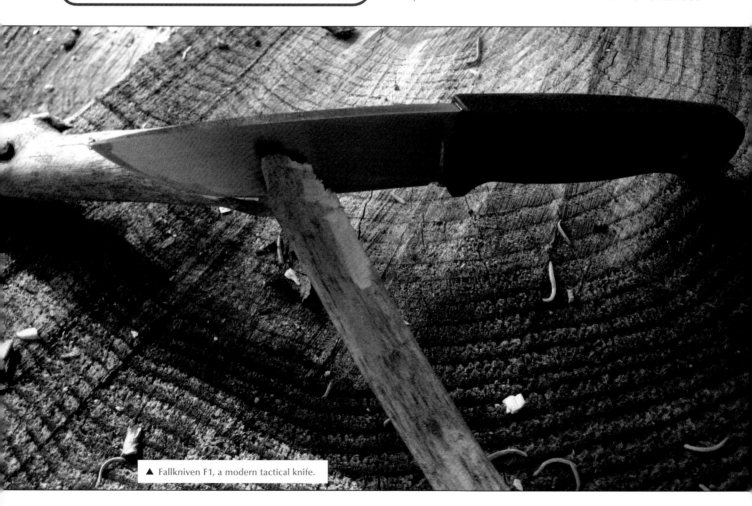

▲ Fallkniven F1, a modern tactical knife.

periods; sometimes, in the event no other tool is available, it must be sturdy enough to baton or chop. An urban survival knife needs to be tough enough to use as an emergency escape device from an earthquake-shattered structure or a building on fire. A combat knife must be suitable for hand-to-hand combat. A war knife must be able to stand up to the hardest usage and worst possible conditions. Sometimes, but not often, all these functions can come together in one knife.

I don't think I have the final word on this topic, so we'll allow for other definitions and continue to explore this question in the following pages. However, this definition will serve to get us started. As an aside, there's nothing really new about tactical knives. The accompanying photos show a selection of tactical knives that span centuries and continents.

• • • • • • • • • • • • • • • • •

In this book, we'll review the history of the tactical knife, discuss standards for field testing tactical knives, and review some of the current and recent offerings in the tactical knife field, all of which have been used extensively, often over a period of years, by me and by friends. These acquaintances come from a wide variety of backgrounds. Some are former special operations people; others are active duty military, para-military,

covert operators and clandestine agents, butchers and chefs who use knives all day everyday, professional wilderness survival instructors, scholars of the knife who work in the field regularly, and my students of wilderness and urban survival, escape and evasion, and martial arts. I listen carefully and analyze the input from these folks, and I have found their contributions to be valuable.

Often I ask this wide range of people The Question—the question that knife people frequently ask each other, the question I am most often asked by students and other interested parties, "If I could only have one knife, which is the best knife?" There is no easy answer to that question. But we're going to spend a good bit of this book exploring it and will come back to it from time to time.

Some of the stories included herein might be considered war stories. They are not intended to promote an interest in violence or to titillate. I have found that stories are often the best teaching tools and what people remember long after all the dry data has faded from the mind. A note about the stories: they're all true. Either I personally experienced them, or people whose word I trust related them to me. For narrative continuity, I have stretched a bit here and trimmed a bit there, but I changed nothing of substance except names and locations to provide a level of discretion.

QUALIFICATIONS

Who am I to write this book? I am not a knifemaker or designer. I have never forged a blade from a chunk of raw iron or stood before a grinding wheel and watched one of my creations emerge from a steel blank. Nor am I a metallurgist. I have, however, been fortunate in learning a good deal about knives from master bladesmiths and knifemakers over the past thirty years or so, during which time I have been an informal but active student of knifemaking. It has also been my privilege to review hundreds of knives during ten years of writing for *Blade* magazine, all of which added to my knowledge about what works and what doesn't for using a knife.

Essentially, I am a knife user. In addition, I am a student of edged weapons and have been an aficionado of the blade for more than a half-century. My military service was with the 82nd Airborne Division and the 7th Special Forces Group (ABN) back in the sixties, which today seems like it was shortly after the invention of repeating firearms. I know of no other contemporary military unit in which the knife was given as much importance as it was then, and is now, than in Special Forces. We learned many lessons about what should go into an effective tactical knife, although we did not use the term tactical in relation to knives at that time. Some of the lessons I learned then, and over the years since, were taught in a hard school. They were hands-on, real-world lessons—the kind that stay with you for a lifetime. That time and place, Special Forces during the sixties, was a crucible for the development of the modern tactical knife.

As a consultant to various governmental and private organizations, I've traveled and worked in more than forty countries, often in primitive conditions, and have been involved in armed conflicts in several of those countries. I have been obliged to defend my life with edged weapons on more than one occasion, which is an experience that gives one a certain perspective on these matters.

As a journalist and amateur scholar, I have visited and worked at museums and archaeological excavations in Europe, North America, Latin America, and Asia with the specific goal of studying ancient edged tools and weapons. As a student of the blade arts, I have trained in Eskrima, both in the United States and the Philippines, in western fencing, and in a number of combat-oriented knife fighting methods, both military and civilian, often by teachers who owed their lives to their skill—or luck—with edged weapons. I have also taught self-defense with edged weapons.

My grandfather gave me my first knife at age five, and I've been fascinated by them ever since. As a kid, I wandered the woods with a .22 rifle and a blade. As an adult, I've successfully hunted small and large game, often with primitive weapons on four continents. I've dressed game, built shelters, chopped kindling, and peeled fuzz sticks for fires. I've made bows and arrows, atlatls and spears, animal and fish traps by the dozens, and other primitive food-getting tools. Knives have been my essential tools for all these activities.

Like everyone else, I've used knives to open thousands of boxes, slice a mountain of bread, and peel enough fruit to feed all of California (well, maybe Los Angeles). I've also cut through a fire door to escape a high-rise fire with a Randall and stopped myself from being swept away by raging waters in an aqueduct with an Ontario Pilot's Survival Knife.

From all this, I've arrived at some conclusions about knives and their usage. My intent in giving you a bit of my history is not to impress you with my background and knowledge, which is meager and undistinguished when compared to many others. Rather it is to let you know that the information in this book comes from someone at least minimally qualified to write on the subject. The information herein is a distillation of my education, observations, and experience. Much that I learned came from people more experienced and wiser than I. It is my hope that you will find something of value herein.

DEDICATION

To my family
To troopers of the 82nd Airborne Division
To Special Forces soldiers
To all the young men who never grew old

ACKNOWLEDGMENTS

Thanks also to

Bela Kahn: Freedom Fighter, fencing master, mentor
Emiliano Patindol: Loyal companion, Eskrimador, a good man in bad places
Romy Gadupa: Fast man with a Kris
Dan Inasanto: For teaching me JKD and the basics of Eskrima
Wayne Goddard: For teaching me most of what I know about what goes into a good knife

Special thanks to

ML Ayres: It would require a book to list it all, everything really
Justin Ayres: For creative, hard work, for hanging in there
Shawn Carlson: For hard work, perseverance, loyalty . . . thanks doesn't really cover it all
Ashley Ayres: He knows why

PART ONE:
HISTORY OF THE TACTICAL KNIFE

Chapter 1

Origins of the Tactical Knife

To find the true origin of tactical knives, we should start a few thousand years ago during the Paleolithic Period, also known as the Stone Age. During this period humans developed knives made from various stones, with flint and obsidian being widely used. The use of stone tools continued throughout the Bronze Age and the early Iron Age, and both stone and metal tools and weapons were in wide use for centuries. Eventually metal tools became widely available, and due to their superiority, stone tools fell into disuse. However, make no mistake—an obsidian knife is as effective today as it was thousands of years ago for our ancestors.

But we're not going to get into Stone Age knives. If we began that far back, this topic could turn into a multi-volume encyclopedia. This is only one book and the point of this section is to provide a little history to show the genesis of the modern tactical knife—both folder and fixed blade—and thereby put the entire matter into perspective. This history is important to provide a foundation for the development of today's knives and those of the future, an example of which is the recent discoveries regarding Damascus steel.

For centuries there have been knives that served functions we now define as tactical. Today, however, we have designs focused on better fulfilling tactical

▲ Early tactical knife blade.

▲ Early versions of tactical blades.

▲ Could these be tactical?

and everyday functions in one package that will fit into our modern daily lives more comfortably than, say, a Roman gladius or medieval scramasax, both of which were certainly tactical. It's also apparent to anyone who takes a look at offerings from today's knife companies that fashion plays a large part in the design of today's tactical knives.

With that in mind, let's skip forward to the Roman era to take a quick look at an early tactical folder. The Romans also had folding knives that served tactical functions. I've handled one that was seventeen hundred years old, and it seemed pretty tactical to me. With its ivory handles, it may have been the first gentlemen's tactical folder.

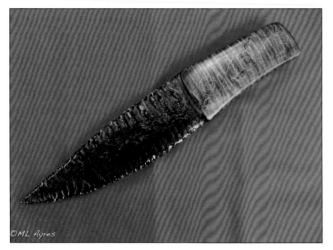

▲ Michael Stafford obsidian blade with a cherry burl wood handle with silver inlay.

▲ Jim Riggs' obsidian blade with antler handle being sharpened with a piece of antler.

▲ Jim Riggs' obsidian blade with antler handle and oak-tanned elk skin sheath.

Chapter 2

Early Tactical Folders

Ancient Steel

Dr. Paul Wagner has the most wonderful tactical folder in the world. It has an ivory handle carved in the likeness of a lioness. The blade is made of ancient steel and has rusted with time. An unknown Roman craftsman made it seventeen hundred years ago.

Dr. Wagner doesn't actually own the knife, but he did find it. The knife belongs to the Landshaftverbund Rhineland, an organization devoted to archaeology and the preservation of archaeological finds. The knife will soon be on display at the Rheinisches Landesmuseum, a new museum in Bonn, Germany. Paul is a regional director of the organization and a renowned archaeologist.

Paul was conducting an excavation of a Roman villa near Bonn when he discovered the knife. Romans settled Germania, a Roman province in the Rhine Valley, over a period of about three hundred years, from the first century AD to the third century AD. The remains of the villas, temples, warehouse, forts, and towns still dot the landscape today. Dr. Wagner, among others, has the responsibility of excavating and preserving these antiquities.

I was traveling in Germany when I met Dr. Wagner and other members of his organization. Paul is a large man with a commanding presence, amiable and articulate in four languages. He was kind enough to personally guide us through the excavation of a Roman villa and invite us to his headquarters, where antiquities are restored and warehoused before being sent to museums.

▲ Ancient Roman folding knife from approximately AD 270 with a carved ivory handle and carbon steel blade.

At the site of the dig, Paul showed us how a modern church had been constructed on the remains of a medieval church, and the medieval church had been built on the site of a Roman villa. The layers of history could be seen plainly in the different building materials and artifacts located at each level of soil.

After visiting the excavation, we went to Landshaftverbund Rhineland's headquarters, which is housed in a restored medieval church and monastery. We sat around a table in the cobblestone courtyard and talked with Paul about the ivory-handled knife. It was a sunny afternoon, but we were in shade from a stone wall built nine hundred years ago. Paul explained that he had found many unique artifacts over the years.

"Although there are many Roman ruins," Paul said, "you must realize that finding something like this only happens once in perhaps ten years. To the best of my knowledge, no more than five Roman folding knives of any kind have ever been found. To find one of this quality, with this excellence in carving and craftsmanship, is a find of a lifetime."

Paul generously allowed me to handle this rarest of knives. He looked at me with a smile and placed it on the worn wooden table. I carefully picked up the piece of history. I don't know if I have ever held so precious an object before. The weight of seventeen hundred years sat lightly in my hand. I turned it back and forth, shifting it from hand to hand and thinking about how the knife would work in actual practice.

I could plainly see that the blade shape was a flat ground spear point with two bevels each about an inch long on the top leading to the point. A simple iron pin holds the blade. The handle is elephant ivory carved in the shape of a crouching female lion. A harness with traces of ancient red paint encircles her shoulders. Her forelegs are broken, her body worn smooth from use. She is snarling, seemingly straining against her harness.

"We have found millions of Roman blades," said Paul. "Daggers, kitchen knives, swords, and blades of all kinds. Literally millions. But in all archaeological finds, I know for sure of only two other folding Roman knives of this quality. Both had carved ivory handles. One was carved in the shape of an ape, the other a sheep. There are reports of some others, possibly five total, but I have not seen them."

The knife is clearly a work of high craft, but it is also apparent that it was a tool made to be used. The blade is about four inches long. Overall, it's the size of today's popular tactical folder and looks as functional as any of them. Its simple steel blade would take a working edge. Although ancient steel would not compare to modern steel in many respects, this folder, this wonderful, incredible folder, would be as useful as any modern folder in actual practice.

"We do not know where this knife, or any of the other folders, was made," Paul said. "None have been found with wood scales. No blades have been found without handles. All have handles of ivory or bone. It is apparent they were made for the wealthy. Perhaps they were all the work of one shop."

One of my companions who was visiting the excavation with me asked, "Would this knife have been used as a weapon?" Paul answered her with one of the most elegant statements I have ever heard on knives.

"A knife is always of many uses. You can cut your bread. You can cut your neighbor. But this knife is too beautiful and too small, when compared to the other knives Romans would have had, to be primarily a weapon. Clearly this is first a work of art and then a tool. This knife was not meant to be a weapon. But I think if you have it with you on a dark night, you will be glad. I think it is a good companion."

There you have it: the definition of a tactical folder.

It was late afternoon, and the slanting sun found us in our shade. All the antiquities were fascinating, but my attention was drawn again and again back to the knife—the simple iron blade, the crouching lioness held back by her harness—that had been made so many years ago when the world was still young. Paul noticed my attention, and before we left he let me hold the knife again for a while. I held it until the ivory grew warm, and I looked long into the lioness's eyes. Paul was right, she would have been a good companion for someone. I wondered who it was.

• • • • • • • • • • • • • • • • • • • •

There is little new under the sun. Some people assert that the tactical folder was first invented only a few years ago. I disagree with that point. Even if we stipulate the modern tactical folder, which is a relatively recent development, the roots of today's tactical folders lie in ancient history.

This is clearly demonstrated by many historical examples. The Turkish yatagan was often made as a folder and used to devastating effect, as were many folders from Europe, particularly in the countries around the Mediterranean.

The navaja is a direct ancestor of the folders we use today. In most examples, it has a clip blade. The clip blade from Mediterranean countries came to New Orleans with French, Spanish, and Creole settlers, and it was arguably this influence that lead to the clip point on one of the most famous knives of all time: the Bowie.

Here are a couple of stories about my discoveries of tactical folders that, by their design and function, influenced modern tactical folders: the navaja and the yatagan.

• • • • • • • • • • • • • • • • • • • •

The Navaja: Spanish Tactical Folder

I was born in a small Midwestern town where nothing ever happened and no one ever visited. At twelve years of age, I had never met a person from another country. Then one day I met a man who spoke English with a slight accent, which I later learned was Spanish. Like many travelers, he had stories to tell.

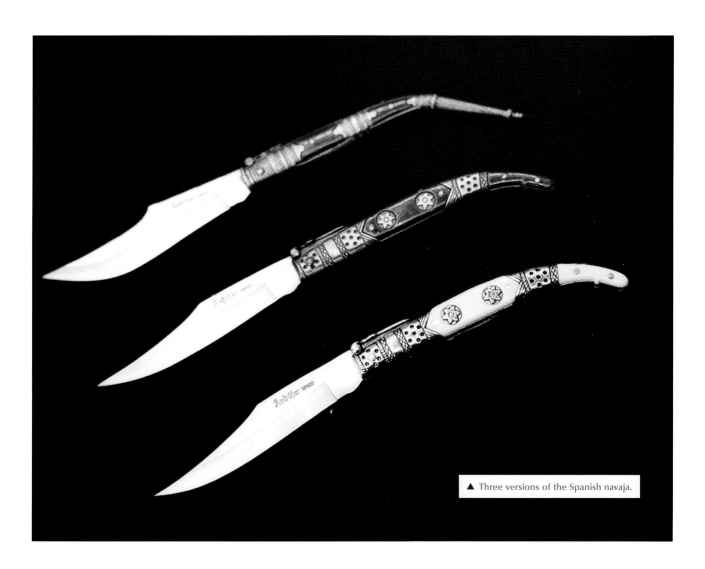

▲ Three versions of the Spanish navaja.

It was around lunchtime when I saw him sitting in the shade of one of the leafy sycamore trees surrounding the county museum, where I used to go to while away the hours looking at dinosaur bones, muskets, minié balls, and—most importantly—swords, knives, and daggers from around the world. He was a thin, quiet man who occupied his space with authority. He was dressed in a black suit, a brilliant white shirt, and a tightly knotted tie. His face was pale and dominated by dark, almost black, eyes. I stumbled on the stairs when he caught me staring at him. He smiled and motioned me to come to him with a curious hand motion, fingers down and brushing the air.

Señor Aguilar introduced himself to me and offered me half of his sandwich. In answer to my questions, he told me that he taught Spanish at the nearby university, that he came from Spain, and that, yes, Spain was very different from Indiana, but that he liked America, and Indiana, very much. After we finished his sandwich, he took a long slender folding knife from his pocket and peeled an apple all in one long spiral, something I had only ever seen my grandfather do.

To a small-town boy he was a fascinating find—a look at the wide world beyond the borders I knew. But it was the knife that really captured me; I begged him to tell me about it. Over the next couple of weeks, I managed to find time to meet him each day at lunch, and little by little he told me his story, the story of his knife, and of his city, Barcelona.

The knife had a blade about five inches long, with a Bowie-like upswept tip. The blade folded into a thin handle with honey-colored horn scales pinned in place. There was a silver tip on the handle and a lock with a lever on the back where the blade and handle joined.

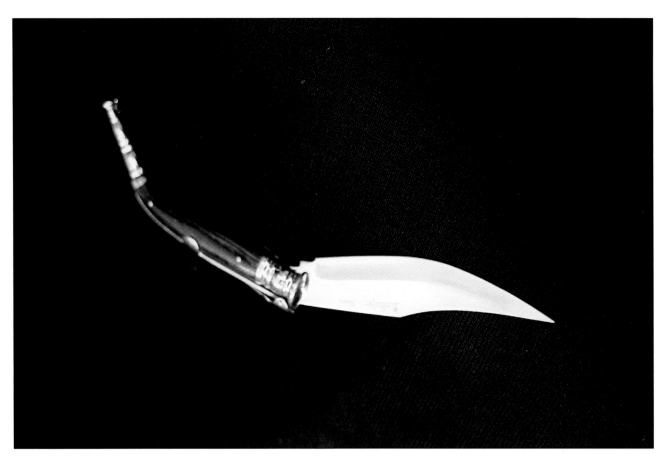

▲ A variation of the Spanish navaja

All in all, it was like no other knife I had seen. I was accustomed to Barlows, scout knives, and my mother's kitchen knives, which I took to the woods when she wasn't vigilant. Daggers and other exotic knives were only to be seen in museums. But here in this dignified man's hand was a knife that spoke of romance, far away places, and events I could only imagine.

"This is a gypsy knife, a navaja," he said. "In the old days, especially during the war, Spain was a very dangerous place, and most people went armed, either with blade or gun. But this knife is more than a weapon. It is a symbol of independence and a willingness to defend your person and pride with your life. We are a very proud people, the Spanish. We have a long history, and steel is part of that history."

He meant the Spanish Civil War, but I did not yet know that. He taught me history as effortlessly as he taught me language and geography. Navaja was the first word of Spanish I learned. His lessons were to become the center of our relationship.

"In those days," he said, "gypsies, poor people, and others who needed a weapon but did not wish to have, or were not permitted to have, a firearm, would obtain a knife like this to protect themselves. Classes were taught in the use of this kind of knife. Swords could no longer be carried, but the navaja could always be with you, companion and protector. In time the navaja, once a poor man's weapon and tool, came to be carried by many classes of society." He smiled, "Of course, you can also peel an apple with it."

"Toledo is famous as the town where the best steel in Spain is made. But there were fine blades made elsewhere. This knife was made in Barcelona, which was once my home. This particular knife has a life of its own. The blade was forged in fire and hammered until there was no weakness in it in the old way with ancient knowledge and magic. It will cut like no other steel. It will bend without breaking and spring back to true. The blade is what we call *acero de Damasco*." It was to be many years before I learned more about Damascus steel.

The knife did look alive. He held it lightly but carefully. Its blade was thin. The handle looked almost fragile. Like a raptor, the long-bladed folder looked as if it might leap from his hand and strike whatever it wanted.

He went on with his story. "I once used this knife to take a man's life and to save a woman's life. It was the life of my mother that I saved and the life of a soldier I took. It was during the war when all of Spain went crazy. The legally elected Republicans were fighting the Army and the Fascists. Republicans were split into many factions, including two kinds of Communists. Anyone who got in the way was killed. My mother was not political. My older brother was a Republican, but not a Communist. That was enough for the Communists to issue death warrants for the whole family. They had already killed my father.

"The Communists came and took my mother one night while I was away. When I returned home, my neighbor told me what had happened. They were holding her at a building not far away. They planned to shoot her at dawn, as they had already shot so many. Everyone in the neighborhood knew where they kept the women, so I had no trouble finding the building where they held her. I went late that night. I climbed across the rooftop, and when the moon was behind clouds, I slipped down into the courtyard. I was only fifteen then. I was small and thin and could move very quietly. I knew there would be no mercy from the Communists, and there was no use in asking for any, not for my mother or myself.

"I hoped to open the door quietly and sneak out with her. But I was only a boy, and I had not thought it all through. There were other women condemned to be shot the next morning. Of course my mother could not leave without them. Nor could I.

"We made too much noise. A soldier who was standing in shadow heard us. You might think that a small boy of fifteen would have no chance against a man with a rifle, but you would be wrong to think that. I had determination and fear and anger for my father's death on my side. I also had a magic knife. Perhaps more importantly, I believed that God was with me. What they were going to do was wrong. It would have been a mortal sin for them to kill my mother or those other women who had done no wrong."

He would never tell me the details of the story, of how he overcame the soldier and escaped with his mother. But the parts of the story he did tell me and the vision of his knife are still with me, even today, more than forty years later.

By any serious definition, Señor Aguilar's navaja was a tactical folder: he peeled apples, sliced sandwiches, and killed with it. A dozen years after I met Señor Aguilar, I rode into Barcelona on my chuffing and rumbling Triumph motorcycle—a blue and white 650cc I bought in England. Along with a small green tent, this motorcycle had been my magic carpet and home for many months. I was in search of one of those slim, deadly knives. Most importantly, I wanted to find the man who forged the knife I had seen so many years ago in Señor Aguilar's hand. I also wanted to see a bullfight and witness a Spain that was lost in time under its Fascist dictator General Franco. I wanted to carry a leather *bota* full of rich red wine, ride my motorcycle to tiny white villages in the Sierra and through lion-colored hills, and see the blue sea from a high mountain pass.

Although twelve years might not seem so many or so long to those of us who are on the far side of the hill, they seemed both many and long to me then. Since I left Indiana as a small boy, I traveled throughout Latin America and Asia, heard shots fired in anger and . . . well, never mind. I had buried friends and was more than a little burned out. I felt old. A childhood quest seemed just the thing.

My first night in Barcelona was laughter and dancing on the sand until first light, when my dark-eyed girl led me back to our room in the Gothic Quarter, just off Las Ramblas near Plaza Real. In those days, they served dinner on the beach in small thatch-roofed buildings—paella in black iron skillets cooked over open fires on the sand from the fresh catch that came in on wooden boats. Wine was drunk from clear glass *porrons* held at arm's length so the clear, cold white wine fell in a smooth stream and ran down your face and into your mouth. El Cordobés, the matador, was the talk of Barcelona and everyone danced until dawn.

I started my search the day after I arrived. I stopped a group of gypsies and asked them if they knew about such knives. They looked at me as if I were crazy and tried to pick my pocket. I heard a rumor of knives forged in the old ways from a friendly waiter with a potbelly who served me *café con leche* each morning. In a knife store I was told that there might be a man making such knives, but no one knew where.

I wandered the crooked streets listening for the sound of a forge. Once I heard the sound of steel on steel and followed the clashing sounds from street to alley to courtyard. But I never found the two men who must have been sword to sword. Whether practice or duel, I will never know.

I talked to the proprietors of knife shops across the city. I learned that everything Señor Aguilar told me about navajas was true. Those knives were just what he said they were to the people of Spain. There were stories told about magic navajas, as there were about certain swords. But there were no such knives to be found. I never did find the man who forged that blade. But life and travel will often bring what you least expect. I did find some healing magic in that city and young love under a star-filled night sky at the edge of an ancient sea.

A few years ago, I returned to Barcelona, this time to make a short film. When the work was done I took a day to myself to resume my search for a man who forged Damascus steel and made navajas in the old way. I would like to tell you that finally, more than forty years after I first heard the story, I found such a man. But I did not. Never in Barcelona did I find that forge or a man who could make magic knives.

▲ One of the author's navajas from Barcelona, Spain.

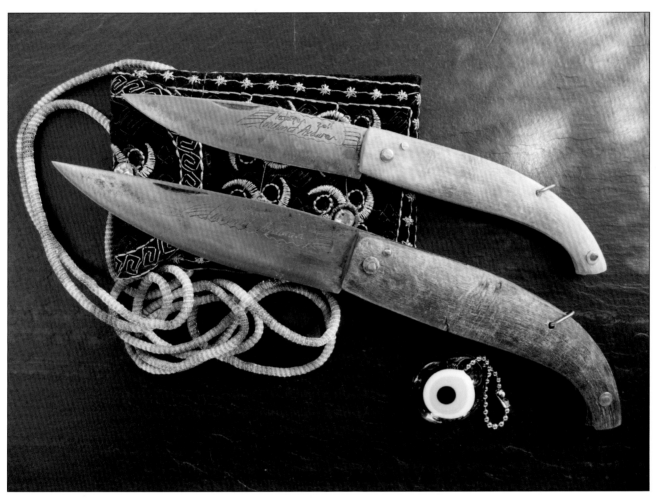

▲ Large and small Turkish folders.

Sometimes I wonder what happened to Señor Aguilar, the professor with the hidden past, the man with the magic knife who couldn't go home again. He told me that there was a warrant for his arrest for killing the soldier, and his brother had been killed before they could get out of the city. I imagine Señor Aguilar, still in his black suit with his mother alive and well somewhere under my Midwestern sky, still carrying his Spanish steel. And I imagine that somewhere deep in the Gothic Quarter of Barcelona, in some secret place, there is a forge where magic knives are made.

• • • • • • • • • • • • • • • •

Señor Aguilar's description of the uses of his folder, "a weapon and tool . . . carried by rich and poor alike . . . you can also peel an apple with it," is the very defini-

tion of a tactical folder. The fact that it was not black and had no saw teeth or tanto point did not prevent its use as a daily tool and life-saving weapon.

The Turkish Yatagan

The folding yatagan is the everyday knife of the Turkish shepherd, the woodworker, the truck driver, sailors and soldiers, Yoruk Nomads, businessmen, and artists; it is an everyman's knife and is used for everything a knife can be used for.

Strictly speaking, a yatagan is a type of short sword used during the Ottoman period. However, the term is in common usage in Turkey for a knife, folding or fixed, or a sword, long or short, and for the iconic folder I've seen all over Turkey. The traditional folding

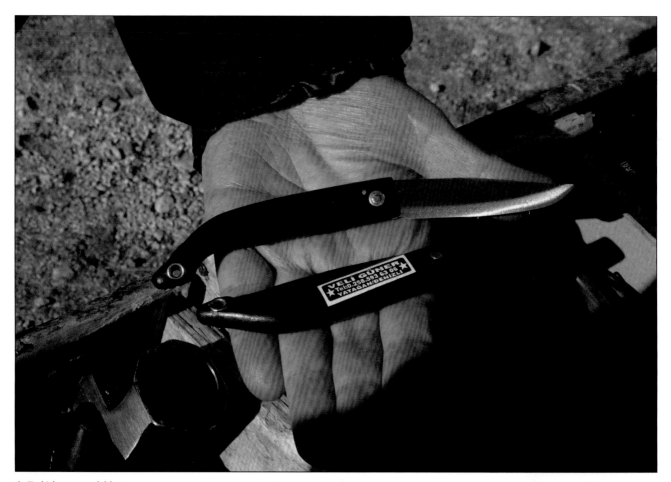

▲ Turkish yatagan folders.

◀ Large and small Turkish yatagans.

yatagan is a friction folder with a sheep or goat horn handle and a thin forged carbon steel blade.

In its various forms, the yatagan shows its heritage in that its blade has a design taken from the tip of light, quick Ottoman sword blades. Anyone who's done a bit of fencing knows critical work is done with the tip of the blade. Thus the yatagan has a defensive function in addition to its daily utility as an all-purpose cutting tool.

I have seen folding yatagans used at village festivals for disjointing whole roasted sheep and goats and cutting meat into chunks for kebab. The villagers work quickly, the blade slicing cleanly and easily through meat, joints, and tendon. I've also seen such knives in local bazaars used for everything from peeling fruit and trimming vegetables to slicing blocks of goat cheese, some with blades worn half away from years of use and sharpening but still in daily use.

Recently I met an amiable traveling merchant, Mohammad, at a bazaar in Southern Turkey. He had a few of the traditional handmade folding yatagans; all were graceful and had the traditional sheep horn handles and hand-forged carbon steel blades I was seeking. As Turkish merchants do, Mohammed ordered tea for me and engaged me in conversation as if he had nothing else to do and had been waiting for my arrival to brighten his day. He had some factory-made yatagans with plastic handles and stainless blades, as you can see in the accompanying photos. They sell for about a dollar and are perfectly functional, but I had

▲ Turkish yatagan showing the maker's mark on blade.

no interest in them. It was the old-school handmade quality of the traditional folders that drew me to his stall. These folders are the essence of primal craft.

Mohammad told me that all of the yatagans I was interested in were made by one man, a craftsman in his late sixties whose shop was in a tiny village about a day's drive from our location. Mehmet, the knifemaker, forged his blades in an open fire, hammered them into shape, and finished them with hand tools—basically files and hammers. He uses no power tools of any kind. He obtains sheep and goat horn for the handles from local shepherds. He also acid etches his name and the date on the blade of each knife he makes. This is his guarantee of quality and customer satisfaction. Little or nothing has changed in the making of these knives for as long as anyone can remember.

Our exchange drew the interest of other merchants and customers, who came closer and joined the conversation. A couple of them took yatagans from their pockets and showed them around. Mohammad asked me about my interest in knives and if I had a knife from America with me. As it happened, I did. My Spyderco Military was very interesting to him and the other men.

Mohammad, with my permission, handled my folder, passed it around to the others, and remarked on the precision of the manufacturing, the lock, and the design. Then, politely so as not to offend, he asked why the blade was so thick. "A thin blade cuts better," he

▲ A collection of Turkish yatagans on sale in the local market in Kaş.

said, looking around the circle. "Everyone knows that." The group nodded in agreement.

Thick is a relative term and given that the Spyderco Military has a flat ground blade that is not nearly as thick as many current tactical folders, I had never thought of this blade as thick. But compared to his yatagans, I could understand his question.

I told him that thicker blades are stronger and resist breaking. He was not convinced. "Never have I broken the blade of one of my knives." Head shakes followed. Neither had anyone else. I suggested that it might have to do with the steel and the temper. I explained that this blade was much harder than the carbon steel blades of his yatagans and that under extreme stress, it might break rather than bend.

"What kind of stress?" he asked. We discussed a few possibilities, including defensive use, but I wasn't getting any converts to the thick blade concept. So, after thinking about it for a few moments, I said that it might be as much a matter of fashion as it was of needed strength.

I bought a few yatagans from Mohamad, gave some as presents back home, and kept a couple to try them out. I discovered that these traditional folders are highly efficient cutting tools and a marvel of low-tech craftsmanship. Mine are convexly ground, as are all of the Turkish blades I've seen in arms museums. They are easy to sharpen and take a scary-sharp edge that cuts like the winter wind off the Taurus Mountains. Mine will slice cucumbers as thin as any sushi knife, easily shave hair, and split newspaper. It will also cut the falling silk scarf—an ancient test of a blade that Mohammad demonstrated for me.

The convex grind supports the thin edge, and the steel is tough and strong beyond what the thin blade would indicate. I've used mine to split kindling, batoning it through thick oak. If you direct your attention to the edge of any knife as it cuts through any medium, you can get a sense of the steel, how it cuts, and its properties. This steel is aggressively sharp and wants to get into a cut, requiring little effort to slice cleanly through roasts, chops, vegetables of any kind, or anything I've cut with it. The blade is about four-and-a-half inches long and the knife weighs only about three ounces.

▲ Turkish yatagan cutting steak.

◀ Turkish yatagan resting after woodwork.

These are simple but sophisticated knives—the design and methods of forging and construction have been worked out over centuries. They require minimal maintenance: a little oil (I use olive oil), sharpening, which is very easy, and perhaps an occasional tap on the pivot pin. These friction folders are held in place at the pivot point with a soft steel rivet. If or when the blade loosens, a tap or two with a hammer or a rock peens the rivet and tightens the blade.

To sharpen mine, which I do not need to do often, I use a piece of 1200 grit carbon paper on the foam pad from my rucksack and strop it away from the edge. One of my Turkish friends, Emel, uses a fine bench stone, which he wets with water. Then, using the same method, he strops the blade away from the edge, first one side then the other. With no more than ten light strokes on each side, his blade is sharp enough to painlessly slaughter a goat, a task at which he is expert.

He leads the goat away from the herd, walking slowly and allowing the animal to graze along the way. Once they are out of the herd's sight, he has the selected goat lie down. He sits next to it, speaks to it softly, and strokes its neck and back. When he's sure the animal is relaxed, he takes out his yatagan, and with a sure and unhurried move slits the goat's neck at the carotid artery. The knife is so sharp the goat doesn't seem to notice it has been cut and quickly loses consciousness as it bleeds out.

Emel also showed me the grip he uses if there's any possibility of the blade closing during use. He firmly grips the handle with his fingertips tucked along the side—not wrapping around the slot where the blade closes.

I've seen a few, very few, yatagans in Bulgaria, a country occupied by the Ottoman Turks for centuries. But your best chance of finding one is in the regional bazaars of Turkey, in the Grand Bazaar, or near the Spice Bazaar in Istanbul. Once, I even found a few with Damascus blades in the shop in the Grand Bazaar, and the dealer claimed they were made in Damascus. If you're an aficionado of steel and you find yourself in this part of the world, seek the men who sell yatagans. You'll find a good knife and a piece of history.

Now let's narrow our focus a little in approaching the fixed blade. Instead of continuing to draw on the worldwide history of cutting implements over the centuries, I'll confine the discussion of earlier tactical fixed blades to American knives. Let's start with colonial America, the crucible that forged our country.

Chapter 3

Long Knives

The long knives used by ranger troops in the colonial period, especially during the French and Indian War (1754–1763), and by long hunters during a similar period were the first knives in America that could be called tactical by our definition. These knives, which were commonly seven to ten inches in blade length with the longer lengths being more popular, were also part of the reason Native Americans dubbed the rangers and long hunters Long Knives. From the Native American perspective, the long knife, carried daily and used both as an everyday tool and fearsome weapon, was a defining characteristic of these groups of daring and adventurous colonists.

The gear and weapons used by the rangers were the same as what was used by the general population; in fact, the rangers were often drawn from and part of the general population rather than a professional military. Their long knives were, generally speaking, the same as the knives used in colonial kitchens, much like those used in kitchens today.

▲ Daniel Winkler Belt Knife with tack decoration and a Damascus blade of six inches. © PointSeven Studios.

Some historians have written that the Native Americans named these men Long Knives because they carried swords. As a result of reading dozens of first person accounts written by long hunters, rangers, and ordinary colonists—including the journals of Daniel Boone, the most famous of the long hunters, and Major Robert Rogers, who formed and led the most famous American Ranger company, Rogers' Rangers—I am convinced this interpretation is incorrect. As a result of reading dozens of first person accounts written by long hunters, rangers, and ordinary colonists, including the journals of Daniel Boone, the most famous of the long hunters, and Major Robert Rogers formed and led the most famous American Ranger company—Rogers' Rangers.

In addition, I have read transcripts of oral history taken from Native Americans, including the Mohawk, Seneca, Iroquois, Wyandot, Shawnee, Potawaname, and Cheyenne tribes, that came into contact with rangers and long hunters and who named these men Long Knives. Over the years, I have visited archaeological excavations and museums devoted to the American history of this period and interviewed archaeologists, historians, and museum curators. The evidence is clear. The Native Americans called long hunters and rangers Long Knives because they carried long knives, not swords.

Officers in the Continental Army carried swords, unlike long hunters, whose gear had to be multi-functional. I have found no instance of rangers being

▲ Daniel Winkler Rifleman's Knife with twist pattern, Damascus eight-inch blade, an overall length of thirteen inches and a deer antler crown handle © PointSeven Studios.

equipped with swords rather than long knives and tomahawks—the only exception being a few ranger officers who carried swords.

The long hunters relied on their knives as both daily tools and weapons. With their long knives, they skinned and butchered enormous quantities of wild game during their extended treks "over the mountains" from Virginia to the "dark and bloody hunting grounds," which are now Tennessee and Kentucky. One account lists the equipment carried by a group of long hunters who had secured 2,400 deerskins. There are no swords on the equipment list. They also used their long knives in hand-to-hand combat. This same group of hunters was returning to Virginia when they encountered a band of Native Americans who objected to the colonists poaching on their hunting ground in violation of a treaty. A fight ensued between the Native Americans and Long Knives, and after the first exchange of gunfire, the fight quickly went to "tomahawks and long knives."

Such armed encounters involving hand-to-hand combat with knives and tomahawks were common on the frontier. So common that Rogers' 28 Rules of Rangering mentions the tomahawk as a weapon. Rogers' Rules do not mention the knife. I think this is due to the ubiquitous nature of the knife; every man had one and carried it daily even if he did not have a tomahawk. Knives were so much a part of everyone's daily gear that they did not need to be mentioned.

Anyone who doubts the primacy of the long knife, that rangers fought with knives, or the effectiveness of their long knives has only to read a few of many original accounts of the rangers' battles. One mission undertaken by Rogers' Rangers shows the importance of the long knife over even the tomahawk.

With a small band of men, the rangers set out to travel on foot and by stealth over two hundred miles through territory occupied by more than fifteen thousand French and their Indian allies. The object of the mission was to retaliate for numerous depredations against colonial settlers and, if possible, to rescue prisoners believed to be held by a band of Native Americans, called the Cold Country Cannibals due to their practice of roasting and eating prisoners.

After more than two weeks of skirmishes, in which the rangers prevailed due to aggressive tactics and fierceness in hand-to-hand combat, and travel through chest-deep bogs and the most difficult terrain, the rangers came upon a village of an estimated five hundred Native Americans. The rangers hid in the forest until the village slept. Then, with the utmost stealth, they infiltrated and dispatched more than two thirds of the warriors with their knives, coming upon them as they slept and eliminating them silently. A general battle ensued when one of the warriors raised the alarm. Since most of the warriors had already been killed in the darkness, the rangers were able to defeat the entire encampment, killing more than two hundred warriors in total. Only two rangers lost their lives. No women or children were killed. The rangers freed five captives and found more than six hundred scalps taken from colonists. It is highly unlikely that the outcome would have been the same if the rangers had not been successful with their tactics: stealth and the silent use of their long knives. Word of the rangers' victory quickly spread through the tribes. Is it any wonder the name Long Knives became a term of fear and respect?

For the most part the knives used by the Long Knives were products of local blacksmiths. With no modern knife-making tools, such as belt grinders, grinding wheels, temperature-controlled heat-treating ovens,

▲ Daniel Winkler Large Rifleman's Knife, with a twelve-inch Damascus blade, overall length of seventeen inches, and elk antler crown handle © PointSeven Studios.

and so on, the blades came directly from the smithy, where they had been shaped by muscle, hammer, and anvil and tempered by the coals of the forge. Deer antler was readily available at little or no cost and made into durable, solid handles with a rough texture providing a secure grip. Blade shapes varied and included clip points, spear points, straight knives, and upswept points. Almost all were single-edged. Many were similar to today's chef's knives. Generally, the blades were somewhat heavier than the knives from England and considerably less expensive, while giving up nothing in cutting ability, toughness, or quality.

Cutting tests and other testing have demonstrated that some of the available examples of long knives from this period were, and are, equal to knives available today. Rockwell testing of surviving examples reveals that some of them were differently tempered. Some had a distal taper. Most had flat ground blades, some had convex blades, and virtually all had convex edges. Before modern equipment was widely and inexpensively available, hollow grinding was used only on fuller swords to reduce blade weight.

I have had the opportunity to handle a number of long knives from the colonial period. One in par-ticular, handed to me by the curator of the Indiana Military Museum in Vincennes, Indiana—the site of one of Rogers' Rangers most famous exploits—caught my imagination with its uncompromising and clearly defined purpose.

The sides of the blade were rough, still marked from the maker's hammer, a textural invocation of primal craft. The blade was ten inches long with a graceful curve from hilt to tip and hefty without being heavy or clunky. It was hafted with antler from a deer taken in the wild forest that once stretched unbroken from the eastern seaboard to the great desert. I imagined thrusting this knife, sheathed in rawhide and buckskin, into the wide sash tied around my hunting shirt as I prepared for an expedition into the green wilderness of the Northwest Territory.

Imagination is all very well, as far as it goes. But it may prove difficult and expensive to acquire ownership of an original long knife. However, it's no trick at all to obtain a replica crafted by hand and forge-tempered by modern day craftsmen who work in the traditional style with traditional materials.

Today there are a number of knifesmiths who have revived the long knife tradition and make replicas that

◀ Replica of a Colonial-era French trading knife.

look and perform like their ancestors. Some of them style themselves as makers of buckskinner's knives, others call their products long knives or camp knives, a term and style of knife popularized by Bill Moran some years ago.

Daniel Winkler and Wayne Goddard are two men who have worked in this style and whose knives I have used and can recommend without reservation. They are both Master Smiths of the American Bladesmith Society. I have used knives forged by both men and found them to be extraordinary, both in appearance and performance. Any member of the ABS can make you a fine long knife that is equal to or better than those carried and used by the American rangers or the long hunters.

Michael Mann, of Idaho Knife Works, is another knifesmith whose work I am familiar with. He makes good knives in the long hunter style. H & B Forge also

▲ Daniel Winkler Lost Lake Camp Knife, forged six-inch 1084 blade with an overall length of eleven inches © SharpByCoop.

works in the old tradition and is well-known among the buckskinner crowd for forging hawks and throwing knives drawn fairly soft so as not to break with the impact of repeated throwing. Some manufacturers, such as Boker and Cold Steel, also catalog knives reminiscent of the era.

A somewhat easier approach to getting ahold of a long hunter's knife is to simply buy a carbon steel kitchen knife. The heritage and linage is clear; long knives were derived from butcher knives. A few years ago, I did exactly this when I lacked a long knife and the need for wilderness was lying heavy on me after a series of long, dull business meetings.

• •

A Long Knife in a French Forest

There is a long knife on my desk as I write, an old chef's knife that was once rusty but now scrubbed clean, a Sabatier with a ten-inch blade. I bought this plain, honest knife deep in the heart of France, in what the French call *La France profonde*. I wanted a long knife as a good companion for a night or two in the forest.

After too many days of smoky rooms and talk, I dumped my computer and other gear in a locker at the Gare du Nord and grabbed the first fast train south with a change of clothing and a few odds and ends stuffed in a small rucksack.

I was headed for the Auvergne region and a national park that sprawls over a mountain range, where stone houses have been abandoned and become ghost villages. Deer herds are everywhere, stepping delicately through the green woods and wandering along broken and unused blacktop roads. Crumbling castles and Roman ruins add to the mystery and beauty. Wild boar—large, red-eyed, and mean-tempered—shuffle and snort through the underbrush. A friend, Henri, hunts wild boar each fall in this area with a spear. I had an encounter with Sir Swine the previous year and wanted something long and sharp by my side for this little excursion—thus the Sabatier long knife.

In a small village store I found my heavy, ten-inch Sabatier chef's knife. Any chef will tell you that the ten-inch chef's knife is the best all-around knife. Forget

▲ Sabatier carbon steel chef's knife with rucksack.

about four-inch paring knives. If you have some real work to do, what you want is ten inches of good carbon steel. The long hunters and rangers knew that, too.

The Sabatier is forged in one piece with handle scales riveted in place. It is strong and durable for the daily demands of professional use. The flat grind produces little drag when cutting. The original design was inspired by a medieval dagger, which served as a weapon as well as a tool in those days. Then it came to America and wound up in the belts of many rangers and long hunters. An integral design such as this from a custom maker will run you several hundred dollars. This masterpiece of ordinary factory steel, if new, would cost you about fifty bucks. This one cost considerably less.

The old knife had been used and neglected. There was rust on the blade. It was covered with dust. It was dull. But the blade balanced well in my hand, and it felt like a knife that could be trusted. I bought it. I also bought a small thick plastic sheet, the kind used for covering cutting surfaces, a roll of tape, and a sharpening stone. When warmed over a stove, shaped around the blade, and secured with a couple of layers of tape, the plastic sheet became an effective sheath for the big blade. A good scrubbing with an abrasive kitchen cleaner removed the rust. Twenty minutes with the stone put a ferocious edge on its carbon steel blade. With my long knife tucked into the back of my belt and a few supplies in my rucksack, I was ready, at least for a walk in the woods.

That night, after a day spent on trails that were centuries old, I camped alone halfway down a hillside. Below me I could hear deer come to water in the small stream. Above, clouds scudded across a full moon, the kind of moon the French call the moon of *loup-garou*, the werewolf. I kindled a tiny fire no larger then my hat in an old stone circle, grilled a venison chop from the village meat market in the coals, and ate it from the point of my knife while drinking a bottle of the rich red wine from Cahors that is sometimes called black wine. The firelight flickered on the big Sabatier blade, and I was glad to have it. There is nothing more elemental to man than a campfire in the forest with red meat cooking in the coals and a sharp blade close at hand while the night shifts and turns. Water splashed over the stones in the stream below and wind rustled the leaves in the trees around my small clearing. Time passed slowly as I sat by the fire and listened to the night.

Moonlight moved across the ruins of a medieval castle on the crest of a ridge on the other side of the small steep valley, and I imagined life as it must have been in the twelfth century. The castle would have been kept in good repair. War was constant then—a clash of steel, screaming horses, and desperate men. I also thought about Rogers' Rangers and their attack on Vincennes after a long trek through a harsh winter.

I held the long blade of the old Sabatier up to catch the moonlight and watched a drop of pearly moonshine slide up and down the blade as I moved it. I drank the last of the wine to keep off the chill and dreamed the fire until it died. This is a term aboriginal Australians use. Dreaming the fire, is staring into the flames and letting your mind wander into Dreamtime, or what I call Tao Space. It's a place where time ceases to exist and all things become as one. I dozed and watched moonrise and moonset, and in the early dawn with a dew-damp blanket from the hotel around my shoulders, I watched a fox lope through the clearing below me.

No, I did not have to fight off a wild boar or a *loup-garou* with my Sabatier. Its actual utility was limited to slicing venison, getting some kindling, and a few other mundane tasks. But I would have been poorer without it. The ten inches of steel came with its own poetry and brought a connection back over the centuries to the Roman soldiers and the medieval knights who walked these hills, sat by fires like mine, ate meat cooked in coals, looked into the night with sharp steel close at hand, and dreamed dreams while drifting and gazing into the fire and wondering what tomorrow would bring. And I remembered a ten-year-old boy who took his mother's kitchen knife to the woods and imagined he was one of Rogers' Rangers.

• • • • • • • • • • • • • • • • • •

The long knives of the rangers and long hunters were also used by ordinary colonists and were important tools and weapons well into the nineteenth century during the mountain man era and the westward expansion. Long knives were often referred to as butcher knives because that was their primary day-to-day function. Game formed a large part of the diet, and the butchering of game was an everyday affair. Long knives were also used for everyday tasks that life on the frontier required, from peeling bark to cutting buckskin for clothing. It was this combination of everyday usefulness and fearsome weapon that made the long knife the tactical knife of its era.

Chapter 4

The Bowie Knife

The Bowie knife occupies a unique, even legendary place in the universe of American knives, and it meets our definition of tactical. The Bowie burst into the awareness of the general public around 1830, and its reputation as a fearsome weapon with unique qualities spread far beyond America. Soon it took on almost magical qualities and became a weapon of legend and something to conjure with like King Arthur's Excalibur.

In fits of hysteria, some municipalities and states outlawed the possession of the newly popular Bowie knife, as if the knife could without human agency leap from its sheath or the drawer where it was stored and attack an innocent person. Other laws clearly stated that the Bowie was being outlawed because it offered an unfair advantage to its wielder—this in a time when duels were common and men brought swords to a knife fight.

A Bowie knife even appeared in Bram Stoker's novel *Dracula*, written in 1897, wherein a Texan uses his Bowie to deal a mortal blow to the notorious fictional vampire who possessed supernatural powers. Was the Bowie knife's reputation deserved? Did it become famous because of the fighting prowess of its developer, James Bowie, or for its intrinsic qualities? It's difficult to separate the man and the legend. How is it that what on the surface seems to be a simple, steel knife is even today regarded with something approach-

▲ J.W. Randall Ranger Bowie © Tammy T. Randall.

▲ J.W. Randall Ranger Bowie with guard © Terrill Hoffman.

ing awe by many? Both the man and the knife played a part in creating the notoriety of the Bowie knife. No doubt James Bowie was an aggressive and highly skilled fighter. But research reveals that the Bowie knife did, and in some contemporary versions does, possess certain characteristics that make it an exceptional weapon, while at the same time retaining its value as an all-around utility knife. More plainly, the Bowie knife deserves its reputation.

Some accounts refer to James Bowie's knife, at least his first knife—there was a progression—as a butcher knife. But whatever the original was, the final knife in the line of development was, by all accounts, a good deal more than a simple butcher knife. In the early nineteenth century in many parts of the United States, knife fights were frequent events and had been

since colonial times. Repeating firearms were not yet available, and the muzzleloading firearms of the era were slow to reload. Therefore edged weapons played an important role in armed encounters. Often knives came into play because they were in everyday use and convenient, whereas the sword was a special-purpose weapon and inconvenient to carry.

In this atmosphere, James Bowie fought in a number of duels and armed encounters. In the encounter that brought the knife that bears his name to fame, three armed men intent on killing Bowie attacked him. According to contemporary accounts, he dispatched all three with massive wounds, cleaving one assailant's skull and nearly decapitating another, each with a single blow. These wounds were reported as horrendous, extraordinary, unprecedented, and partly what sparked

▲ Daniel Winkler Southwest Bowie with a 5160 blade of 11⅝ inches, overall length of 16½ inches, and an elk antler handle © PointSeven Studios.

the notoriety of the Bowie knife. The encounter was widely reported, along with the nature of the wounds sustained by Bowie's attackers. Soon everyone wanted a knife like Bowie's. The business of James Black, the Arkansas blacksmith who made Bowie's knife, exploded, and shortly thereafter every knifemaker and cutlery factory in the United States and England was producing Bowie knives.

Given that fights and duels with edged weapons were common, many people had seen the results of knife fights. Doctors well understood how to treat knife wounds. Yet there are no accounts of the kind of wounds inflicted by Bowie in other knife fights. The effectiveness of knives used in combat by American rangers, including the famous Rogers' Rangers, are well-documented. But nowhere, except in accounts of Bowie's encounters when he fought with his famous knife, do we read of extraordinary wounds from any knife. What was the difference between a long knife and a Bowie?

By all accounts, Bowie's blade was nine to ten inches in length. No ordinary nine- to ten-inch butcher knife, regardless of the ability of its wielder, would have had the features required to inflict the wounds reported in Bowie's notorious and deadly encounters. Therefore, the preponderance of evidence indicates that there were unique features to the Bowie knife that made it a formidable weapon. James Bowie may well have been the most extraordinary swordsman or knife fighter since King Arthur. But he could not have caused the wounds described in the histories with an ordinary butcher knife.

What, then, were the characteristics of this extraordinary knife? James Bowie fought with more than one knife and was constantly in the process of developing the best knife. According to legend, Bowie carved the final version from wood and gave the model to Arkansas blacksmith James Black, who produced the knife Bowie ordered along with a version with a sharpened clip, which was the final version chosen by Bowie. Most experts acknowledge that this knife had a blade nine-and-a-half to ten inches in length with a clip point. It was this knife that Bowie used in the fight described above. Unfortunately, many of the finer details of the design remain a mystery and are a subject of some dispute among scholars. Black kept his methods secret and went so far as to work behind a leather curtain when he was forging and tempering his Bowie knives. There were many rumors, including

▲ Russ Andrews Bison, named for its hump, multipurpose knife for camp and hunting chores. The blade is hand-forged W2, mounts are four bar twist Damascus, and handle is sambar stag © Hans Holzach.

▲ Russ Andrews Bowie with a random pattern nine-inch Damascus blade made of 1084 and 15N20 steels, two bar twist Damascus guard and ferrule, Missouri black walnut handle, and a sheath by the maker, which was hand stitched with a snake skin insert and Damascus frog button © SharpbyCoop.com.

◄ Russ Andrews Bowie with a ten-inch blade of W2 steel, 416 SS mounts, fossilized walrus ivory handle, and a sheath by the maker with a shark skin insert © SharpbyCoop.com.

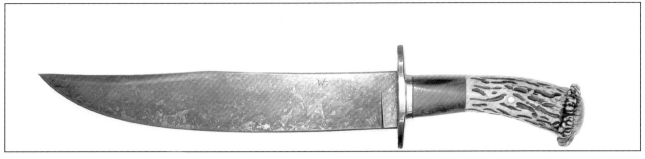

▲ Wayne Goddard Scagel-style Bowie with an eleven-inch forged blade of 5160, mustard finish, bronze guard, desert ironwood, and deer antler handle © Wayne Goddard.

one that Black used ore from a meteorite to create his seemingly magical knives. Was it his secret method of forging that gave the Bowie its extraordinary abilities, the secret in the design, or a combination of all aspects of make?

According to some statements attempting to describe the qualities of a Bowie knife, it was said that a Bowie had to chop like ax, pierce like dagger, and cut like a razor. But accounts differ when it comes to actual specifications beyond the basics of blade length and style.

The advent of affordable, reliable, repeating firearms, in particular Colt revolvers, signaled the beginning of end for the edged weapon's importance. Although many continued to carry Bowie knives as backup weapons, and the Bowie and other large knives continued to be important as tools, over the next few decades the Bowie faded from common usage. The

▲ Cold Steel Laredo Bowie.

▲ A beautifully executed Mace Vitale Coffin-handle Bowie.

▲ Mace Vitale Coffin-handle Bowie. The blade is eleven-and-a-half inches and the spine is one-fourth of an inch at the guard for a total length that is a bit more than seventeen inches. The blade steel is 1095 heat treated with clay, fittings are wrought iron with a curly maple handle, and a nickel-silver pin.

once famous and fearsome Bowie even became an object of some derision due to lurid dime novels and drugstore cowboys who carried Bowies and pretended prowess and experience they did not possess.

In recent times, the Bowie has enjoyed a resurgence partially due to the efforts of Bill Bagwell, a controversial bladesmith who wrote prolifically about the Bowie and advocated its use as the ultimate fighting knife, while also promoting its primacy as a utility tool. Bagwell also claimed to have defined the characteristics that made the Bowie an exceptional weapon. Although Bagwell did not claim to have determined what steel Black used or details of his heat treat and forging, he did state that he had determined certain characteristics that made for an exceptional knife. In addition to the general specifications, they are: a pronounced distal taper, which provided balance, speed, and power; a convex profile and edge, which gave

the Bowie its cutting ability; a differential temper with a soft back and hard edge, which also contributed to cutting ability but, more importantly, made for a tough blade able to withstand shock and flex; and a sharpened clip, which allowed the back cut, a decisive move taken from saber fencing.

Is Bagwell correct? Did the original Bowie as forged by James Black have these features? I have no idea. What I do know from using Bagwell's Bowies is that the Bowies crafted by Bagwell outperform, in certain critical ways, any other knife in its size range that I have used.

Some years ago, in addition to Bagwell Bowies I owned Bowies from seven ABS Mastersmiths and a dozen or so from stock removal makers. All were made according to similar specifications as above, although each differed considerably in actual execution and the individual craftsman's interpretation. I, and others,

▲ Ontario Knife Co. Bagwell Bowie, called "The Gambler".

▲ J.W. Randall Bowie with a blue giraffe bone handle © Tammy T. Randall.

▲ J.W. Randall Historical Bowie © Tammy T. Randall.

▲ J.W. Randall Radial Bowie © Tammy T. Randall.

used them for all the usual outdoor functions, as well as trying them out in the kitchen and cutting carpet, softwood, hardwood, and rope. All were excellent knives and exceptionally efficient wilderness tools. Some of them surpassed eighteen-inch machetes and small hatchets in woodcutting. Most were agile and useful for precise tasks—altogether a surprising collection of abilities from a relatively short blade. If I had to choose one knife, and only one knife, for wilderness use, it might well be a hand-forged Bowie from an ABS Mastersmith.

I also evaluated all of these Bowies as weapons. In addition to my personal evaluation, I brought them to a well-regarded Eskrima master for his review and to others in martial arts with combat experience. Our evaluations included cutting tests in appropriate materials, training exercises, and *mano a mano* matches with the edges taped. On one occasion, I hosted a small group of knife users at my home and conducted a blind testing of all my Bowies. The maker's marks were taped over so they couldn't be identified. A con-

sensus emerged from all this testing and evaluation. The overall balance and sensibility that Bagwell gets in his knives reflect an exceptional understanding of the uses of edged weapons. For daily tasks, Bagwell's Bowies were in the top four in every instance, but they were not superior to others from the ABS Mastersmiths in general cutting tasks. However, we agreed that none of us had ever used a better version of the Bowie as a weapon than those from Bagwell's forge. They were agile and light. That speed, along with their other features, combined to create a weapon that was devastating in the right hands. James Black may well have possessed a secret forge and steel that added to the reputation of his knives—a secret that remains undiscovered. But possibly Bill Bagwell discovered some of his other secrets.

Today you can obtain excellent Bowies from any ABS member. Whether Journeyman or Master, any ABS knifesmith can run you up a hand-forged, differential tempered, distal tapered, convex edged Bowie that will surprise you with its performance. Many Knifemakers'

▲ Daniel Winkler Cowboy Bowie, forged with a nine-inch 5160 blade, overall length of fourteen inches, and elk antler handle © PointSeven Studios.

Guild members also custom craft excellent Bowies, some of them to similar specifications.

Wayne Goddard, an ABS Mastersmith, has told me that he can create a stock removal Bowie or any other blade, that will equal the performance of a forged blade. Over the years I have learned to never doubt Wayne on knives. There are almost certainly other makers out there who can do the same. Many stock removal makers also get excellent results and provide Bowies of exceptional quality. Many manufacturers today provide excellent factory versions of the classic Bowie, notably Cold Steel. Unfortunately, the Ontario Knife Company has discontinued production of its excellent interpretations of Bagwell Bowies.

The basic design persists and has become the basis for hundreds of derivative designs in sizes ranging from a relatively short six inches up to twelve inches. It can be argued that almost any clip point today has derived from the Bowie. The KA-BAR of World War II fame was based on the Bowie, as were the methods of fighting with it, which were based on saber technique and are still used today. The famous Randall Model One and Model 14 and 115 are also Bowie patterns.

The romance also persists. The Bowie has appeared in countless novels, including *The Difference Engine* by William Gibson and Bruce Sterling and in *The Jaguar's Heart*, a novel by the author. There was even a movie, *The Iron Mistress*, based on a novel about James Bowie's life.

There are many who say you can get by with a little knife, and that's true. But you can't go wrong with a good Bowie, which is perhaps the finest tactical fixed blade ever designed.

▲ Hawthorne PC Blade with a 1084 & 15N20 ladder pattern, Amboyna burl handle supplied by client Steven Garsson, 416 SS mounts, and a sheath by Paul Long © Buddy Thomason.

Chapter 5

World War I and World War II

There was little development in tactical knives in the United States between the mid-nineteenth century and the American entry into World War I in 1917. This period saw rapid development in repeating firearms, from machine guns on the battlefield to vest pocket revolvers and automatic pistols available to civilians. The obvious advantages of reliable, repeating firearms rendered edged weapons all but obsolete, except for those who lacked access to firearms.

The development of tactical knives during World War I was virtually nonexistent; there was simply no need. The "war to end all wars" was one of static, set battlefields and fixed lines with little movement and few units operating outside of normal supply channels. Although a variety of trench knives were issued and used in hand-to-hand combat, trench knives were essentially daggers and intended as weapons with no utility function.

Unfortunately, World War I did not end war at all and instead set the stage for World War II. World War II was worse than anything politicians and generals could had projected—a war on civilians with death camps, the bombing of cities, and unimaginable horrors. World War II, significantly, was one of swiftly changing battlefields and fire-and-maneuver battle tactics. In the past, infantrymen were in close contact with a long supply chain, or tail, and war was fought according to lines of enemy or friendly occupation. In World War II, this was often no longer the case. In many theaters of operation, supply lines were broken and troops ran out of ammunition, and as a last resort they turned to knives and entrenching tools to combat enemy soldiers.

World War II was also a war of partisans and guerillas, thus new types of units were developed and deployed. Paratroopers were dropped behind enemy lines, began their fight surrounded by the enemy, and had to rely on whatever resources they jumped with or could forage. Modeled on Rogers' Rangers and the British Special Air Service and Special Boat Service, Darby's Rangers were formed and carried out lightning strikes in Europe without the benefit of artillery, air support, or resupply. Marine Raiders attacked Pacific islands in small units. The precursor to the CIA, the Office of Strategic Services (OSS), was formed and infiltrated teams into enemy-held territory. Many of these troops and operatives needed specialized knives, including the clandestine and covert units. The tactical knife now became important and the subject of much study and development.

What few may realize is that knives, bayonets, and their aggressive use by American soldiers proved decisive, not only in individual encounters, but also in a number of fiercely fought battles, such as the ranger attack on El Guettar in North Africa and the night combat jump into Sicily by the 505th Parachute Infantry Regiment of the 82nd Airborne. During the Allied invasion of Sicily, the night the 82nd troopers jumped in became a series of small unit and individual hand-to-hand engagements in which knives and grenades, which wouldn't give away positions and draw return fire, were used to devastating effect. This was also true of battles at Anzio, during which troopers of the 504th Parachute Regiment of the 82nd were called "devils in baggy pants" by a German officer for their aggressiveness and readiness to engage in hand-to-hand combat with the blade. Both the paratroopers and rangers used Fairbairn–Sykes daggers, World War I trench knives, other specially designed fighting knives, and Randalls. In the Pacific Theatre, the KA-BAR used by US Marines and soldiers who could get them, became famous. Based on its popularity with the troops and its widespread fame, the KA-BAR was in many ways the tactical knife of World War II. In fact, the KA-BAR's influence and widespread use carried over into the Cold War era.

It was not only soldiers and marines who needed knives. Covert operators, such as the SAS (British

▲ KA-BAR USMC Fighting and Utility Knife.

Special Air Service), needed knives as well. The Fairbairn–Sykes was much favored by the SAS. Clandestine agents, including the OSS, used various specialized knives, such as lapel and sleeve daggers, in addition to their Fairbairn–Sykes and a wide range of personal knives. These developments during the first two World Wars formed the foundation for what followed.

Chapter 6

The Cold War and Vietnam Era

The nature of the Cold War was determined by the desire of both East and West to avoid nuclear war. The concept of mutually assured destruction (MAD) helped to prevent a nuclear war and at the same time promote small scale brush wars and wars between client states of the United States and its enemies. The Vietnam War grew to become the largest and most well-known of these conflicts. The Cuban Missile Crisis was only the tip of the proverbial iceberg in the Caribbean Basin and Latin America, where guerrilla warfare, urban and rural covert conflicts, and revolutions raged all across the southern continent, as well as in Central America and Mexico. Cuban guerillas even deployed to Africa to raise Communist-led revolutions. There were small wars, secret wars, and undeclared conflicts on every continent. Revolution was in the air everywhere.

It became clear to US leaders that unconventional warfare would be the most effective method of engaging a dispersed and elusive enemy. New units were formed, the most famous of which were the US Army Special Forces, popularly known as the Green Berets. As an aside, a Green Beret is a hat, not a person. SF soldiers were, at that time, commonly known as Sneaky Petes or Snake Eaters in the military community. The Navy SEALs were also formed during this period, drawing on the old frogman concepts from World War II and expanding their role.

During all this change and development, it was found, sometimes from tragic experience, that the individual SF soldier had a high likelihood of being separated from his unit in enemy territory. The nature of many of their missions required them to operate for extended periods in small groups with no support or contact with their supply chain. Covert and clandestine agents or operators, who were sometimes recruited from the military, worked without the kind of communications and backup available today and were for the most part on their own. The new units and agents, or operators, needed new equipment and knives.

Therefore, the combination fighting and survival knife concept began to loom large. In World War II, a survival knife was seen as a tool for a downed aviator. A good example of this is the Pilot's Survival Knife, a five-inch bladed sturdy piece of steel with a stacked leather handle and a sharpening stone in the sheath; it is still in production and makes a good traveler's or survivor's knife. The KA-BAR, similar in construction but with a seven-inch blade, was viewed as a fighting knife, although it was also used as an all-around utility knife.

The idea of the survival knife, or the modern tactical knife, that emerged in the sixties was a relatively compact package in which the SF soldier, and certain others, would have a tool and weapon allowing them to rip their way out of a downed helicopter, build shelters, make primitive food-getting tools (such as traps, bows, spears, etc), and serve as a silent weapon. The knife had to be reasonably compact, or it would not be carried at all times. Troops, Special Forces or not, will discard anything that's not useful, especially if traveling on foot. It had to have day-to-day utility for the same reason. Specialized edged weapons were seldom used and often discarded. It had to be sturdy. It had to be maintainable under field conditions.

Then, as now, top brass and the military supply chain gave little attention to knives for the troops; battles were not fought with edged weapons and hadn't been for more than a century—with certain exceptions, some of which are mentioned in other chapters. This point of view failed to take into consideration that individual soldiers are not as concerned about the big picture as they are their own survival. Every combat soldier or clandestine agent can visualize a hand-to-hand fight to the death wherein an edged weapon might well save his or her life. They aren't wrong to do so. Even in today's high-tech warfare, with batteries for various electronic devices weighing down rucksacks and radios that can call in all manner of destruction from the air, blades can and do save lives. There are many stories today and in the recent past of hand-to-hand combat with naked blades.

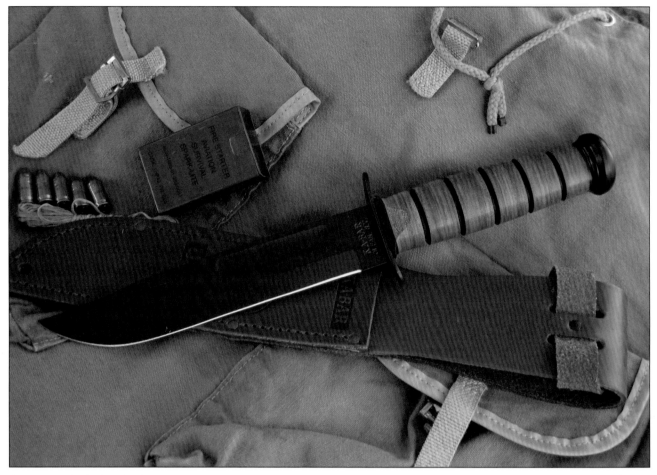

▲ KA-BAR with a leather sheath.

As always since World War II, the Marines had their KA-BARs. The Army only had bayonets, which were poor substitutes for field knives, even if the decision makers at the Pentagon thought otherwise. The issue bayonets were of soft steel that was made to withstand impact, not to keep an edge, thus they were virtually useless as utility knives. Quite a few soldiers got their hands on KA-BARs, and that was fine, as far as it went. But it didn't go far enough for the needs of some of the new soldiers. What was a paratrooper, a Sneaky Pete, a covert operator, or clandestine agent to do? We bought our own knives.

I was at Smoke Bomb Hill, the home of Special Forces, in the early sixties and later in the field when these requirements were being defined. I served with the 7th Special Forces Group and the 82nd Airborne Division and was also engaged in nonuniformed service. In many ways, my personal experiences mirrored those of others in the community and perhaps can help explain the development that went on during that period of tactical knife development.

In our group, we bought virtually every commercial knife available. Almost all fell short in one way or another. We learned that there was nothing commercially manufactured that met all our needs in one package. Machetes were awesomely destructive weapons and terrific tools for the tropics but too large to carry at all times. The Scandinavian knives were good cutters but with too little strength, and they lacked handguards or grips that allowed hand indexing, at least one of which is needed if the knife is to be relied on as a weapon.

The KA-BAR was a good all-around utility knife and, as many World War II–era Marines testified, a reliable last-ditch weapon. There must have been fifteen or twenty KA-BARs floating around my small unit. Some were quite strong and worked just fine. Unfortunately, others bent easily, and quite a few broke at the tang-blade intersection. Also, the tips broke off or bent on quite a few of them. Many of the KA-BARs in use at that time were of World War II vintage, and I suspect the problems we experienced were partially due to how the KA-BARs had been manufactured by many different companies and quality control varied during wartime. Or it could have been due to the kind of testing we did on our knives. In any event, some of us went off to war with KA-BARs, and I never heard about any of our customers complaining about being rendered *hors de combat* by a KA-BAR. But many of us were looking for something more.

Chapter 7

Knife Testing and Training at Smoke Bomb Hill

I have no idea what, if any, knife testing was done in World War II. But in the early sixties we put our knives through a wide range of what many would consider extreme field tests—the kind of things I have heard many knifemakers criticize as unrealistic, inappropriate, and abusive uses of a knife. I view those comments as uninformed and coming from people who have no experience of armed conflict or harsh field conditions or from those who do not wish to stand behind their knives as advertised. Such comments are valid only if the maker advertises his or her knives to be used solely for dressing game, kitchen use, or as collector's items. Any knife billed as combat knife or survival knife should bear up under severe use. Otherwise it isn't worth the weight of carrying it. Worse, a knife that fails when you need it might cost you your life. At that time and place, we wanted knives we could rely upon. We wanted knives for extreme situations because sometimes our lives were pretty damn extreme.

Some of the testing we engaged in and a little bit of the training is described below. I am NOT advising anyone to do these tests. In fact, DO NOT DO THESE THINGS. If you do, it's your responsibility, not mine. Some of the gnarly old vets got a good laugh out of our hijinks. We were young, extremely physically fit, loaded with testosterone, and soon to put our lives at risk. This combination makes for guys who can be . . . well, a little reckless and high-spirited. Maybe you were thinking of the Quiet Professionals, as Special Forces soldiers came to be called? That came later, as did much else, including the loss of some high spirits and the proof of the value of our testing and practice with the knife.

I REPEAT: DO NOT DO THESE THINGS.

One of our favorite tests was to take a knife in each hand and leap into a vigorous airborne pushup, the kind where both feet leave the ground and you do a handstand, landing on the tips of the blades with soles of your boots facing the sky, sort of like jumping over a large imaginary barrel blades first. Often we did this with only one knife, landing in the position for a one-handed push up. Mostly we did this in the dirt, on wooden walkways, or on blacktop streets. Occasionally we tried it on concrete sidewalks, although this, more often than not, produced a broken blade or tip. In our small group, anyone at any time could yell, "Hit it!"—an ingrained jump school command—and everyone was expected to hit it and land with their knife, or knives, point first.

Another favorite was to run full speed and tackle a tree—knife first. Sometimes we used a knife in each hand, but more often we used only one knife. We did this both with a reverse grip for an overhand stab and a forward grip, as in a thrust, albeit a flying thrust. The full impact of our bodies traveling at speed concentrated a terrific amount of force on the tip of the blade. Think of a linebacker hitting the ball carrier as hard as he can. Only in our case, the ball carrier was an immovable tree, and we hit with the point of our knives, not our shoulders.

These activities most often took place at night—occasionally when we'd had a drink or three and spirits were running high. I am informed that today's SF soldiers are all quiet professionals who never drink or get out of hand. Be that as it may, we were a rowdy bunch and often raised three kinds of hell between sunset and sunrise. Anyway, the idea behind these tests was that the impact would be similar to that of a hard thrust into an opponent's chest, maybe through web gear containing loaded magazines, and would serve as good training. Or something like that. We broke a lot of knives, got some cuts and bruises, and learned which knives would absorb this treatment without breaking and how to execute powerful thrusts.

We also used knives in Escape and Evasion practice to rip out the mortar between the blocks in cement block and brick walls using the back of the tip to remove the blocks or bricks and escape the room. We jimmied open various kinds of locked doors and went to the junkyard to cut through trunk lids of abandoned cars—from the inside—each of us taking a turn with the other guys outside the junked car yelling encouragement, taking bets on time, and holding the lid closed. We quickly learned that no matter how good the knife, it took a lot of muscle to cut through a car, that auto bodies are tough, and that it was more efficient to jimmy open the lock. Of course we knew we could simply kick out the rear seat from the truck. But the idea was to simulate being taken prisoner. We wanted to try all options. We did the same thing with junked refrigerators. We drove knives into trees and stood on them. We pounded them between rocks on the sides of cliffs to serve as emergency pitons.

One of my friends, a little guy but very strong, who had been a gymnast in school was able to climb the side of a wooden barracks using two knives as climbing devices. He would stab one into the wall and support himself on that one, then stab the other higher up and pull himself up to it. He repeated the process until he reached the roof of our old wooden barracks buildings, all the time looking stylish, as if he were in a gymnastics competition. A few others not so gracefully managed to follow our gymnast up the sides of wooden buildings, then brick buildings, by wedging blade tips into the space between bricks to serve as climbing aids.

The whole thing turned into a game. Many of us carried our knives at all times, even off duty, and took every opportunity to find new ways to stress them. Stabbing a blade into any available surface and doing pull-ups on it was an everyday pastime. We're talking fixed blades here. No one ever considered doing any of these things with the folders of that time. We might have been a little crazy, but we weren't stupid. Well, not that stupid.

We also threw our knives. Yeah, I know. You're never supposed to throw your knife. We did anyway. You might also if you thought you might ever need to do so during a hostile encounter. We threw knives at trees, walls, scrap sheet metal, and junked auto bodies—anything we could make them stick into. Sometimes when spirits were running high we threw them at each

other in a kind of dodge-em game. Then one bright lad got the idea of using handheld boards as targets. That was fun. We threw knives while sitting on our bunks, sitting cross-legged on the ground, and lying on our backs or sides. We threw from standing positions and while running, from somersaults, body rolls, and PLFs (parachute landing falls)—daytime, nighttime, it was all the same to us. We also practiced diving over obstacles, rolling right into a full thrust or a series of slashes. Of course we did a similar kind of training with handguns, but that's another story.

Little of this was part of the standard training program, which at that time was still in the process of evolving. Most of it was done on our own time. We figured it was a good idea to invest our spare time in what might turn out to be survival skills. We got some encouragement in this pastime and our other knife-related activities from a surprising source.

During this period there was a good bit of semi-formal training conducted by various experts. For example, my first instruction in knife fighting came from a former member of the Hungarian National Fencing Team. There was an afternoon class and a night class for the three or four of us who were more dedicated. We used metal tent stakes for our full speed, full power sparring and collected many scrapes and bruises. We also learned caution and developed excellent reflexes when we later used live steel blades.

A few of the old hands who were originally from Hungary or other Eastern European countries and had escaped from the Soviet Block encouraged us in our efforts. Some of them had been Hungarian Freedom Fighters who had attacked Russian tanks with bottles of flaming gasoline on the streets of Budapest. Others had fought in various wars and revolts. One old fellow—he must have been almost forty years old, which was ancient to me at that time—told me the Russians had a top secret unit they called Spetsnaz that was something like SF, and they did everything we were doing and more in their training with heavy emphasis on unarmed combat and combat with edged weapons. He told a couple of us some graphic tales of Spetsnaz activities and encouraged us to get as much training in these things as we possibly could. Considering that there was an excellent chance of our facing the

Spetsnaz in combat, we were inspired and motivated to do exactly that.

The knives we used were from many makers, but few stood out in any way. Buck knives of that era were tempered hard and outstanding at holding an edge. However, that edge holding came with a high price; the blades were brittle and broke with little lateral pressure. The ability to take a keen edge is paramount, but holding that edge was not as important to us as strength. We could sharpen our knives, but a broken blade was a disaster.

Later on—in the late sixties, as I recall—Gerber got a horse in the race with its wasp-waisted dagger. It was modeled on the Fairbairn–Sykes dagger, a killing knife not a utility or survival knife. There were a fair number of double-edged daggers around during the early sixties, some from various European makers, others unmarked. In general, double-edged daggers had few takers among my friends and acquaintances, except those who were impressed by the looks of one or had a need for a single-purpose knife. There were those who favored daggers for "night visits" and some who carried daggers in addition to their utility knives, reasoning that it was better to save one knife for actual hand-to-hand use to keep its edges razor sharp and untouched. As well as the current production knives (or replicas—I'm not sure which), there were a few original World War II–era Fairbairn–Sykes and V44

▲ Randall with a SF Beret.

daggers in Group, but those were in the hands of the older vets.

Some spoke well of the dagger as a killing weapon, others did not. I knew one older vet who always kept a Fairbairn–Sykes close at hand in uniform or civilian clothing, on or off duty. Another World War II vet told a story about a Fairbairn–Sykes that "broke off in a Nazi," and he thought they were total junk. It is my understanding that wartime production of the Fairbairn–Sykes, like that of the KA-BAR, varied a great deal. Still other Fairbairn–Sykes were treated as legacy items or, considering that some of them had been bloodied in combat, as revered relics.

The general run of commercial hunting knives failed in one respect or another. Almost all of them broke easily, and some wouldn't even take a good edge, let alone hold it. Many of the designs had upswept trailing points, which limited their utility. The stainless steel of that time was, for the most part, miserable stuff that was hardly able to take a decent edge and useful mainly for getting a brilliant shine on a blade to impress the consumer and preventing rust in a household dishwasher. Plain carbon steel kitchen knives provided all-around better service than most so-called hunting knives of the period, at least those we got our hands on. But kitchen knives were not strong enough for our purposes.

Chapter 8

Randall Knives at Smoke Bomb Hill

uring this period of relentless testing, the knives from the W.D. Randall shop emerged as *the* knives. Randall knives were made in a semi-custom shop with a few highly skilled workers that was operated by one man, W.D. "Bo" Randall. In addition to our personal experience, Randall's knives were well-known in the community and had gained acclaim during World War II. Stories about hand-to-hand fights from World War II and more recent actions had became part of unit verbal history and were passed down to my generation, often first-hand. Therefore, the need for a reliable combat knife was well understood by those of us who paid attention to the veterans, which I made a point of doing.

Further, during the run up to the Vietnam War, there were many small actions wherein knives were decisive. The reports from the field—Latin America and South East Asia mostly—were unequivocally in support of the Randalls. Virtually every experienced NCO (noncommissioned officer, i.e., a sergeant) at Smoke Bomb Hill carried a leather-sheathed Randall on his belt, not on his equipment harness, so the knife would stay with him if he became separated from his gear.

A young soldier had to cut deep into his beer money to save up for a Randall, which was a considerable hardship. A Model 1 was priced at thirty-six dollars, a princely sum when commercial hunting knives were available for five bucks. Jump pay was only fifty-five dollars a month, thus paying for a Randall was a stretch. When I was still in training, more than one veteran told me, "You better get yourself a Randall." I did, and I never regretted it.

The Model 14 Attack was a popular choice. With its 7.5-inch Bowie-style blade, overall sturdy construction, and well-thought-out design, it was a knife user's knife. So too was the Model 1 All-Purpose Fighting Knife, a slimmer Bowie-style blade with a thinner tang and antecedents going back to World War II. The Model 1 more or less embodied the entire concept of a tactical knife in its name. It was an all-purpose

knife and a fighting knife. The Randalls were forged of quarter-inch tool steel or well-tempered stainless. Although Randall's stainless was accepted by many, the only broken Randall I ever saw was made of stainless.

Due to the high demand during this period, Randall had contracted with a firm in Solingen, Germany, to make blades, many of which were stainless. These blades were then fitted out at the Randall shop in Florida. The Solingen blades were clearly marked, but after all these years I have no recollection of whether the broken Randall was one of those with a Solingen blade. In any event, I have chosen only tool steel blades for my Randalls and have never been disappointed.

Both Randalls were used for making shelters, traps, bows, spears, and other primitive weapons and tools and in training for knife fighting and killing with the knife. In this combination of use they had no equals. The Model 14, with its thick, full tang construction, was the stronger of the two, easily capable of slashing through helicopter skin or ripping a man-sized hole through a barracks wall in fewer than ten minutes, as a certain fellow demonstrated one night after a sufficiency of whiskey during a discussion of Escape and Evasion methods. We didn't manage to break a Model 1 either, but not for want of effort.

• • • • • • • • • • • • • • • • • •

The Cuban Connection

A guy I used to know well, let's call him Jesse, carried a modified Randall Model 1 concealed under his shirt while he was in civilian service. He was assigned a mission during the United States intervention in the Dominican Republic. The US Marines and 82nd Airborne had landed. There were firefights in progress, and Special Forces units were in the country for various missions, but most of the island at that time was relatively free of armed conflict.

Jesse had recently been discharged from the military and had taken service with a civilian organization closely related to the military. His first assignment was a solo mission to circulate in waterfront and beach areas and "acquire actionable intelligence" about the possible presence of Cuban provocateurs who were thought to be behind, or taking advantage of, the attempted coup and civil unrest that had sparked the US invasion. There was even the possibility that the famous Cuban revolutionary Che Guevara might be on the island.

The young ex-paratrooper was given a fishing rod and some fishing gear as part of his cover as a deep-sea fisherman who was looking for a cheap charter to take out in search of marlin. His superior decided that Jesse's 9mm Browning automatic couldn't be adequately concealed under tropical civilian clothing, was inconsistent with his cover, and he "wouldn't run into any trouble anyway."

Jesse hit the waterfront armed only with a cut down Randall Model 1 in a clip sheath under his Hawaiian shirt, a collection of large fish hooks, a rough working knowlege of Spanish, and knowing nothing whatsoever about marlin or deep sea fishing. He was uncertain of his best approach. Should he just go into a bar and ask, "Dónde está Che?"

What? You thought all clandestine agents are equipped and trained like James Bond and those shadowy government agencies and intelligence services are ruthlessly efficient? We're talking government agencies here, folks. Think Social Security Administration, DMV, or IRS.

To make a long story short, the young agent ran afoul of some bad guys in a waterfront bar. There were four of them. He didn't know if they were Cuban Communists, Dominican rebels, or run-of-the-mill barflies. He tried talking his way out of the situation but got nowhere with his fish stories. They tagged him as a gringo spy. They had guns. He did not, which might have saved his life.

The shooting started in the barroom, and Jesse ran up the stairs to rooms on the second floor where ladies of the evening plied their trade. On his way to a window, out of which he planned to jump, he encountered three more men. One them pulled a revolver from his waistband, and another one reached for something in his pants, which could have been anything, or nothing. The third one was behind the first two, and Jesse couldn't see if he was armed.

In a split second, Jesse decided to do what all paratroopers are trained to do. He attacked. He got his Randall in hand and managed to slash a way through the three men and to the window, where he did another thing paratroopers are trained to do—he jumped. Again drawing on his training, he executed a good PLF (parachute landing fall) and ran. Paratroopers, even ex-paratroopers, are really good at running. He ran for about two hours, losing his pursuers and eventually returning to report to his superior, "There might be some Cubans here."

• • • • • • • • • • • • • • • • •

The Randalls were unique in their day. The designs were almost perfect. Forged of tool steel and tempered fairly soft, they were virtually unbreakable. The soft temper required them to be sharpened more often than the Bucks and other knives with a harder temper. But that was no problem because they were easy to sharpen with a small stone, even under field conditions. The Randalls hit the sweet spot—light and compact enough to carry at all times, strong enough to withstand extreme use, capable of taking a razor edge, and highly functional as a utility knife or a killing weapon. We didn't call them tactical knives, as we had never heard the term, but that's what they were. This nexus of need still defines the fixed blade tactical knife of today.

One thing that became crystal clear and remains true today is this: if a knife was not useful for everyday tasks, odds were it would be left in the barracks when on a mission or field training. I saw many more Fairbairn–Sykes daggers that lived in footlockers than were used, although one man, who had used his in combat, wouldn't leave the barracks without it. Also, no matter if you could use it as a piton or a wrecking bar, if it was too big or heavy, it got left behind. Even then, soldiers were burdened with massive amounts of ammunition, weapons, radios, rations, water, and personal items.

Chapter 9

Knives of the Sixties, Tactical and Not So Tactical

At that time, folding knives also mattered. Almost everyone had one or two, but they were not seen as being mission critical like the fixed blade. There was an Army-issue Schrade switchblade that had been in use since World War II, but they were in short supply and no new requisitions were being made. The Schrade had the virtue of opening with one hand, which was vital for a paratrooper entangled in his lines and equally so for countless other uses, but it was not very strong and saw little use as a utility knife. Also, it was kind of fiddly to operate in that the blade would close if you didn't at once remove your thumb from the button after pressing it, which was hardly something anyone wanted to fool around with while under pressure. But it was what we had, so we used it.

I carried mine secured by a lanyard in my left flapped and buttoned shirt pocket, where I could reach it with either hand while rigged in full jump gear. I also found the Black Cat folder, one of the first, if not the first, front-locking lockbacks. Made by Linder in Germany, the Black Cat was inexpensive (dirt cheap, really), had decent steel in the blade, and was reasonably strong and thin. With a little practice, I could open it with one hand, right or left. I had flat slip sheathes sewn into the tops of my Corcoran jump boots and carried one in each boot, reasoning that if I were to break one arm in, say, a bad tree landing, I could reach the other one with my good arm. I also had slip sheaths for the same purpose sewn into my jungle boots when we switched over to them.

A fixed blade boot knife would have been a better choice in terms of function and strength. But these folders fit flush with my boot top and were therefore not subject to getting tangled in lines during a jump, and they were so thin and light as to be unnoticeable in a boot, pocket, sock, or almost anywhere else. Besides, I had my Randall if I needed a fixed blade.

With the Schrade, I now had three small folders, none of which weighed more than a couple of ounces, and all of them were close at hand when I exited an aircraft in flight. I also had a Randall Model 1 on my belt, relatively inaccessible under a parachute harness but easily reachable after I landed and shucked off my parachute. Other guys in my military units and in non-uniformed service also used Black Cats.

• • • • • • • • • • • • • • • • • • •

Black Cats Save the Day, or at Least the Agent

One fellow I knew, I'll call him Jake, carried two Black Cats secured by nothing more than a strip of adhesive tape in locations only the most diligent search would locate. In this instance, he was not concerned about a parachute jump gone wrong, but the possibility of needing defensive weapons in a situation where he could not have a firearm or even appear to be armed. He kept them hair-splitting sharp and did not use them for utility purposes.

Jake was assigned to penetrate a communist cell in Paris, France. The cell members were functioning as provocateurs among idealistic, naïve college students and organizing violent protests in hopes of violent reprisals, which would make both the French and US governments look bad and lead to destabilization. His cover was that of an American foreign exchange student.

Jake identified and exposed an instigator from the Eastern Block who was a communist government agent rather than the diligent student of his cover identity. This drew suspicion to Jake, who had previously been the subject of jokes and had laughingly been called an American imperialist. Now the jokes turned serious. One night Jake was cornered in a student crash pad by five guys who Jake described as "dedicated communists determined to do me great bodily harm." They did not have firearms but were armed with knives and improvised clubs.

Jake said he went for his Black Cats and used them "aggressively and without hesitation." With one in each hand, he cut his way through the crowd and out of the room, sustaining some wounds of his own and leaving a trail of blood and wounded men behind him. He ran down the stairs and kept going. He did not return to that group and went on to similar assignments.

• • • • • • • • • • • • • • • • •

In both of the previous stories, the men involved were in mortal danger. Note that neither one engaged in a knife fight or a duel. Both were threatened by a group of hostiles, and both used their knives as a force multiplier and thus escaped and evaded, something they might not have accomplished without the aid of their tactical knives. One used folders, the other a fixed blade. My guess is that these stories would have turned out about the same if they had swapped knives. Also, and I think this is an important point, neither knife presented the image of today's tactical knives: black blade, tanto point, saw teeth, etc. Yet their knives functioned tactically by any measurement. Another point illustrated by these stories is that knives matter, but the person's abilities and determination matter more.

Linder still makes the Black Cat, and you can buy one for about twenty bucks. They're no match for today's tactical folders, but they are a bargain in the world of three hundred dollar factory knives. Randalls

▲ Knives of the sixties, both tactical and not. From center top to bottom: Opinal, Puma Boot Knife, Henkels lockback.

are still being made in Orlando, Florida, and cost considerably more than twenty dollars. Both will work as well today as they did back then.

In the late sixties and early seventies, still in civilian service, I sometimes replaced the Black Cats with stag-handled lockbacks by Hartkopf and Henckels, depending on my profile. The stag-handled folders were gentlemen's pocketknives, and if spotted, they were acceptable in almost any company. This was also true of Laguiole folders and the twist-lock Opinel. I first discovered Laguiole and Opinel folders in a small French village and have usually had one or the other in my bag or pocket ever since.

The Opinel, a simple, inexpensive folder manufactured since the 1890s, is familiar to many. With a little practice, its twist lock can be manipulated with one hand and locks up solidly. Its plain but handsome beechwood handle is unassuming, clearly a working-man's knife. It is, however, an ingeniously designed and executed folder. The thin carbon steel blade is an excellent all-purpose design, and it takes a fierce edge—one you really can shave with. (I've done it.) At about twenty bucks, they're also one of the best bargains in knives today. The Opinel has achieved iconic status in France, as in much of Europe, and even in the United States in certain circles. Other companies now make similar knives with the twist lock, including Nontron. The Nontron knives are finished a little nicer and come with various wooden handles in a number of configurations, some with decorative carving, and at a higher price. If the day ever comes when I'm restricted to only one folding knife, I could get by just fine with an Opinel.

The Laguiole is a traditional French folder that comes in many varieties, all of which are nonthreatening in appearance. Laguioles do not have a true lock blade,

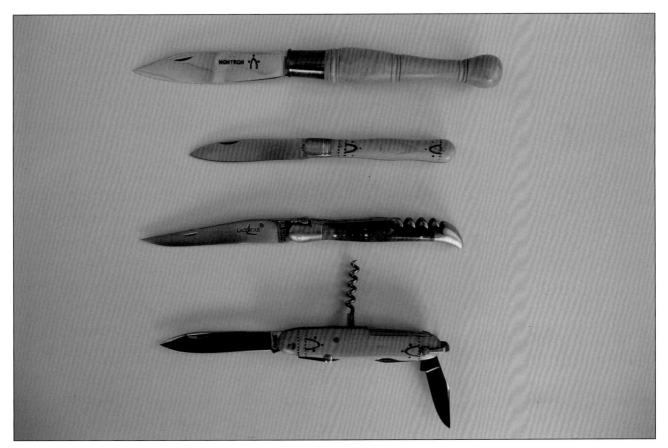

▲ Three Nontrons and one Laguiole.

▲ Three Laguioles ready for action.

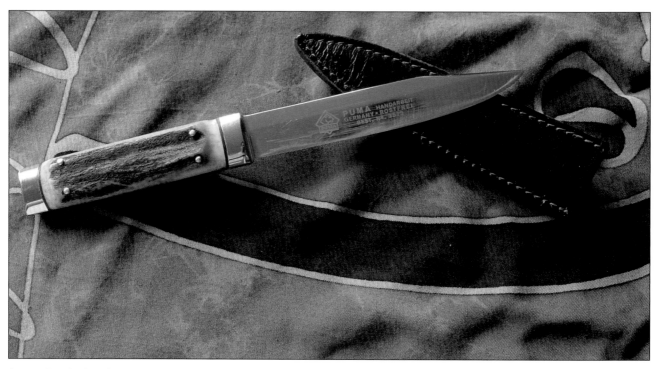

▲ Puma boot knife and sheath.

▲ Laguiole ivory knives (left to right): H. Viallon, P. Graveline, N. Crocombette © Gibert, Thiers.

rather they have a deep detent and a strong back spring that, with reasonable care, will keep the blade from folding while in use, even fairly hard use. The better ones are made from good steel and take a good edge. Many Laguioles also come with a corkscrew on the back, a feature that defines their primary purpose as a picnic knife but is a feature I consider of primary tactical importance. Sometimes, the most tactically intelligent thing to do is to pull a cork, pour a glass, and wait for the problem to resolve itself.

A couple of the people I knew back then carried lapel daggers similar to those first designed during World War II; they were tiny slivers of sharpened steel designed to be highly concealable and quick to hand so they could be deployed in an emergency where an operative might have to cut and run. There were also some sleeve daggers and a variety of small edged weapons in use with civilian clandestine operatives, all of which could be deemed tactical. I never carried any such signature knives while in civilian service. A stag-handled folder was something anyone might have in

his or her pocket and thus aroused no suspicion with border guards, foreign custom agents, or anyone else with an interest in my activities. This was also true of the Laguiole and the Opinel. If something like a lapel dagger was needed, a single edged razor blade and a scrap of tape could fulfill that function, which was a trick learned from criminals and used by more than one person employed by our government.

During this same period, when it seemed like something more robust than a folder might be needed and a Randall was out of the question, I carried a stag-handled boot knife made by Puma rather than a sleeve dagger that screamed weapon. In many places, including the Europe of that time, a stag boot knife was seen as an ordinary accoutrement for a traveler who was also a hiker or outdoorsman, especially one who always had a small rucksack and a few camping items packed in his suitcase or duffle bag.

The Buck 110 Folding Hunter was released at this time. With its sturdy construction and needle-sharp clip point, this folder broke new ground in folding knife design and introduced the concept of heavy-duty folders. About a million civilians and quite a few soldiers and sailors purchased the Folding Hunter. In the Buck 110's favor was the fact that it was an excellent tool for daily tasks. It took a razor-sharp edge and held that edge for a long time. It did not rust in normal use, even in tropical environments, and it had an excellent warranty. The Buck company, which has always set the highest standard for customer service, backed it up.

However, the 110 never gained much of a following with Special Forces, at least not among the guys I knew or anyone I knew in civilian service. SF soldiers work their blades hard, and the 110s I tried shared the sixties' Buck flaw of being too brittle for extreme usage. I have seen many 110s with broken tips, some no doubt from being used as screwdrivers, others from ordinary use. In all fairness, the knife was and is billed as a folding hunter, not a folding survival knife. Also, the Buck 110 was, and still is, a heavy folder; it is actually much too heavy to carry in a pants pocket, thus requiring a belt sheath, which then came into common usage across the country among military and civilians alike. The big folder in a belt sheath was convenient for daily carry and easy to access.

But the folding knife in a belt sheath got no traction in my admittedly small crowd. The reasoning was that if you're going to have a belt sheath, you might as well have a fixed blade that offered more utility by an order of magnitude. Also, in civilian service there were many reasons not to be seen with a knife and few to be seen with one. The belt sheath with a large folder was much more obtrusive than, say, a boot knife in an inside waistband clip sheath or a lighter folder carried in a pocket. Also, for all its weight, the 110s were not any stronger than the much lighter German lockbacks.

These knives, folders and fixed blades and their uses formed the foundation for what came next.

PART TWO:
MODERN DEVELOPMENT OF THE TACTICAL KNIFE

Chapter 10

The Emergence of the Contemporary Tactical Knife Concept

The matter of tactical knives remained the same for a decade or so. During this period, there were changes in mission concepts for both the military and the covert and clandestine services, but essentially we were still in Cold War mode with brushfire wars popping up around the globe and the need for a response to those conflicts. But there was no particular need to revise the conclusions that had been reached regarding military and related service knives. What we had worked.

There were, however, considerable changes in the civilian world. I started seeing American travelers in developing countries where formerly the only Americans were a few intrepid adventurers, often ex-military, and those engaged in specialized activities. The jumbo jets had started flying, and airfares were at an all time low. Global travel became more common, first among young backpackers and adventurers. Then, a few years later, everyone who had the price of a plane ticket and the desire to see the world jumped on the jumbos. In a few hours, they found themselves in Europe, Asia, Africa, or Latin America.

One result of all this travel to far away places with strange sounding names was that these new travelers often found themselves in situations they were not prepared to handle; situations that formerly were only encountered by those in Special Forces or in professions, such as archaeology and anthropology or NGOs (nongovernmental organizations), all of whom had some preparation. Some of those situations were life-threatening and could happen to anyone.

• • • • • • • • • • • • • • • •

A Thriller in Manila

In the mid-seventies, I was working in South East Asia, including the Philippines, and had come to Manila for a meeting. My contact insisted we meet at a new hot spot, a revolving restaurant on the top of a high-rise building. While we were seated in the dining room, I noticed smoke coming from the kitchen. Then the kitchen doors burst open and billows of smoke flowed into the dining area. Cooks, waiters, and other restaurant employees started running around and yelling. In the middle of all the confusion, a man I took to be the manger deployed fire extinguishers and got his people moving in the right direction to control the fire. In spite of that, I thought it was time to go. So did others.

A crowd mobbed the automatic elevators, which would not open their doors. I hit the stairs, pushing my contact in front of me with what seemed like about fifty screaming panicked people behind me. By the time I got to the ground floor, my guy had almost passed out from exhaustion. He wasn't exactly an athlete. Those behind us were strung out over the twenty or so floors.

I thought we were home free. Then I saw the door to the outside had been chained shut in violation of every fire regulation in the civilized world. Later I learned that this was a common practice and an attempt to foil the thieves that plagued Manila. Right about then, I started getting a little concerned. The mob was thundering down the stairs and closing fast. I didn't think I could fight my way through them to try to get to the door on the second floor that might or might not be unlocked, especially not while dragging my guy with me.

Remembering all the fun and games at Fort Bragg cutting through walls, car trunks, and so on, I got my Randall Model 1 from its slip sheath under my shirt and drove it through the chained up fire door, which was filled with what appeared to be asbestos. Then the mob started piling up behind me, yelling, shoving, and doing their best to push me through the closed door. I stood and turned to the crowd. Luckily I was about a foot taller than anyone else, so they could all see and hear me when I unleashed my best drill instructor command voice and told everyone to STOP! They stopped.

I told them we would be out of there in a couple of minutes if they would all settle down and stop shoving. Then I got one of the women to give me her platform shoe—this was the seventies, remember. I used the thick wooden sole of her shoe to baton my knife and cut out a triangle about four feet in height. Few of the people in the crowd were much over five feet tall. Then everyone scrambled through the makeshift door. After they were all out, I ducked through the opening to applause. It was kind of cool being the hero of the moment and all that. But it was really no big deal since I had a good knife and some experience cutting through unusual things. I had returned the shoe to its owner and was standing on the sidewalk waiting for fire trucks with dozens of people now scrambling out of the fire door, when a young American—actually he was about my own age, but seemed a lot younger—asked me what kind of knife I had and how was it that I had such a big knife. I had noticed him before in the restaurant—shorts, t-shirt, open-faced, and smiling at his girl—had to be American. Without getting into background, I explained that I had been a Boy Scout and had taken that organization's motto to heart: Be Prepared. I advised him to get a good knife, learn to use it, and keep it with him. I still think that's good advice.

• • • • • • • • • • • • • • • • •

Judging from the print media and general scuttlebutt of that time, many others had similar questions. Magazines ran stories about travelers lost in jungles, mountains, and deserts and kidnapped in developing cities. Many Americans had got up from in front of their televisions and headed out into the world, much like their ancestors had left the old world and come to America. Some, like their ancestors, got arrows in their back. It was during this period that the topic of survival knives came to be a subject of discussion in adventure magazines and around campfires and traveler's hostels. For many the answer was to trust in a SAK,

or Swiss Army Knife, the traveler's all-purpose tool chest. This was fine as far as it went. The SAK is plenty of knife—until it isn't. I have nothing against SAKs. I always have one in my bag. But the notion that a SAK can take the place of a fixed blade is simply wrong.

I met one young, adventurous American traveling in the middle of a guerilla war in a Central American country. He hadn't noticed the war, which was an intermittent sort of conflict. He was camped in a cave overlooking a gorgeous blue lake. He had a US Air Force Pilot's Survival Knife and appeared to be a competent outdoorsman, judging from the good edge on his knife and his organized camp. He was also a prudent traveler. When I informed him that there were guerrillas operating in the area, he packed his rucksack and caught a bus into town with his survival knife under his shirt.

The concept of a knife that combined the functions of tool and weapon had seeped into civilian life. Interest in wilderness survival was at an all-time high, even in the United States, where there is little actual wilderness left. Articles began to appear about disaster preparedness. There was much discussion in print and in conversation about the pros and cons of survival knives. Two of the burning issues were size. Which was better, big knife or little knife? Thick or thin? Sharpened pry bar or thin sliver of razor steel? That discussion continues today. More on that later.

The survival knife discussion continued with much sound and, every now and again, a bit of fury from one advocate or another. More custom makers appeared on the scene. A few new folder designs emerged from the factories, but nothing groundbreaking. The concepts were floating around, and the perceived need was there. Many thought we needed something new in knives. But it was unclear what was needed. So not much changed in terms of available knives until . . .

There is a saying among scientists to account for a particular phenomenon. Once one person makes a breakthrough in a particular field, an avalanche of development ensues. The saying is, "When it's time for rockets, there will be rockets." In the world of tactical cutlery, the late seventies was the time for rockets.

Chapter 11

The Development of the Modern Tactical Folder

Al Mar: The Eagle and the SERE

Al Mar, a former paratrooper, SF soldier, and brilliant knife designer, started his own company in 1979. Previously he had been chief designer at Gerber Legendary Blades. While with Gerber, he designed the Mark I and Mark II. After starting Al Mar Knives, he designed and manufactured some of the best-designed factory knives ever seen.

One of his early folding knife designs was called the Eagle, a handsome, graceful lockback that balanced beautifully and was incredibly strong for its light construction. I first bought an Eagle based on eye appeal and used it as an everyday utility folder. After handling and using the Eagle, it became apparent that the designer of this knife knew something about using knives—something I have found to be uncommon. It appears to me that many knives are designed by those with little or no field experience with knives.

I called Al to say hello, compliment him on his work, and talk knives. I discovered we had served in the same military unit, although not at the same time. We got along well, and I felt I could question him about the strength of the Eagle without insulting him. In the first of many conversations, Al told me about a guy who threw his Eagles, sticking them into the hood of a junked car without damage. He assured me I could do the same if I could throw a knife, and if my knife broke, he would replace it. I tried it. From ten feet with a hard throw, my Eagle pierced the hood of a junked VW Squareback with no observable damage. It did so more than once.

Yes, we've agreed that you aren't supposed to throw any knife, least of all a folder. Everyone agrees on that

◀ Al Mar Eagle with ivory Micarta handle— a classic.

point. On the other hand, refer back to my earlier comments about knife testing and training at SBH. (Just don't do it!) Of course, I was now older and in theory more responsible, so I would never even consider doing such a foolish thing as throwing a folding knife unless I was testing a knife or had no other choice. Then it's good to know how. Al understood that well.

I bought two more Eagles, which immediately replaced my stag-handled lockbacks for daily carry. Besides strength, grace, balance, and good looks, the Eagle had certain characteristics that made it uniquely suited for clandestine tactical use. It had no protuberances or false guards to impede penetration; it also had a straight feed from point to heel. With a proper hold, this four-inch bladed folder could penetrate up to six inches in soft material and up to three inches more given material compression—even deeper if retrieval wasn't a concern. The Eagle and others in the series, the Osprey and Falcon, were nicely turned out gentlemen's knives. The Eagle in particular would also serve as an excellent weapon, the best I had ever seen in a folding knife. Al told me none of this was by accident, and he had worked all this out before production.

Later I gave one of my Eagles to a friend in need. One got lost in a faraway place. The other one just plain wore out after a decade or so of constant use. They were fine knives, and I'd love to have another of the out-of-production beauties. Although they were essentially the same technology as the German lockbacks, they were its ultimate refinement.

Then, in the early eighties Al—he was the artist of knife design of his era—worked with Colonel James "Nick" Rowe to create the first purpose-designed Survival, Evasion, Resistance, and Escape (SERE) folding knife. Colonel Rowe is famous in the SF community, a true hero who survived five years of captivity during the war in Vietnam and escaped his captors under his own power.

Years after these incidents, Colonel Rowe accepted the role as commanding officer of the SERE training school. At the time he met Al Mar, Colonel Rowe had defined a need for a new kind of knife. He wanted something smaller and more easily carried than any fixed blade but stronger than any folder. As it turned out, he had come to the right person.

Many soldiers who aren't SF have a tendency to dump their web gear, packs, and weapons at every opportunity. Usually their fixed blade, if any, will be attached to their web gear instead of their person. As a result, the soldier is then completely unarmed and unequipped, without gun, knife, grenade, entrenching tool, canteens, or rations. Any survival gear he or she may have is usually also on his or her web gear. Effectively, the soldier is naked in the world. Given his personal experience and his understanding of the soldier's mentality, the need for a strong, compact knife that could and would be carried on the person rather than as part of web gear figured largely in Colonel Rowe's intention to improve the American soldier's chances of survival.

The result of Colonel Rowe and Al Mar's collaboration was the SERE, a heavily constructed folder that was meant to serve the isolated solider as his last ditch and only tool and weapon. The SERE was a thing of beauty, as were all of Al's knives, and an excellent knife that lived up to Colonel Rowe's concept. Here was a folding knife that was stronger than any other folder yet developed. It had a solid front lock and, in one version, a nonslip handle. The blade was of an excellent tough steel tempered a little soft so it wouldn't break at the tip or chip out, and it could be easily sharpened with a rock if need be. Now anyone could easily and conveniently carry a serious survival tool and emergency weapon at all times. Although the SERE was meant to be carried in a belt pouch, as such pouches were now common, and it was thought that a solider would be willing to have it on his belt or carry it in a uniform pocket. In effect, they had created the first tactical folder. This was to the benefit of countless soldiers, covert operators, and civilians alike.

In one of our conversations, Al told me of his design education and how his artistic skills and vision combined with his military experience in each of his knives. Al's company, Al Mar Knives, continues, but Al passed on some years ago, still a young man and still unsurpassed as a knife designer.

While the SERE was a leap forward, it did not break new ground technologically speaking. In my view, the most important thing the SERE accomplished was to ignite a revolution in thinking with one simple question: can a folder replace a fixed blade? That question and concept drove the development and design of an entirely new class of knives: the modern tactical folder. As we now know, Colonel Rowe was prophetic. Virtually every soldier today and about ten million or so civilians carry what has become known as a tactical folder. Although the original SERE has been surpassed technologically, its place in the history of tactical knives is secure.

The Liner Lock

During the following decade, folding knife design exploded. Dozens of variations were tried, and many were discarded. New locking systems were developed. One locking system that became central to the development of this class of knives, the liner lock, was reintroduced and repurposed by a custom knifemaker, Michael Walker. The liner lock was tried by many, perfected by a few, and in time became a standard locking mechanism. It is still in use. Many believe the liner lock to be intrinsically stronger than the lockbacks. Discussion on this point continues today, and many new locking systems have been introduced.

Sal Glesser: Pocket Clip, Spyder Hole, Serrations

I first met Sal Glesser, the founder and CEO of Spyderco, at a gun show, where he showed me three of his innovations in one small knife: the pocket clip, a hole in the blade to facilitate opening with one hand, and the serrated edge. A new genius had arrived on the knife scene. All these innovations have become standards of the tactical folder. Of these, from my point of view, the most important was the opening hole, followed by the pocket clip.

Until now, all folders except automatics, which were generally of poor quality and in short supply, were designed to be opened with two hands. This was true of the seminal Al Mar designs, as well as the century old Opinel and my Black Cats. True, you could find a way to open all of these folders with one hand. But it was sometimes a fiddly and unsure proposition.

One-handed opening is important to the person who needs to get a knife into action to defend himself and to just about everyone else. Try opening a standard two-handed folder on the front deck of a pitching sailboat at night in Force Eight conditions to cut free a

▲ Spyderco Endura—similar to the original Spyderco model of the sixties © Spyderco.

▲ Pat Crawford Kasper folders, four-inch blades with titanium handles © Pat Crawford.

fouled sheet, and you'll immediately see the need for a one-handed knife. More prosaically, it seems that you always need your knife when it's in your pocket and you have a twelve-pound trout in hand. There had been a couple of previous attempts in this direction, but nothing had really worked out. Now everyone tried developing one-handed opening systems. Thumb studs of all sizes and descriptions sprouted on knife blades like mushrooms on a foggy morning.

Creative Explosion

There was a good deal of creativity in the industry during this period. New materials were tried, like titanium for handles and exotic steels for blades. Clips appeared for tip up and tip down carry, along with

much discussion about which was best. As I recall, Bob Terzuola was the first to bring together some of these elements in a folding knife that broke more new ground. I bought one of Bob's first prototypes at a custom knife show. It was a titanium-handled liner-lock with a thumb stud and a blade of high-tech steel. It locked up more solidly than any folder I had ever seen.

A little later on, I met Ernest Emerson at the Solvang Custom Knife Show. Among other attractive offerings, Ernie displayed his first liner-lock, a handsome knife with, I think, rosewood scales. Ernie later went on to create a liner-lock folder with a tanto point—an innovation introduced by custom maker Phil Hartsfield—that became the foundation of the company he built, which is famous for its tactical folders. Sal

▲ A useful collection of tactical folders.

Glesser continued to innovate, and he built Spyderco into one of the most respected knife companies in the world. Bob Terzuola is now a justly famous custom knifemaker commanding top dollar for his excellent work.

But all that was yet to come. Back then, the explosion of creative energy through the custom knife community quickly spread to knife manufacturers, and it is still expanding today. We now have the strongest, most innovative folding knives the world has yet seen. Tactical folders in some ways now define the tactical knife both for military and civilians. I am informed that industry statistics show that folders are purchased twenty to one to fixed blades. This is understandable. Few civilians will carry a fixed blade in their daily rounds, and most of these knives sold are to civilians.

However, today most military people also select the folder over the fixed blade, often in addition to the fixed blade. This is due to the nature of the conflict zone, current strategy and tactics, changes in logistics and communications, and the fact that today's folders can stand in for many functions formerly limited to fixed blades. Tactical folders are everyday utility knives, survival tools at need, and weapons in an emergency.

Chapter 12

The Development of the Modern Tactical Fixed Blade

While all this development had been going on with folders, fixed blades also developed, though not so much in basic design concepts as in formulations of steel, refinements of proven designs, and experiments with new designs that were influenced both by designs from countries around the world and historical knives. In folders it's a different order of reality, as opposed to with folders, where it seemed the mothership landed and emissaries from another planet said, "You need new folding knives." In fixed blades, the changes have been evolutionary rather than revolutionary and were stimulated by all the action in folding knives.

With all the noise about tactical folders, you might think they have altogether replaced fixed blades, but this is not so. However undeniable the virtue of today's folders, the thing that makes them convenient to carry and ensures they will be at hand for daily tasks and emergencies is also their greatest weakness: they fold. No folder can be made as strong as a fixed blade. No matter how strong today's locks, and some of them are extremely strong, none can match the strength of a straight slab of well-tempered steel. Fixed blades can pry open doors and rip through materials that would cause the strongest folders to fold. Many who live in the world of covert and clandestine action prefer fixed blades or have them in addition to their folders.

During this period, new knives appeared, and old factories expanded their focus. Lynn Thompson founded his company, Cold Steel, with a line of knives that was focused almost entirely on the emerging tactical market and its need. His Tanto, which I think Thompson designed himself, was the first factory-made fixed blade with what was to become known as a tanto point, which is essentially a squared off chisel grind. Phil Hartsfield had been the first to introduce the concept of a chisel point to the American knife-buying public. Phil's knives sold well but, being custom creations, were priced out of the reach of most consumers.

Cold Steel's Tanto was soon seen everywhere. I have no idea how many were sold, but the Tanto probably set sales records for fixed blade tactical knives. It also stimulated an avalanche of competition. Soon tantos, from both custom makers and factories, were springing up like daisies in springtime. The success of the Tanto and Cold Steel's other tactical fixed blades showed that there was a large untapped market for tactical fixed blade knives. Soon many factories began to expand their product line from sporting knives to include tacticals.

This expansion and development led to many innovations and the market we see today, which is one inundated with tactical fixed blades. Judging from the knives offered for sale to the public, a visitor from another planet—or even one from a developing country with limited communications—could be forgiven for assuming that Americans held Friday Night Knife Fights as an alternative to football or basketball games. However, all this activity has been beneficial for knife buyers since there are more choices than in the fifties and sixties.

◄ An old favorite fixed blade, Spyderco's Bob Lum Tanto.

Benchmade CSKII—a handy, all-around tool to have in ► your bag.

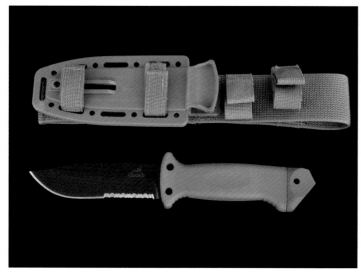

◄ Gerber LMF II ASEK© Justin Ayres.

Chapter 13

Materials and Design of the Contemporary Tactical Knife

This is not a technical treatise. Professional knife-makers, metallurgists, and others spend years acquiring their knowledge, both through formal education and hands-on experience. What I will cover here is a once-over light survey of technical information that might be of interest to the tactical knife user.

Many years ago, master bladesmith Wayne Goddard told me that the three most important things in making a good blade—one that will perform and not just look good—were:

1. Selection of steel
2. Heat treat appropriate to the steel being used
3. Geometry of the blade

He further said that a maker must have all three factors working right, not only one or two, to produce a good knife. In many discussions over the years, I have found that virtually all knowledgeable knifemakers and industry experts agree with this statement. My experience has also shown the wisdom of this statement. How these factors come together in a particular blade determine its performance characteristics.

Steel and Heat Treating

Since steel selection is at the top of virtually every discussion on tactical knives, let's first take a brief look at the heart of every blade: steel. There is a continuing quest for better steel for blades. This has been going on since about 2000 BC, well before the end of the Bronze Age and the widespread adaptation of iron and steel at beginning of the early Iron Age, about 1200 BC. As one might imagine, there have been quite a few developments and improvements in blade steel over the past four thousand years. Much of this improvement is due to competition and the desire to improve tools and weapons.

The rise of the Hittite empire around 1500 BC was made possible by the superiority of their iron weapons.

Later, the Israelites waged war on the Philistines to obtain iron-working technology. Today's commercial competition is considerably less violent but still quite intense. As a result, today we have a wide range of superior steels available to knifemakers that can be ordered from a catalog.

Steel available from steel manufacturers that is in use by knifemakers today includes: 1095, 01, A2, W2, D2, L6, 440B, 440C, ATS34, 5160, VG-10, CPMS30V, and CPMS35V. In addition, many bladesmiths still forge or re-forge their own steel, some from used files, sheer steel, ball bearings, stock billets, and various other sources. There are many different steels in use because mills offer them and individual knifemakers have individual opinions as to which offers them optimal performance. Further, many knifemakers use a variety of steels, choosing each one for its best properties and the customer's intended use.

Some knife factories also use a wide range of steels, again depending on what optimal performance they seek. Another factor in steel choice can be popularity. Sometimes a customer will read or hear about the properties of a certain steel and request a custom knifemaker use it or choose a knife from a manufacturer's product line based on what he or she thinks is desirable. In fact, we often see knives marketed as being superior products by virtue of the steel used in their manufacture.

Which is the best steel for a tactical knife? Given that steel performance is dependent on heat treat, blade geometry, and the maker's skills, as well as the intended use for the knife, there does not appear to be a conclusive answer to that question. I wouldn't select a knife based on steel type alone, nor should you. As knife users, we don't buy steel. We buy knives. Every knife is a manufactured product that is the result of a long supply line and the craft and skill of everyone behind it, from the mine that extracted the ore through the steel mill and on to the maker of the finished

▲ Fred Perrin at the forge © Fred Perrin.

don't think much of it at all. Again, it all depends on the skill, craft, and science of the knifemaker. I have some knives made of S30V that take a terrific edge, hold that edge for a long time, don't show rust even if I deliberately leave them out in the rain for a few days to test for rust resistance, and are tough. I also have knives made of VG-10 and 440C about which similar things can be said. On the other hand, I had a knife of 440C shatter on impact with another blade made of crude steel forged in a nipa hut in the Philippines and S30V blades that chipped and fractured along the edge when cutting pine wood. I have VG-10 blades that I couldn't put an edge on with hours of work.

So, what's up here? Shouldn't there be consistency in steel performance from maker to maker? No, not so much. It's the package that matters: heat treat, grind, and the maker's skill all go into making a knife. It's not just the steel. It's also who makes the steel and how. If you would like to learn about the technicalities that go into making a knife—steel, heat treat, geometry—I recommend a book by Wayne Goddard, *The Wonder of Knifemaking*. I know of no better primer on the topic.

Meantime, here's a quotation from another master-smith, Daniel Winkler, a man who knows knives and steel and everything that goes into them, who says, "Steels are only as good as how a maker treats them from the beginning. A maker that does his research and tests can get great performance out of mediocre materials, while the best steel can be screwed up with poor handling." Believe it: it's the maker, not only the steel.

product. There are many variables in each step along that supply line, each requiring decisions that only someone schooled or trained in the topic can make. Every factor in every step of the process plays a role in the final result—the knife in your hand.

At knife shows, in retail outlets, and around campfires, I have heard and taken part in many discussions about the properties of various knife steels. I have come to the conclusion that beyond certain basics, such discussions among nonprofessionals amount to the same thing as a discussion about how many angels can dance on the head of a pin.

S30V is now highly thought of by many makers with whom I have spoken. This steel was designed and made specifically for knives, which is unusual. Is it the best steel available? Maybe, maybe not. Other makers

▲ Elsa Fantino demonstrating heat treat of steel.

Geometry, Designs, Grinds, and Forging

The third critical component of any knife, after steel and heat treat, is the geometry of the blade, or how it is ground. Beyond questions of thick and thin blades are concerns related to the nature of the grind itself and the profile of the blade. In common use today are the following profiles: hollow, flat, convex, saber, and Scandi, which is a variation of saber. Many knives have combination grinds, such as Randalls, but in general whatever grind is predominant is the one by which the knife is described.

Each grind has its advocates, each its detractors. I have seen good performance for virtually all grinds when handled properly by a skilled maker. However, as a general statement, it is my experience that a full convex profile from spine to edge produces the best all-around performance for a tactical and survival knife. The flat grind with a convex edge comes in second. However, the other blade profiles have their place, and I have seen amazingly good performance from hollow ground knives from talented makers, such as Chris Reeve.

The saber grind used on, say, a KA-BAR brings the full thickness of steel the length of the blade, which makes it strong. And the straight saber grind, such as the Scandi, places a good deal of steel behind the edge to support it. In general this makes for a strong blade—one that's easy to sharpen by using the flat as a bevel guide.

The hollow grind was originally used to make fullers. Contrary to popular belief, those grooves that run along some blades, especially on swords, are not blood groves; they are fullers, which are meant to lighten the weight of the blade. During the Industrial Revolution,

▲ (L-R) Mora knife with a Scandi grind; Spyderco paramilitary with a flat grind; Chris Reeve Professional Soldier with a hollow grind; Wayne Goddard Camp with a convex grind © Justin Ayres.

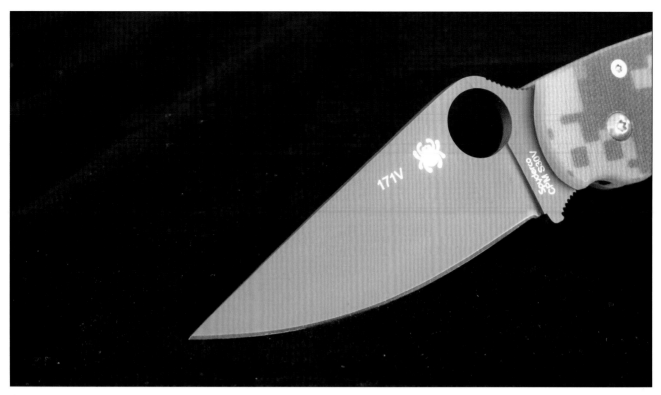

▲ Flat grind blade on a Spyderco Para-Military with a digital camo handle © Justin Ayres.

▲ Chris Reeve Professional Soldier with a hollow grind blade © Justin Ayres.

▲ Randall Model 1 knife with a choil.

▲ Leverage advantage of knife with no choil.

▲ Mora 2000 model with no choil.

when factory-made steel became readily available, grinding wheels also became available. Round grinding wheels produce a hollow grind and allow for rapid production. This is good for razors and other blades that need to be sharp but have little need for strength. That said, I have seen hollow ground blades from some makers that perform well and are tough.

The Choil

I remember when I first saw a choil. One of my training sergeants had a knife that he let me examine. As I handled it, I asked him what the cut out in front of the guard was for. He told me it was for your index finger, so you could choke up on the blade to get more control.

Let me get this straight, I thought. I'm supposed to put my finger, my *trigger finger,* next to the razor-sharp edge in front of the guard, which is designed to protect my fingers, to get more control over the blade. Well, I about choked up myself. The thought of putting my

trigger finger up against the edge, maybe at night, maybe when it's cold and my fingers are not very sensitive, the thought just . . . well, no. Not gonna happen. Nope. If I want more control, I will extend my finger along the top of the blade the way a butcher or chef might do. I have never seen a butcher knife, any commercial working knife, or any knife made before the twentieth century, for that matter, with a choil, and I have no idea what they're good for.

I see the choil as a waste of valuable edge. The edge right in front of the guard is where you can bring the most pressure to bear to cut resistant materials, and it is helpful for press cuts, shear cuts, and notching. The edge an inch or so in front of the guard requires about four times as much force for a given cut. I'm sure that some of my readers may be iron-wristed Rambos who would never have such a sissy consideration. But for the rest of us, that spot is very useful. Try the Frost or Fällkniven knives, the RAT RC-4, or any knife without a choil, such as a kitchen knife, and press cut a sapling or shave hardwood and you'll see what I mean. Some choils, due to their design, can get snagged and hung up while cutting soft materials, which could be a bad thing.

Stock Removal or Forging

The folks who make knives by stock removal often refer to bladesmiths as the heat and beat crowd. There is an ongoing debate on the merits of forging versus stock removal. I'll leave the final answer to the experts and will only note that of all the knives I have owned, the ones that performed the best came from master bladesmiths of the American Bladesmith Society.

PART THREE:
CHOOSING A TACTICAL KNIFE

Chapter 14

Who Needs a Tactical Knife?

Who needs a tactical knife? If I need a tactical knife, which one is best for me? Do I need more than one tactical knife? Let's deal with the first question first. I think pretty much every self-reliant person needs one. It's the most basic and versatile tool we have.

Watch television news for an hour or glance through any newspaper or online news source, and you will be confronted with news about numerous acts of violence, terrorism, various natural disasters, accidental injuries, and deaths by misadventure. Cars crash and trap their passengers. Earthquakes shatter buildings. People are kidnapped and assaulted for various reasons. Fires sweep through homes and offices. Floods overwhelm . . . Well, you know what I mean.

Some sheltered friends tell me that such events are aberrations that disturb the calm natural order of our daily lives. Nothing could be further from the truth. Disaster is normal. Disaster is common. Disaster is part of daily life—for someone.

Those same friends tell me we can and should rely on the police and fire department to protect our families. Today, popular media and many of our institutions support this point of view and would have us believe that individual responsibility no longer matters. I don't buy that.

Those who offer their lives in our defense can't be everywhere, and there's no way to predict when, or if, disaster will strike. If there were, we could arrange to not be present for fires, floods, plane crashes, robberies, and other calamities that happen somewhere to someone everyday. There's no need to bunker up or travel in an armored Hummer with gun ports. We have dealt with all these things throughout history. However, being prepared in a general sort of way isn't a bad idea.

Think ready. Be ready. Personal skills and abilities are different for everyone. All of us cannot be as physically fit as a paratrooper, nor do we need to be. But we can all act when we need to do so. We have all heard stories of the mother who lifted her wrecked car to pull her child to safety or the man who ran into a burning building to save his elderly neighbor. Ordinary people do extraordinary things. I think this is important to all of us; I've even written a book on how to acquire extraordinary skills titled *The Tao of Survival*.

On the scale of importance, equipment comes well down on the list. But gear does matter. The right tool at the right time can save a life. Next to my desk is a daypack I am currently using as a laptop case and briefcase. In addition to my laptop, pens, a writing pad, and other daily necessities I take with me when I go traveling, it also contains a number of items that could mean the difference between life and death in an emergency.

▲ A small sampling of tactical folders.

▲ Zero Tolerance Model 021 with a fixed blade.

There is a small first aid packet with a trauma dressing, a space blanket, a couple of butane lighters, a flint stick, a full water bottle, a pocket-sized survival kit, nylon cord, duct tape, and most importantly a couple of knives. All this gear is potentially useful, but I could lose it all without a backward glance—except for the knives.

Inside the bag is a large, tough knife. In an outside pocket, there is a Swiss Army Knife with a locking main blade, a saw blade, and the usual selection of tools. Today I happen to have a tactical folder in my pocket. What if an earthquake hit or a riot started up outside my office; both events have happened within the past few years. How would these knives help me? I don't know. And that's the point.

I don't know if I'll need to hack through a door in a burning building, cut a jammed seat belt, slice a piece of carpet to use as a smoke shield, or cut up some stiff cardboard to make a splint for a friend's broken arm. But if I do need to do any of these things, as I have in the past, at least I will have a tool handy for the job.

I don't know if a knife will save your life or mine. But I do know this: a good tactical knife is the best all-around tool that we have. You can use a cell phone to call for help, and that might work, if the cell network is functioning. You might have a full-on, end of the world, four-wheel drive in front of your house that will enable you to escape a city in the middle of a riot if someone doesn't steal it before you get to it.

You might choose to ignore any number of personal threats. You might not even have an extra bottle of water at home or a wrench to turn off the gas in the event of a broken pipe. But if you feel any need to prepare for whatever life might bring you and if you have any tool at all, make it a tactical knife. What the heck,

▲ A few fixed blades to consider (left to right): Wayne Goddard Custom, ZT, Benchmade, Chris Reeve, ZT, Fållkniven.

everybody uses knives for something. Might as well make at least one of them a tactical knife.

• • • • • • • • • • • • • • • • • •

Okay, so you've decided to get a tactical knife. Which one is right for you depends on your needs and what you can comfortably and legally carry. Later in the book is a review of specific knives. But first let's consider which type of knife is best for you. This can best be determined by analyzing your needs and by considering what kind of work can be accomplished with various categories of tactical knives.

Do you need a lightweight knife to accompany you on long backpacking journeys in wilderness areas, one

that can serve your daily needs, as well as function as a survival knife? Are you active duty military preparing to deploy to a war zone? Will you be leaving in a couple of weeks for a month-long trip in the African bush, the South American Altiplano, or the jungles of Asia? Do you have a job teaching English in a foreign city with a reputation for crime, overcrowding, and substandard buildings that collapse without warning? As we go along, I'll give you my opinions and those of other professional knife users. We'll consider the various options: big knife or little knife, folder or fixed blade, thick blade or thin blade, and so on. After reading this book, you'll be able to make your own decisions regarding tactical knives.

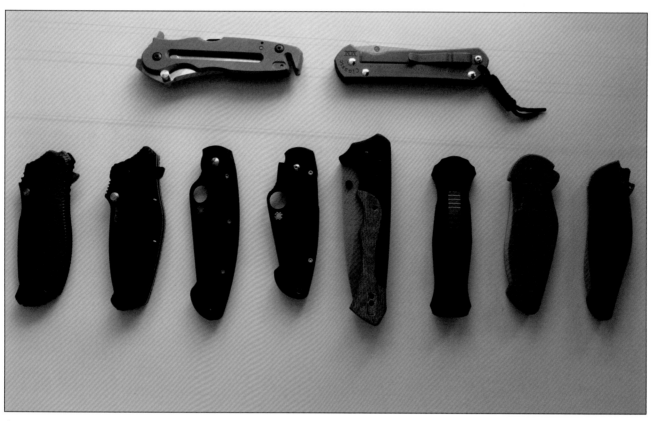

▲ Any one of these folders would be a good choice for your tactical knife.

◀ Folders (left to right): Benchmade Rukus, Spyderco Military, ZT, SAK Rescue Tool, ZT, Chris Reeve Sebenza.

Chapter 15

Big Knife or Little Knife

As far as I can tell the little knife versus big knife argument got started with Nessmuk, an outdoorsman and writer of the early twentieth century. Nessmuk, whose work I much admire, advocated for a thin, four-inch fixed blade as the best all-around working knife for the outdoorsman. The thing is, Nessmuk always had a hatchet with him, and he was focused on life in a relatively benign forest. If you're going to tote around a hatchet, you can get by with a handy little blade in a temperate forest, no problem. If you don't have that hatchet, a machete in the tropics, or a pry bar in an urban setting, you might need something more substantial to deal with events you encounter in today's world. Nessmuk never had to deal with a high-rise building coming down on his head.

During the past few decades the big versus small argument has gotten downright silly. A large crowd of folks who unfortunately have a good deal of influence take a vehement position, against all common sense, that all anyone ever needs is a little knife and that big knives are an indication of that Freud thing—you know, big cigar, little . . . whatchamacallit. I've been told that all you need is a pocket-watch-sized folder for any job, that lockbacks are for sissies who don't know how to use a knife, and that any cowboy can dress out a beef critter with a razor blade. Yeah, right. All you need is love too, until you want dinner. There is a reverse machismo thing going on here—mine's littler than yours.

I can dress out a deer with a sharp rock, maybe not as well as our Paleolithic ancestors, but good enough to get to meat. That doesn't mean stone knives are the best butcher's tools. If they were, there would be a big business in selling stone knives to butchers, chefs, and other professionals. What a small knife has going for it is convenience of carry. At the end of the day, that's quite a bit. It may mean the difference between having

▲ Moras (left to right): Model 2010, Model 2000, 780 Tri-Flex, 840 Clipper, and 840 Carbon. Handy, sharp, and affordable.

▲ Cold Steel Bushman—a handy knife to have in the bush.

a knife and not having one. But that doesn't mean a small knife will do the job any better or as well as a big knife.

Ask any professional chef which knife he would select if he were limited to one. Invariably it will be a ten-inch chef's knife. Professional butchers will chose a ten-inch butcher knife if pushed to use one knife. In every climatic zone on our planet where people live close to the land, they use big knives as their daily tool: machete, bolo, or parang in the tropics; the Leuku or Sami in the Artic. When I was trained in survival, the dogma was big knife, small gun—normally a .22 target pistol—if you were down to basics. That's worked for me and many others decades, and it still applies today. Check out the SERE training sites and you'll see it's still big knife, small gun. That's because the combination still works.

My daily carry is often a tough, four-inch fixed blade. With it and a baton, I can go through fire doors and auto bodies. I can construct a shelter, cut some firewood, and dress game. But I could do all that and more with, say, a ten-inch Bowie or camp knife and do it faster. However, in an emergency I probably won't have that big knife at hand. My big knives reside in my bag, not on my person.

Occasionally I attend gatherings of survival experts from around the world. Usually an interesting crowd shows up: archaeologists, anthropologists, Native Americans, mountain hippies, active duty Special Forces soldiers on leave, retired military, primitive skills people who live as aborigines, sometimes actual aborigines, and all manner of outdoorsmen, hunters, and trappers. At one gathering, I decided to ask everyone their opinion on the big knife, little knife question,

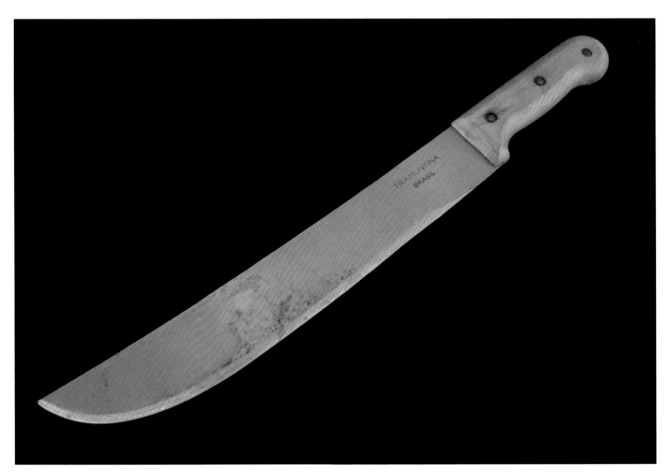

▲ Tramontina machete with a twelve-inch blade.

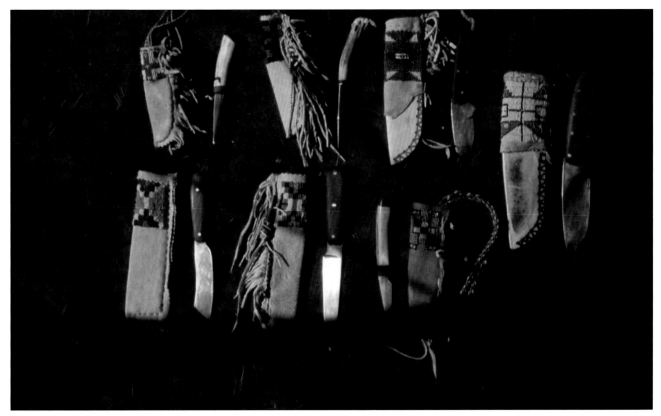

▲ Knives of Winter Count.

partially because I was curious about their answers and partially because I'm just nosey and wanted to know what knives everyone was carrying.

Everyone had knives. There were long knives, short knives, big knives, and little knives. There were knives with beautiful horn handles, inexpensive utilitarian blades, hand-forged works of art, high-tech marvels, and low-tech stone knives. There were machetes from Brazil, laminated blades from Sweden, and jackknives from old-line American manufacturers. Everyone had at least one knife, and most people had two or three. Everyone, even the students who came for basic classes, knew the importance of a good knife. For many of the instructors, survival conditions are just how they live. These folks know a good deal about using knives.

The primitive skills folks can get by without any kind of knife. They just chip a sharp edge out of a handy rock, cut down a sapling, and haft a larger sharpened rock to it. Now equipped with knife and ax, they can

set up housekeeping and fix dinner just about anyplace on the planet. But given a choice, they have knives. They know that a good knife will save labor and make life easier in the field.

There were more than one hundred instructors at that event, and I talked to at least seventy of them. So what do they use? What is the answer to the big knife, little knife question from those people's points of view?

Hawk Clinton makes knives and uses them daily at his remote desert residence. He codesigned a bush knife with Tai Goo that is in wide use as the big knife among survival instructors. Tai forges the blades, and Hawk makes the handles and sheaths. Hawk prefers simple carbon steel and horn or wood handles for his knives, and he carries a lot of knives. As we talked, he showed me his neck knife, a boot knife, and a belt knife. My impression was that there were probably a few others tucked away somewhere in his buckskins. If he would let you hold him upside down and shake him (unlikely), you would probably get enough knives

▲ Chris Reeve Sable with a handle wrap by Rob Withrow.

to open a store. Hawk doesn't leave home without his big knife.

Albert Abrvil served with Phoenix SAR (search and rescue) for twenty years. His Apache heritage guides his approach to the natural world. When it comes to knives, he is very perceptive. "These guys know what they are doing. If you look at the common factors in their choices, you will see that they are in agreement more than in disagreement. The big knife is

it—because it does more with less effort. But the small knife is always with them."

Albert has one tool he won't leave home without: a modified Tramontina machete. By re-profiling the point into a spade shape, he has a tool that will chop, pry, and dig with equal efficiency. "In the desert, you need to dig for water. Also certain roots are primary food and medicine items. This works for everything." Many of Albert's modified machetes were in the hands of other instructors, and I brought one home myself.

Karin Drechsel is a museumologist who works with archaeologists. From Köln, Germany, Karin has worked on digs around the world, including in Israel, where she discovered some of the oldest examples of stone knives in the Middle East. She spends much of her time in the field and always travels with her four-inch bladed Helle knife. It is of traditional Scandinavian design with a laminated blade, wooden handle, and leather sheath. "This is my indispensable tool. I use it every day in the field. Besides being the most functional knife I could find, it is also nonthreatening. I travel many places where political tensions are high. This doesn't look like a weapon." She also has a twelve-inch machete in her bag. Although Karin is not a survival instructor, she is a highly intelligent knife user who spends a great deal of time in the field in locations around the world.

Although the one hundred instructors had at least three hundred knives of considerable variety between them, their choices were consistent. Everyone agreed that a big knife, nine to twelve inches, was it. In a survival situation, if you could choose one knife, take the big knife. Although everyone knew how to baton a small knife through a pile of lumber and could dress out Godzilla with their utility knives, they agreed that the big knife would do the small knives' chores much easier and faster then the reverse. It was also understood that in an unexpected emergency situation rather than a planned trip to the field, they would probably only have a small knife with them. For that reason, most of them had both. The small knife is handier for small work, and it has the critical advantage of being highly portable and easy to carry. It is also more acceptable in today's world. The machetes and the like live in rucksacks and duffle bags. So, curiosity satisfied. I wasn't becoming delusional in my advanced years. Big knives

▲ Swiss Army Knife with a fire starter.

▲ Karin Drechsel at Winter Count survival camp in Arizona holding a Helle fixed blade.

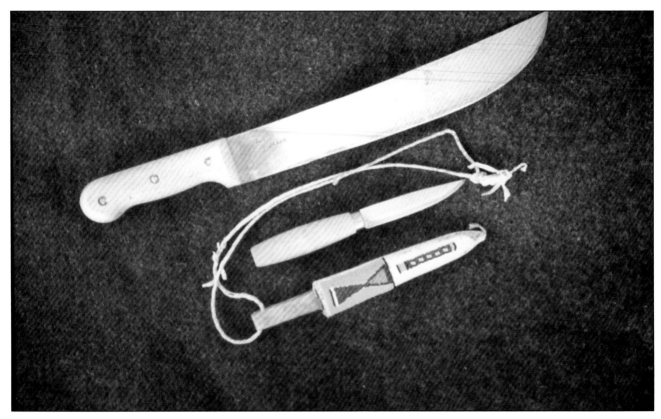

▲ Winter Count tools: Tramontina machete and Mora knife with a beaded sheath—most popular knives at Winter Count.

are it. But there's a big caveat: little knives get used the most because they're more portable. Little knives are mostly what people have with them. It's not really one or the other. Both are needed.

But wait, I hear someone asking, "What about medium-sized blades, the ones in the six- to eight-inch range, the ones the military uses, the Randalls and KA-BARs and . . ." Well, that brings us to the next chapter, where we will deal with that question, plus another topic that bedevils many discussions among knife people: do we need thick, tough knives, or is a slim slicer with better cutting efficiently the best knife? The two questions are closely intertwined.

Chapter 16

Sharp Pry Bar or Slim Slicer— The Medium-Length Knife

edium-sized knives in the six-to-eight-inch range are neither fish nor fowl. Too small to be big knives with chopping ability, too big to have the carrying convenience of small knives—what is their purpose? This size knife came into widespread use as a result of extensive studies done by the American and British War Departments during World War II to find a replacement for World War I trench knives. The trench knife was seen as too large and cumbersome for modern soldiers, who were armed with repeating rifles and had to cover a great deal of ground on foot, often quickly. However, it was clear that a need for a fighting knife existed. The studies showed that a seven-inch blade was the minimum length required to reach vital organs through uniform clothing. Both the KA-BAR and the Fairbairn–Sykes designs were influenced by these studies, as well as many of today's designs.

Even if today's designers don't know the antecedents of their own designs, they continue to build on the previous generation, turning out seven-inch knives for soldiers. They are not wrong to do so. The studies that were carried out seventy years ago are still valid. Longer knives will serve better in actual hand-to-hand combat, no disagreement on that point. But since such conflicts are relatively rare in modern warfare, soldiers won't carry big knives, certain special ops units aside. They will, for the most part, carry a KA-BAR or something else in that size range. However, given the oft-changing nature of warfare, that may change. As related in a previous chapter, a marine dispatched an enemy with his four-inch bladed tactical folder. Others have done similar things. I recently heard a story from a reliable source about a solider who overcame a fully armed enemy combatant with a concealed fixed blade fewer than three inches in length.

In the civilian world, there is little reason to recommend the medium-sized knife. Most civilians will be better served with the little knife, big knife combination as discussed in the previous chapter. The medium-sized knives I carry and use these days are those that are exceptional in some way or because I like them and they are old and familiar. I will admit that after many years of toting small utility blades, I'm trending back toward the medium-sized blade, but the jury's not yet in on that point. Most of the professional knife users I know who use the seven-inch length are, like me, former military, and for the most part we're operating from habit and experience more than current necessity.

The thick versus thin question also got started with the military in World War II. It was well understood that a thin-bladed knife would kill as efficiently as one with a thick blade, perhaps better. After all, they had centuries of experience to guide them. If you ever have the chance, visit the arms and armor collections in Paris and London. The swords and daggers of the sixteenth century up to the age of the firearm were not thick or heavy. They were thin, light, and quick in the hand. So are the Kris blades forged in Mindanao today, short swords that can take a man's arm off with little effort.

One problem facing the war departments of World War II was the difficulty of producing the enormous quantities of steel needed for the war effort. High quality blade steel was almost unobtainable. The solution was to use lower quality steel and make up for the lack of quality by using thicker blades.

There was an additional reason to use thicker blades. Given that bladed weapons were no longer primary in warfare, a knife issued to the troops would also have to serve as a utility tool. Thin, whippy swords do not make good tools for ripping open ammo crates, cutting steel packing bands, opening C-Ration cans, or tearing through building walls. Thus the KA-BAR was born, a combination weapon and utility tool. This legacy influences knife design today. I think that's a good thing.

Not everyone agrees. At one of the survival gatherings I described in the previous chapter, I introduced the topic of thick and strong blades versus thin, more efficient cutters. Which is better? Is there a happy medium? Is it possible to have cutting efficiency and strength for prying and ripping in one blade? I thought the answer to that question was yes. But I tossed it out to the group for consideration and inadvertently ignited an emotional controversy. We had previously agreed that the most common carry knife was a four-inch utility. So, I started with two four-inch knives and two opposed camps.

According to the various voices in the group, they were the best of knives, they were the worst of knives, the Mora was the perfect knife, the Reeve was the perfect knife, the Mora was a cheap and flimsy paring knife, and the Reeve was an overpriced, sharpened pry bar. A woodsman from the North praised the Mora; a mountain man from the West praised the Reeve. The Mora was weak, the Mora was strong, the Reeve

wouldn't cut, the Reeve cut like a razor. You could trust your life to the Mora, but not to the Reeve, you could trust your life to the Reeve, but not to the Mora. It was clear to the masters of the woods and the mountains that these matters were settled forever.

The knives in dispute were the Mora and the Chris Reeve Shadow III. The two knives are as different as chalk and cheese. The only thing they have in common is size; they both have four-inch blades and handles for an overall length of eight inches. The Mora is a thin-bladed, wooden-handled knife with a stick tang and a design as old as a square-rigged sailing ship. The Reeve is a one-piece, hollow-handled piece of A2 tool steel as contemporary in design as an F14 fighter. The Mora is made in a factory by the thousands, and the construction looks a little sloppy. The Reeve is made to machine shop precision in

▲ Mora with buckskin sheath and flint stick pouch.

virtually custom quantities. The Mora costs about as much as a hamburger with fries and a milkshake. The Chris Reeve will set you back the price of dinner for two in a fine restaurant in a major city, wine included. Both are purported by their advocates to be the perfect tactical knife.

A woodsman showed me his Mora, which he carried on a thong around his neck. He said the Mora was the perfect survival and tactical knife. It was perfect for all forms of woodcraft, took a sharp edge, and was easy to sharpen. He also told us a good test of a tactical and survival knife was to drive it with a baton point first into a tree and then stand on it. He stated unequivocally that this could be done with the Mora and that the blade would not bend or break.

During a conversation with a mountain man, I asked him what he thought of the Mora. "It's a great little carving knife," he said. "But it's no tactical or survival knife." I asked him what he used as a survival knife.

He opened his shirt and showed me a Chris Reeve Shadow III suspended from a thong around his neck.

Both of these men were highly experienced outdoorsmen, yet their opinions were diametrically opposed. While at the event, I had many conversations with others on this topic. Some were experts, some had no experience whatever; all had strongly held opinions. They tended to fall into the two camps; it was either the Reeve or the Mora that was the perfect tactical and survival knife. Both knives offer advantages over a folder and are small enough to carry everyday, local legalities aside. Both easily fall into the category of the knife you have with you.

My family was with me on this trip, and despite my warnings, my sons took to the woods and out of my sight, drove one of their Moras into a tree, and stepped up on it, as the northern woodsman had assured them was safe. Luckily neither one was injured. They brought me the remains of the knife with its bent blade and broken handle. If the blade had broken instead

▲ Chris Reeve Sable with a handle wrap by Rob Withrow—a good medium-sized knife.

of bending and my son had tried to cling to the tree instead of pushing away, he may have cut his leg badly. The woodsman looked pretty hefty, but maybe he weighed less than he looked, less than my ninety-pound eleven-year-old son. Or maybe he had an anti-gravity device.

We discovered that the blade geometry of the Mora was excellent for wood work: making triggers for deadfalls, carving wedges to split logs, shaving fuzz sticks for fire starting, and a dozen daily tasks, such as slicing veggies and meat for a stew, trimming the ragged edge of a torn pant leg, and so on. The woodsman was correct when he said the carbon steel blade took a fierce edge and was easy to sharpen. The Moras have the Scandinavian grind, which is basically a saber grind with no secondary bevel. By laying the bevel flat on a sharpening stone and using the bevel as a guide, it's easy to get a hair-popping edge. I like the Mora knife. I like its laminated carbon steel blade, its comfortable handle, and its overall geometry. It's also tough enough to use with a baton. With its wood handle, nicely formed blade, and leather sheath, it makes a handsome package. And for the price, it's a terrific bargain. But is it the perfect tactical and survival knife?

During the week, we also used a Chris Reeve Mountaineer I, which differs from the Shadow III only in having a clip point instead of a spear point. The hollow steel handle made for a handle-heavy knife, but this didn't affect its use. The only downside to the round handle was that it rolled off a table when I put it down. In cold weather, I would wrap the handle with tape, but in the mild autumn it was comfortable to cut with, even after some hours of whittling bows, atlatls, and other primitive tools. We used the Reeve for the same kinds of jobs as the Mora and found that it served equally well, except for precise woodcarving, where the Mora was more efficient.

My son found he had a harder time getting a good edge with the Reeve, since it didn't have the bevel that served as a guide. But after some additional instruction, he caught on and was able to bring both knives to a shaving edge.

Undeterred by their earlier experiment, my sons asked me to see if the Reeve knife would pass the tree

test. I agreed to try it, with the stipulation that I, not one of my sons, would put my weight on the knife. With the aid of a tree limb, I drove the Reeve into a pine tree and carefully, a little bit at a time, put my weight on it, while supporting most of my weight from another limb. The Reeve flexed but did not break. I stepped down and the blade sprang back to true.

Some of the advocates of the Mora witnessed this experiment. "That's silly," one said. "You'll never need a knife to do that." Leaving aside the fact that their guru had clearly stated this was the test for blade strength, let's examine the need for blade strength in a tactical and survival knife. Let's also go back to our original notion of a tactical and survival situation.

A survival or tactical situation is not camping, hanging out in the woods or mountains, or engaging in various woodworking crafts. It is one in which you must act to save your life wherever you might be, wilderness, city, or anyplace in between. Strength in a blade is a good thing. Strength without cutting ability is useless. If you have strength without losing functionality, you've got a tactical and survival knife.

As I mentioned earlier in this book, I once had to cut through a locked fire door with a six-inch bladed Randall Model 1 to get out of a high rise in Manila when a fire broke out. I once used a military issue Air Force Survival Knife with a five-inch blade to stop myself from being swept away by icy cold rushing water in an aqueduct where I was swimming when someone opened the sluice miles away. These were potential survival and tactical situations.

How would the Mora or the Reeve have worked in those situations? I wouldn't want to try and cut through a fire door with the Mora. I know the Mora won't bear my weight, so I surely wouldn't want to use it as an arresting device. I know from actual experience that the Reeve will cut through the roof of a Honda and bear my weight. It also carves wood well, if not quite as well as the Mora with its purpose-designed geometry.

Eventually, I realized that tree test aside, these two men, both true experts in their areas, were using different definitions of the term tactical and survival knife. To the woodsman and his followers, survival takes place in the woods and involves the construction of bow drills for fire making, shelters, traps, and various

▲ Mora cutting an oak limb.

◀ Chris Reeve Mountaineer with a fixed blade.

primitive tools from wood. The Mora will do this kind of work with ease, even elegance.

The mountain man is a combat veteran, as well as an outdoor guide and survival instructor. To him a tactical and survival situation is anything that threatens your life and can happen without warning any time or place. He wants a knife that will do for woodworking, serve as an emergency weapon, and have a reserve of strength for extreme situations—emergency uses that would destroy the Mora. I don't consider this a failure on the part of the Mora. Those uses are outside the design parameters of the knife. The Mora was designed as a cutting tool, and it serves that need admirably. The Reeve was designed to a completely different set of specs and achieves its goals. The Reeve is a tough knife and a good cutting tool.

This bring us to a class of knives that I think are about the most useful all-around knives made today, aside from folders.

Chapter 17

The International Traveler's Tactical Knife

*L*et's follow the logic of what we have learned in the previous chapters. Big knives are great but won't be carried on your person. Medium knives, around seven inches, are still too big for convenient civilian carry, and in most cases we don't need their war function. Small woodcarving and wilderness-oriented knives are not strong enough for emergency use. What does that leave us with, folders aside? If we want a tactical and survival knife, one suitable for daily carry in all kinds of conditions, we're looking at knives in the four-to-five-inch blade range with reserves of strength. This category of knives is one that for years I have called traveler's knives.

I do so because I have lived much of my life as an international traveler, and after thirty years, six continents, and more than forty countries, after five star hotels and jungle camps, war zones, third world slums, and palm-fringed islands, I have found this to be the most essential tool and emergency weapon I can have with me. That's aside from firearms or a SatCom that would allow me to call in an air strike and an extraction team. (Joke. Mmm, not really.)

Anything can happen on the road and often does. I have thought about this topic at length and considered the needs of others I have encountered in my travels,

some of which I have written about in earlier chapters. Recreational travelers, especially the international adventure traveler, might experience any climate or terrain. A traveler might encounter emergency situations or have a walk in the sun. He or she may travel alone or in company, friendly or unfriendly. In all cases, he or she should be self-reliant. His or her primary knife must serve planned and unplanned needs in all circumstances and environments. It might be the only tool available in an emergency.

A traveler is far from home and often unable to replace broken gear. He or she also should try to travel as lightly as possible. Therefore, the traveler's primary knife must be useful for a wide range of everyday tasks and have a reserve of strength for extreme situations. It must take a good edge and be easy to sharpen. It must not break. It must be useful for everything from slicing tomatoes and ripping coconuts open to arresting a slide down the slimy interior wall of an aqueduct. For the knife to be available, it should be on the traveler's person, except when it is checked with luggage for flying or in other secured areas. It seems to me that most of this also applies to the person who only travels a few miles from home. Who knows what will happen when you step out of your door? As Bilbo Baggins said in J.R.R. Tolkien's *The Fellowship of the Ring*, "It's a dangerous business, Frodo, going out your door. You step onto the Road, and if you don't keep your feet, there's no knowing where you might be swept off to." *The Lord of the Rings* is a fantasy series, but that message demonstrates wisdom. So where does all this take us?

Right back to where we started. A tough, sharp fixed blade about four to five inches in length, essentially a small tactical and survival knife, is the best compromise between function, size, convenience, and social acceptability. My experiences have led me to realize the wisdom of equipping US military pilots from World War II on with the Pilot's Survival Knife. It is, in all essentials, also a traveler's knife and will serve a traveler's needs well.

▲ Traveler's knives.

No folder, even an automatic, is faster to open than a fixed blade that's already open. No folder can be as strong as a tough fixed blade. The shorter blade will do almost everything the longer blades will do, and it will be there when you need it. And if you travel far off the beaten track, you will need it.

You'll find many good choices in this category when you get to the review section. But for now, here are a few examples of knives I have used and been satisfied with.

On an extended trip a few years ago, I carried a Chris Reeve Mountaineer I daily. I used it for food preparation and daily chores in camp and around town. While visiting an archaeological excavation in France, I was trapped underground when the staff left and locked the security door—the only way out—behind them. I

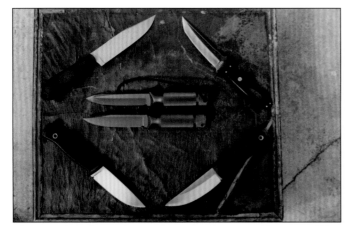

▲ Chris Reeve Shadow III, Chris Reeve Mountaineer I, Fällkniven F1, Fällkniven H1, Spyderco Bob Lum, and Spyderco Fred Perrin.

was in no immediate danger, but I was facing a long, hungry weekend before anyone returned on Monday morning. The excavation tools—shovels, picks, etc.— were stored in a shed aboveground. The only tool I had with me was the little Reeve.

I decided to attempt jimmying the security door open. I had doubts that the small knife would survive the effort or open the door, but dinner beckoned. I slid it into the crack near the lock and slowly applied pressure. Bit by bit the door gave. Bit by bit the blade flexed. I thought the diminutive blade might break, but I continued to apply pressure. Finally the door popped open, the blade sprang back to true, and I escaped in time for some roast duck with a nice Beaujolais.

This story is an illustration of the value of a fixed blade and the have it with you principle. The strongest folder I have ever seen would have folded up if I had tried to pry open that door with it. If I had not had the knife with me, there would have been no roast duck and no Beaujolais, just a long weekend underground with some recently excavated skeletons. The other version of this tiny powerhouse, the Shadow III, is just as strong, perhaps more so since its spear point has more steel close to the point.

Fällkniven have two models in the short and stout category. The H1 and F1 are both about eight inches overall, full-tang knives made of V10. Both knives have survived without damage the depredation caused by groups of teenagers in survival classes. Their convex grinds provide efficient edge geometry and strength. I've been using the H1 and the F1 for years and like

▲ Fällkniven F1 and H1 with traveler's gear.

▲ Benchmade Nimravus.

▲ An old favorite fixed blade, Spyderco's Bob Lum Tanto.

▲ Spyderco Fred Perrin Street Beat, the perfect traveler's companion.

▲ Bud Nealy Cave Bear II © Bud Nealy.

▲ TOPS Travelin Man 2, a reliable, tough example of a traveler's knife.

both of them a great deal. These are excellent examples of what the traveler's knife should be.

Benchmade's Nimravus is another good choice, although I would prefer if they offered the knife with a plain blade instead of a black one, which can draw unwanted attention in civilian use. At nine inches overall, it is a bit longer than the Reeves and Fällknivens but still a handy size. The Nimravus also survived the terrible teens during a shelter-building class. No joke. Untrained teenagers can destroy a piece of equipment faster than anyone but a parent would think possible. Benchmade also catalogs a shorter version of the Nimravus called the Cub. It should also work fine for the traveler.

Spyderco's Bob Lum Tanto is also a good choice for a traveler's knife; its VG-10 blade is strong, takes a good edge, and holds it well. Fred Perrin's Street Beat and Street Bowie, both in the Spyderco versions and Fred's handmade versions, are excellent traveler's knives. Our group has used both over a period of years, sometimes well outside of their design parameters, and has found them to be reliable, handsome, comfortable, well balanced, and all-around great knives.

Check out the Bud Nealy knives in the review section to find some nice traveler's knives. Many of Bud's knives have a self-defense focus, but they are equally useful as basic tactical, survival, or traveler's knives. Bud also has a new batch of models specifically designed for backpackers and outdoorsmen that will work well for travelers.

These are not the only knives suitable for the adventure traveler, but they are good examples. To evaluate a knife for extreme use, you might want to try some of the things I outline in the section on reviewing knives.

Still, let's not forget the utility of the big knife. A big knife of some kind is indispensable in the bush, but more or less useless in the city. If you know you will be traveling in the bush, it is worthwhile to pack one. Otherwise, for spontaneous trips afield, I buy a parang machete, bolo, or something similar at the local market.

As a traveler to far away places, you might also want a little back up. One of the tiny lockbacks pioneered by Spyderco, such the Cricket or Dragonfly, clip to any part of your clothing, open with one hand, lock solid, and cut like miniature chainsaws. The serrated models will easily slash though a seat belt. They provide much greater utility than their size might indicate.

You might also want an Swiss Army Knife. I don't really think of SAKs as knives; they're more like pocket tool kits. A small, simple one is best. But an SAK without a corkscrew is no SAK at all. Be prepared, right? Who knows when a bottle of Beaujolais or Bordeaux might happen along?

You can load yourself down with a dozen knives and a hundred pounds of gear before you hit the road. But after a while you will find that you only need a minimum of equipment. A few years ago, I walked across a good bit of Italy with a ten-pound pack and a Fällkniven F1. Some time back, I carried even less while island hopping for months in the Southern Philippines. I have found that travel has a way of bringing you to simplicity and clarity about your needs in life, as well as on the road. If you travel off the beaten track, take a small, strong fixed blade. Don't leave home without it.

Chapter 18

The Tactical Folder

Okay, you don't buy it. You don't want any kind of fixed blade. Can you get by with only a folder? Maybe. Many do. Over the past decade or so, I have used and tested more than two hundred of what we now call tactical folders. Today's tactical folder is not your grandfather's pocketknife. In many cases tactical folders can, and do, stand in for the small fixed blade utility knife. They can even serve as lifesaving weapons. Here is one marine's story that serves as an example of this fact.

• • • • • • • • • • • • • • • • • • •

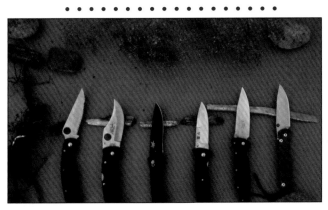

▲ A useful collection of tactical folders.

▲ Kershaw, Ken Onion design tactical folders.

Death Among the Reeds

On January 29, 2005, the day that the first democratic elections were held in Iraq, a professionally trained insurgent mortar squad dispatched from Baghdad and took up position to rain fire, death, and destruction on Camp Fallujah, a military base about ten kilometers southeast of the city of Fallujah.

This mortar squad had hit the base previously. In response, a team from Marine Sergeant Heath Lanctot's platoon had set up an observation post (OP) about two kilometers from the marine base near a point where they suspected the mortars would be placed to fire on the base again. "We wanted to catch the insurgents in the act and ambush them," Sgt. Lanctot said. Lanctot's team was designated as the Quick Reaction Force and held in reserve at the Marine base. The QRF's responsibility is to respond to calls for immediate assistance.

At about noon, Sgt. Lanctot's team received a call from the OP saying that the enemy had set up mortars right in front of the OP and that the OP team had opened fire on the enemy mortar crew before they could fire on the base. Lanctot's QRF sped from their base in open-backed Humvees. Seven minutes later, they leaped from their vehicles at the OP and joined the fight.

The OP team had killed one of the enemy with their Squad Automatic Weapon, but three other insurgents fled using the nearby canals and surrounding berms, part of the Euphrates River system, to cover their retreat. The insurgents then took up position in one of the canals concealed by thick reeds.

Sgt. Lanctot and two of his team members charged the canal firing their M4 Carbines as they ran. "We hoped to draw their fire from a distance, but it didn't work out that way. By the time they fired, we were on top of their position. The enemy opened up from a concealed position three meters from us. One of my teammates was hit and went down. I dumped three magazines into the reeds. Then, while my other teammate laid down covering fire, I ran down the berm and pulled my friend out of the kill zone. But it was too late. He had been killed instantly."

There were at least two of the enemy still at large, but the firing had stopped and the enemy was not to be seen. Maybe they had fled the area. Sgt. Lanctot went into the canal to retrieve the enemy body and search for any evidence. The water was chest deep and icy cold. Lanctot retrieved the enemy body and returned to the canal when he noticed a trail through the reeds.

In the matter-of-fact manner of a professional marine, Sgt. Lanctot told me, "I followed the trail, and, having left my weapon, ammo, and web gear on the berm, I pulled out my Columbia River Knife and Tool folder. I made my way along the canal and into the reeds. Suddenly one of the enemy popped up and grabbed my right arm."

There, cut off from any possibility of help, Sgt. Heath Lanctot fought his enemy as men have done since the beginning of the human race—with hand weapons—to the death. The water was deep, the reeds were thick, and the bottom of the canal slippery. Footing was unsure. During the course of the desperate, furious fight, Sgt. Lanctot dispatched his enemy with two knife thrusts to the neck.

Lanctot was climbing out of the canal when he heard a cough from the reeds. Without thought for his own safety, he immediately went back into the canal with his knife, ready to face another enemy. As he again moved into the reeds, the thick reed wall parted. He could see the enemy's eyes. But this time some of his buddies were on the berm above and behind him. The platoon corpsmen fired right over Lanctot's

▲ Benchmade Nagara.

shoulder, killing the insurgent and eliminating the need for Lanctot to engage in another hand-to-hand fight in the canal.

That was the last enemy Heath's unit engaged that day. This insurgent mortar squad would kill no more marines. They would never again attack Camp Fallujah or any other American or Iraqi base.

A knife used as a weapon is different than a firearm in that it puts your life and the life of another person in your hands—literally in your hands. You feel the heat of your opponent's body as he struggles to take your life. His breath mingles with yours. You smell his sweat and fear, as well as your own. When a knife has been used in terminal personal combat, that knife takes on a talismanic quality. In your mind it becomes the magic weapon that saved your life. I asked Sgt. Lanctot if that was true for him or if he regarded his CRKT folder as just another knife.

"No," he said, "it's not just another knife. I still use it for everyday things, but I plan to put it aside, maybe in a shadow box, when I get home. I wouldn't have been able to do it without the knife. I bought the knife in the PX (Post Exchange) when I first came to Camp Fallujah. Operation Iraqi Freedom Certified is engraved on it. But the guys in my unit will tell you that mine is the only one that is actually certified. Many of the guys in my unit have now bought one just like it."

"Did you have a KA-BAR?" I asked Heath, trying to understand how he came to use that CRKT in combat. "Most Marines I know do. And if you had one, why didn't you use it instead of your folder?"

"Yeah, I have a KA-BAR. But my folder was right there and quicker to get to," Heath said.

Sgt. Lanctot's response is all the reason anyone who has been in harm's way needs to understand. Experience shows that a last ditch weapon close at hand can save your life. Time compresses in combat and speed can determine who lives and who dies.

Men have fought with swords, knives, and other hand weapons in the Euphrates Valley for all of recorded history, and conflict continues there today. The outcome of Heath's fight might have been different there in that ancient land, that day in cold water among the reeds, if Heath had not had his folder clipped to his pocket when he went into the canal. It was a fateful decision to buy a personal knife at the PX. But what most occupies Heath's mind is grief for his fallen friend and the sorrow that the family and friends of his buddy feel at their loss.

"I like to believe it helps, knowing those responsible will never harm another American serviceman or-woman. The mortar team we took out turned out to be the major players in our area of operation. Locals identified the team as being the most feared in the area. It was an honor and privilege to get them off the streets."

Although Sgt. Lanctot bought his knife at the PX, Doug Flagg, a vice president at CRKT, donated a number of knives to a soldiers' knives program that we initiated. Those knives are now in the hands of service people in Iraq. Hopefully, none of them will need to be used in mortal combat. But it's good to know that they can be relied upon when fate rolls the dice and your number comes up.

Many armchair experts tell us that there is little need for knives in today's military because supply lines are more efficient and troops are less likely to run out of ammunition. Therefore, these experts say, the notion of a knife as a weapon is as outdated as swords on today's high-tech battlefields. But few of those so-called experts have ever heard a shot fired or felt the fear that rises in your chest when you are alone, unarmed, and facing an armed enemy.

▲ Desert tacticals from CRKT. © CRKT.

The troops in the field disagree with the experts; they buy personal knives. One of them, Marine Sergeant Heath Lanctot, of First Platoon Bravo Company, Second Recon Battalion, Second Marine Division, is alive today because he disregarded the experts' point of view. More importantly, he's alive because he embodies the finest traditions of the American fighting man and the Marine Corps: Semper Fi.

• • • • • • • • • • • • • • • • • •

Tactical folders are good for more than fighting to the death; they can help to save your life in other ways. For some years I provided survival training free of change to many young people who pursue outdoor recreation. Most of them were city kids who have no idea how quickly things can go wrong in the wilderness. These kids have seen the value of tactical folders. Influenced by fashion and social pressures as much as practicality, these kids totally refuse to carry a fixed blade while skiing, snowboarding, backpacking, white-water rafting, hunting, fishing, or a dozen other outdoor activities that have the potential for disaster. They will carry a folder. With proper technique and training and good folders, these kids have built one hour shelters good enough to protect them, and me, from a winter storm in the Northwest. They've made rabbit sticks and fish traps and started fires with their folders and sparking rods.

▲ Chris Reeve Sebenza.

They have learned to survive, and their tactical folders worked for them. Here's a short story about one such group.

• • • • • • • • • • • • • • • • • •

Home Away from Home

Three students from one of my previous classes asked me if they could take the next step in the process and apply what they had learned in a real world setting. I agreed. They would have to construct a shelter that would keep us all safe, if not comfortable, through a wet, cold Pacific Northwest winter night. They would have only a folder and the contents of their pockets or purses; no backpacks, tarps, tents, sleeping bags, stoves, or chainsaws were allowed. Ashley, who had previously taken a number of my classes, had the foresight to carry his ready bag. This was within the rules of the exercise, since the bag was his everyday carry bag, essentially a small shoulder bag no larger than a woman's purse.

Each of them borrowed a knife from me for the exercise. Ashley, the most experienced of the group, chose a Chris Reeve Sebenza. Nika chose the Al Mar SERE for its comfort in the hand. Kory, the youngest of the group, liked the Benchmade McHenry Williams.

My three volunteers followed me a few miles into an area of mixed second growth and underbrush that is typical of Pacific Northwest coastal forests. The distance and the nature of the undergrowth and terrain was enough to make the two more inexperienced members of the group feel they were in true wilderness. Then I gave them the following scenario:

The four of us were out gathering mushrooms. We got a little bit turned around. (I do not get lost.) Then I klutzed out, fell, and broke my ankle. With only two hours before nightfall, it was too late for any of them to walk out and get help. My size and weight was too much for them to carry. Being good-hearted kids, they were not going to leave my sorry, ancient self to freeze during the fast-approaching night. We would have to spend the night in the forest, and then the two strongest would go for help in the morning. The tempera-

ture was falling fast. Standing water was already freezing over. It was going to be a cold night. We would probably get snow or sleet. The three of them would have to build a secure shelter for the four of us and get firewood for the fire pit they would make inside the shelter.

I designated Ashley as team leader, and he instructed Nika in how to gather and trim the evergreen boughs for the classic bough bed that we would sleep on that night. Kory, being larger and stronger, was assigned to gather the saplings that would be used for the framework of the shelter. Ashley decided to cut saplings for the framework until they had enough of them to start construction. Then he would start the actual construction of our home for the night while the others fed him materials. I gave them about ten minutes additional instruction on how to use their knives most efficiently to accomplish these jobs without cutting themselves and while working against a deadline.

Since I was "injured" and unable to help, I sat on a log and watched as these young folks went to work. Ashley went through a stand of birch like a beaver on espresso. He would place the Sebenza at a diagonal, strike it carefully and accurately with his baton, and be onto the next tree before the first one hit the ground. Nika used her SERE to strip branches from large limbs with surprising proficiency for a city girl who had never done any of this before. Kory used his Benchmade to baton his way through pine, birch, and alder. They also learned that an easy way to cut down

▲ Kory cutting branches for the shelter in the woods © Justin Ayres.

saplings was to bend them to one side and cut into them on the outside of the bend. They used downed wood as available.

After the framework was solid, they thatched a roof about two feet thick with pine branches. Then they gathered some kindling by reaching into the lower branches of pines and snapping off the dead branches. There were not nearly enough of these branches to get the fire hot enough to burn damp wood, so some larger wood had to be split to get to the dry wood inside. They split logs by batoning their folders first into the edges, stripping off sections about an inch thick, and then working their way to the center. There was a bit of friction between the kids, as is normal when people are thrown together and stressed, but they worked out their minor problems and continued. One hour and five minutes after they started, we stopped for a short break. The temperature had now fallen well below freezing. The shutter of my camera froze and stopped working at this point, and I was unable to take any photos of the completed structure with fire pit.

In another ten minutes, we had a floor of pine boughs about two feet thick, a small fire pit inside the shelter, and a supply of firewood—all in all, a secure place to spend what was shaping up to be a harsh night. Three people, two of them with no experience with folding knives or the outdoors but with proper instruction, accomplished this in about an hour and fifteen minutes.

We were a little chilled as the sleet started to sting our faces, and we crawled inside the shelter. But thirty minutes later we were sitting around the fire laughing about how Kory got a load of ice water down his neck when he pulled down a sodden branch. It was so warm inside we all had our jackets off. For dinner we shared the only food in the group. Nika had brought nothing. Ash had a can of sardines, some sea crackers, and a bag of trail mix in his ready bag. Ashley also had in his bag a small survival kit that I had designed. The Global Survival Kit weighs about twelve ounces, will fit in a large pocket, and food can be cooked in the container. Ash brewed some tea, and we all had a warm drink. Kory had a squished Snickers bar in his pocket, so that was desert. I had deliberately brought nothing and was prepared to go hungry with the kids to help teach these lessons. It was clear to the kids that we could safely, even comfortably, spend the rest of the night there in our warm shelter. I would have been okay if I had really broken my ankle. The lessons had been learned.

Ashley also has some sugar packets that could be used to bait traps, as could the sardine oil and some other items in his ready bag. But this was not an extended exercise, just a quick lesson on how to use a tactical folder to build a shelter. Along the way, we all also learned some other things. Kory learned how to cope if he got lost snowboarding. Nika, who was soon returning to college, learned that a city girl could get by in the woods if she needed to. Ashley refined his

▲ Using the Chris Reeve Sebenza to build a shelter in the woods.

▲ A well-built shelter © Justin Ayres.

knowledge about taking care of others. I learned that today's kids are just as resourceful and willing to learn about the outdoors and personal responsibility as were the kids of my generation. You just have to give them a chance. So a little after midnight, we dowsed the fire and crawled outside.

Nika and Kory were surprised at how cold it was away from our little fire and outside of our forest home. They all checked to make sure their folders were secure in their pockets. We pulled on our jackets and started the long walk home under a full moon. We made our way through the trees and around ice-covered bushes gleaming in the moonlight and walked back to the old truck, crunching through frozen puddles and across a frost tipped field under a million icy stars.

• • • • • • • • • • • • • • • •

Can you get by with a tactical folder instead of a small fixed blade? Well, as we have seen, you can fight for your life with one. You can build a shelter and save yourself from freezing with one. Obviously, you can slice bread and spread peanut butter with one. Thousands of people have substituted tactical folders for fixed blades, including many in active military. So my answer would be yes, with one caveat: no folder can be as strong as a fixed blade. If you need a really tough knife, go with a fixed blade. That said, odds are a tactical folder will do the job—if you don't have to do anything that would cause it to fold.

▲ Nika Butler relaxing in the shelter © Justin Ayres.

Chapter 19

Tiny Tacticals

The term tiny tactical is a term I created to describe a category of knives that I do not think has been adequately recognized. The fixed blades in this category are often called neck knives, which tells us nothing about them except the intended method of carry. The folders are not called much of anything, expect whatever individual name the maker assigns to them. As a class, I know of no name that describes a little folder with a blade of two inches or less and has tactical potential. I believe that both small folders and fixed knives are worthy of attention and should be considered on their own terms. First, lets take a look at the folders.

Tiny Tactical Folders

It's generally agreed that a tactical folder is a folding knife with features that make it tactical: a reliable blade lock, strong construction, exceptional cutting ability, one-hand opening, and a clip to attach it to your clothing. Most tactical folders have blades of about four inches or, in smaller versions, blades of about three inches. A tiny tactical has a blade of no more than two inches.

This category may seem a bit overly specific, but there is a considerable difference between the social acceptability of a folder with a two-inch blade and

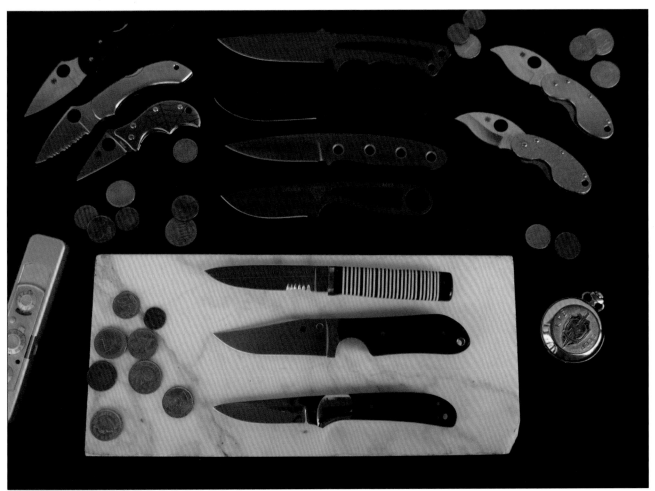

▲ A collection of tiny tacticals, both folders and fixed blades.

one with a four-inch blade. Like it or not, we must deal with issues of social acceptability. Also, there are many places, more and more these days, where we are not legally allowed to carry a knife any larger than what amounts to a penknife. Moreover, a tiny tactical is much more useful than any penknife. In order to qualify as a tiny tactical, the knife must meet the same criteria as the large tactical, folder, except for its size.

How useful is such a small blade? Very. Our ancestors survived and thrived with such small blades as a starting point, so to speak. As an amateur student of archaeology, I have learned that stone age hunting and gathering cultures got along quite well with tiny stone knives with an average length of about two inches. Ötze the Iceman, who was discovered in the Alps in 1991, was found with a flint knife of just this size. From his possessions it is clear to scholars that he made his bow, arrows, and other tools with his two-inch flint knife.

Jürgen Weiner, a friend who is a respected archaeologist and recognized authority on lithic, or stone, tools consulted on the Iceman excavation. Jürgen tells me that Neolithic hunters relied on small blades for most of their work. They made stone axes for chopping down trees and other heavy work. But for day-to-day skinning, game processing, wood crafting, and other basic tasks, they relied on short (at least by our standards) stone blades. They also killed each other with them, as has been proven by the examination of hundreds of fossilized skeletons. In addition, they used their small blades to make larger tools, such as bows, spears, baskets, and the other stuff of everyday life. In other words, Ötze's gear was the standard Neolithic outfit for a hunter–warrior.

Over many millennia, our ancestors learned what worked best, and those little blades were it. They could, and did, make larger blades, but those were used mostly for ceremonial purposes or to impress the neighbors—Neolithic conspicuous consumption. We may not have to wrest a living from the wilderness, but we can learn something from our ancestors. If they could build an entire culture with such small blades, and if they decided that such a small blade was the best tool for most jobs, maybe we should consider that our modern tiny tactical folders might be the right tools to take care of many daily tasks. They can also help us get out of a tight spot when needed.

I have dressed out game with a Spyderco Dragonfly, a tiny folder with a two-inch blade. Recently my son tied his Spyderco Cricket onto a long bamboo pole and cut a ripe orange from an out-of-reach tree branch for one of the neighborhood children. My wife uses her Cricket daily to open boxes, trim threads from garments, and a hundred other tasks, including slicing a baguette. Often she uses her tiny folder to prepare dinner in spite of having a kitchen full of knives. And trust me, our kitchen is full of knives.

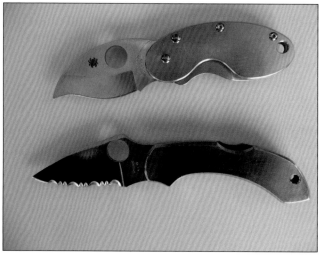

▲ Spyderco Cricket and Dragonfly.

▲ Spyderco S knife.

I have used the plain-edged Dragonfly to plane the flats on a quickie bow, much as I would have used a flint planer. I've also used the Cricket to make notches for arrows and dig out a spindle holder for a bow and drill fire set. Jürgen Weiner and Jim Riggs, another expert in lithic arts, instructed me in the technique of using stone tools. I simply substituted the Dragonfly to try it out. It worked great, as it did for other primitive craftwork and most anything else.

These homely tasks show the utility of the short blade, even for wilderness survival. But what about a real world survival situation in a city? What use would such a small blade be in an extreme situation, say a high-rise fire—something that only sounds unlikely until you find yourself in a burning building?

Think of the two-inch blade of a tiny tactical as the tip of a larger tactical folder. Most blade work gets done with the first couple of inches anyway. If your tiny folder meets the tiny tactical criteria, it can cut a fire shield from a carpet or baton through a stuck door almost as well as its larger cousins. With proper technique you can do some amazing things with a tiny blade. A tiny tactical is not just any small folder. To meet the standard, it must be strong. It must have a solid reliable lock. It must take a razor-sharp edge. A clip is so useful, it amounts to a necessity, particularly in the case of these little guys. Clipped to a waistband, with the clip behind a belt, your miniature folder is all but invisible. Attached to a sock, sleeve, or undergarment, it becomes part of your clothing.

There is much to be said for a serrated edge on a tiny tactical. Harking back to our ancestors, all stone blades are serrated. The serrations on a stone blade have a lot to do with their exceptional utility. Stone blades are made by flaking off tiny chips until a sharp edge forms. The result is an edge that cuts more aggressively than a plain edge of the same overall size. Serrations are not required for a tiny tactical, but they do ratchet up its overall effectiveness, albeit at the loss of the ability to do fine woodcarving. But everything is a trade off. I use both.

Spyderco has been the pioneer in developing this category of knife. Their Dragonfly and Cricket define the category and are available is a variety of finishes and handle materials. We have used both models extensively over the past years and have found them unexpectedly useful. ML, my ever-resourceful wife, snatched the first Cricket she saw before it was even out of the box. That was some years ago and she hasn't been without one since. At present, she uses her pretty little engraved Cricket for everything. However, do not get the idea that the Cricket is useless for anything but domestic chores. It has a wicked little recurved blade and point and is capable of doing serious damage in a self-defense situation.

I used to teach seminars on self-defense with edged weapons. I actually preferred using tiny tacticals for these particular classes. My intent was to teach defense, not offense, and little knives are effective for that purpose. In addition, their appearance is inoffensive and no one objects to carrying them. Some are so small as to be unnoticeable until needed.

Some years ago, Spyderco cataloged the Co-Pilot, back when you could still carry a small knife onto an airplane. I bought a half-dozen Co-Pilots and distributed them to students in a class I taught back then for certain people who needed a means of emergency defense in restricted areas. I wish Spyderco would bring back all their little folders—I think they had two or three other similar models—and offer them as a series: Tiny Tacticals.

Now other companies are making tiny tactical folders. Al Mar's SLB (Stout-Little-Backup) seems to qualify. Kershaw's Ken Onion Chive and Small Eros, as well as

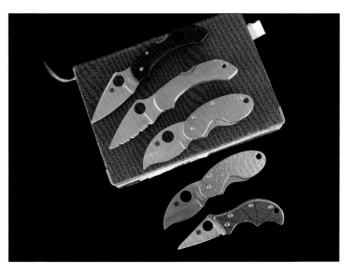

▲ Spyderco collection of tiny tacticals: Dragonfly Lightweight, SS Dragonfly, SS Cricket, Etched Cricket, and the SS Spin Etched.

some models from CRKT look like good candidates. Check out the current factory catalogs. You'll probably find quite a few tiny tactical folders, even though they won't be listed by that category.

When you find one you think will serve, try it out in the kitchen. Kitchen usage is a true test of utility. Then, if you value preparedness, test it for extreme usage. Perhaps baton it through an old door, or cut up a piece of sheet metal. Use some common sense and caution while doing these things. Don't slip and cut yourself. Don't do these things at all if you are not sure you can handle a knife safely.

If you wreck the knife while dressing out an old Honda, do not complain to the maker. Do not ask for a refund. It is your responsibility to test your gear, and no manufacturer should be expected to bear the cost for that. The destruction of a folder is a small price to pay for the security of knowing the limits of your equipment. After you are satisfied that your choice will serve your needs, buy a few of them. These are not expensive knives. I consider my Dragonflys and Crickets to be all-time bargains. I use them daily and am not afraid to use them up if need be.

Tiny Tactical Fixed Blades

You can hang any knife around your neck and call it a neck knife. A butter knife on a string might be a neck knife, but it sure isn't a tiny tactical. There are two main differences between a tiny tactical fixed blade and a folder: one, it doesn't fold and is therefore stronger, and two, it's a little larger because . . . right, it doesn't fold. In order for a fixed blade to be considered a tiny tactical, it must be tough; it must take an excellent edge; and it must be small, with no more than a three-inch blade and about six inches overall length.

Many folks wear Moras around their necks, and they're certainly sharp and reasonably strong. However, Moras run to blade lengths of about four inches, overall about eight inches, which puts them into another category and size range. So by these standards, Moras aren't tiny tacticals.

These knives do include: the Buck/Mayo Kaala, the Becker Necker, the Chris Reeve Professional Soldier (a little oversized for this category, but it's close), the ESEE Izula, the Spyderco Fred Perrin Street Beat, Fred Perrin's Neck Bowie, and the Spartan Blades Enyo. There are others, but these are the ones I have recently reviewed. All of these tiny tacticals are tough. All come sharp and stay that way, are well designed, and are easy to carry. Basically, these knives define the category of tiny tactical fixed blades. You can do anything with these knives that you can do with the folders and more, including prying, twisting, tearing, ripping, and stabbing—all things you want to be careful about when using a folder.

▲ ESEE Izula with arrow quiver from Borneo.

▲ Chris Reeve Professional Soldier and the Becker Necker.

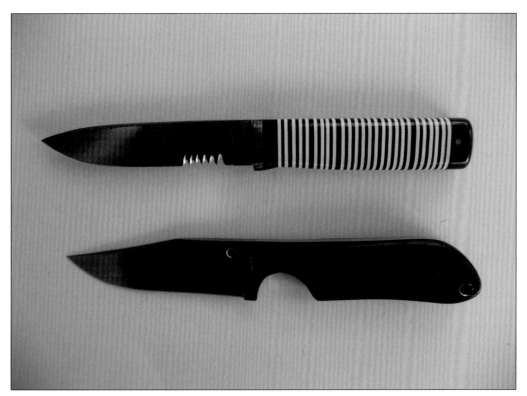

▲ Wayne Goddard LBK and Spyderco's Fred Perrin—two fixed blade tiny tacticals.

▲ Spartan Blades Enyo making a fireboard.

They vary a good bit one from one another. The Reeve is made of S35V steel, as is the Enyo. The Becker and the RAT are 1095. Of course, each maker has his or her own heat treat, so steel choice isn't definitive. The Becker and the RAT are both flat ground. The Buck is deeply hollow ground. The Reeve has a sophisticated combination of grinds. They are all in the same size and weight range. Check out the reviews in the makers' sections for details on these terrific little blades. In general, they're all good to go.

With its fine finish, nicely contoured handle, and polished VG-10 blade, the Spyderco Fred Perrin Street Beat is the class act in this crowd. The blade is a little longer at three inches, and it straddles the category between tiny tacticals and traveler's knives. We've used this one hard and extensively, and it has performed way out of its class. So has Perrin's smaller but just as useful Neck Bowie. See Spyderco in the review section for more information on the Street Beat and Fred's section for more info on the Neck Bowie.

Either one of the folders or the fixed blades would make an excellent back up to a bigger blade. Or they can stand on their own. As small as they are, you could easily carry both a folder and a fixed blade or more than one of each. One of my correspondents, a contractor who worked the past few years in hot, dry places where lots of bad guys blow things up and kidnap people, carries two Spyderco Crickets clipped to his underwear. This is in addition to his primary shoulder weapon, a handgun, a hideout pistol, a large fixed blade, and a tactical folder. He told me, "You will *not* be seeing me on the Internet being beheaded."

On a lighter note, anyone with a modicum of skill and a healthy dose of determination could wander off into the wilderness and survive, in fact thrive, with only tiny tacticals. Our ancestors did for hundreds of thousands of years.

PART FOUR:
USING YOUR TACTICAL KNIFE

Chapter 20

Basic Skills

*I*t drives me slightly nuts when I see someone in a restaurant sawing away at his or her steak and shredding it into ever-finer shreds. Likewise, when I see someone hacking at a chunk of wood with a folder or small utility knife. I witness this kind of thing all too frequently. Of course you know how to use a knife. But in case you have some friends who do not, here is a review of the basic cuts to aid in the instruction of your friends.

Cutting

The Draw Cut: Place your edge on the surface to be cut and draw the edge across it while maintaining downward pressure. This is not sawing. Sawing is the ineffective method of drawing a smooth edge with no saw teeth back and forth over the intended cutting surface with no downward pressure. Press down and draw. This will do for most any steak.

The Push or Press Cut: Place your edge on the thing to be cut and simply push down.

The Shear Cut: Anchor the tip of your knife so it does not move. Holding the handle in one hand, use the secured tip as a fulcrum and press down with your edge on the material to be cut.

▲ Leverage advantage of no choil with a press cut.

▲ Gerber LMF II illustrates a press cut.

The Slash: Move your edge to and through the material to be cut, usually done with speed. The combination of a slash and a draw cut is taught in certain blade arts and is a highly effective technique.

The Stab: Secure the handle firmly and drive the point of your blade into that which you wish to penetrate.

The Chop: Swing your edge with force into the material to be cut. A chop with a small knife is futile and damaging to the edge of the knife. Even medium-sized

▲ Cutting veggies with a draw cut.

▲ Mora knife making a shear cut into a hardwood limb.

▲ Stab with ZT fixed blade.

blades of around seven inches are miserably ineffective as choppers. Use a chopper, such as a machete or other big knife, to chop.

Batoning: If you need to chop things and have no chopper, use a baton. A baton is anything used to baton, or strike, the back of your blade. This is an effective technique for cutting large things with a small knife. Correctly done, it will not damage the knife. Simply place your edge onto the thing you wish to cut and strike the spine of the blade directly over the cutting surface—lightly, not like you're hitting a home run. Repeat.

▲ Close-up of an orange tree limb slashed by Mace Vitale's forged camp knife.

Since it's a critical survival skill, we're going to cover batoning in a little more detail. A baton is anything sturdy that can be used to pound a blade through a resistant medium: a chair or table leg, a large or small Maglite, even a hard-soled shoe will serve.

Hold the baton in a loose pivot grip so that it can rotate around the junction of your fingers where you grasp it. Hold the knife with a loose but firm grip so that it can pivot around the axis of your thumb and second finger. The other fingers should be somewhat loose. The knife must be able to pivot to avoid stress in the event of a misplaced strike. Use the edge to cut if you're using a folder. No folder should be driven through a resistant medium point first, whereas a fixed blade can be. If using a folder, the key thing is to not put direct stress on the lock.

Strike the back of the blade directly over the place where the edge is in contact with the surface to be cut. By striking in this spot, you transfer the force of the blow through the blade and into the object you are cutting with little stress on the blade. Correct baton technique will stress your knife far less than chopping with it, since the edge must absorb the energy of the strike when chopping. Chopping with a folder or small knife is ineffective in any event. If you use proper technique, batoning wood should not damage your knife, either fixed blade or tactical folder.

To cut through a flat surface, say a door, place the belly of the blade, the part just behind the point, on the surface. Again, strike directly above the contact point. Since you are using a curved part of the edge, the cut will be a bit easier than when you use the straight part of the edge.

When would you use a baton? When there is no ax or machete available and you need to cut saplings for an emergency shelter, through a locked door to escape a burning building, or open a car body to extract a trapped passenger. I read a story about one of the firefighters who

▲ **Batoning** a folder.

was near Ground Zero on 9/11. He was running from his car to the scene when he heard cries from inside a shipping container where a woman had been trapped when the container was flipped over by the blast. The firefighter was alone. He had none of the tools of his trade with him. He used his folder and his flashlight to make two diagonal intersecting cuts, pulled the sheet steel out of the way, and rescued the woman. His folder was a tactical from one of America's leading manufacturers. Cutting through steel like the firefighter did may destroy your knife, but a knife is a small price to pay for a life.

If you want to be ready in an emergency, practice this skill before you need it. Don't wait until a building is burning down around you before you try to use a baton. Reading about how to do something is not the same as actually doing it. Be inventive; use expedient batons. See how effective a flashlight is compared to, say, the hard heel of a shoe. Obviously a sneaker would be less effective as a baton than a table leg. However, in a recent test a small woman was able to cut through the roof of a car with a tactical folder and one of her boat shoes.

Try cutting different things, such as tree limbs, discarded doors, plywood, and junked car bodies. You will learn about the resistance of various materials and become proficient in the skill. If you go at it seriously, you may make a few mistakes and you may wreck a knife or two in the process. But that's a small price to pay to acquire a valuable skill. Don't complain to the knifemaker if you wreck a knife while learning. Consider it the price of education.

Sharpening

Some knives are easier to sharpen than others. Some steels respond to the stone better than others. Ease of sharpening is related to, but not entirely determined by, the hardness of the steel. Other factors, such as the grain, texture, or the nature of the steel play a part, as do how the blade is ground, the sharpening material, and method.

I will try to simplify the matter and describe a general process that can apply to virtually all common steels and knives. In general, I have found that the stainless steels are harder to sharpen than carbon steels, either because stainless is heat treated to a harder level or due to the nature of the material in general. I only mention it because it's possible that you might be doing everything right, but because it is taking so long to get an edge, you might think your method is incorrect. It may be, but even if you're doing everything

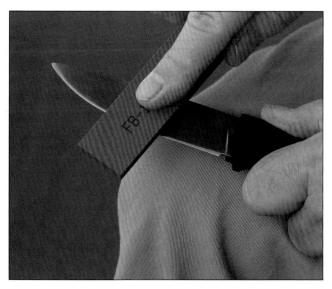

▲ Using a Norton pocket stone to sharpen this Fällkniven F1.

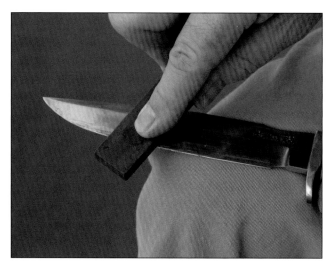

▲ Pocket India stone being used to sharpen the Randall Model 1.

▲ Spyderco Tri-Angle Sharpmaker.

▲ Another view of proper usage of the Spyderco Tri-Angle Sharpmaker.

▲ Using a Lansky pocket touch-up sharpener on this Lone Wolf Harsey.

▲ Using the Scandi bevel as a sharpening guide.

▲ Sharpening a convex edge by drawing away from the edge.

▲ Sharpening Fällkniven F1 with a convex edge by drawing away from the edge.

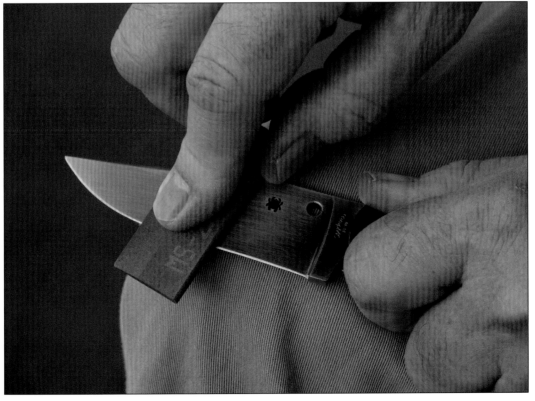

▲ Using a slip stone to sharpen this Spyderco fixed blade.

right, you will probably find that it takes longer to get a sharp edge on, say, a blade of 440C than one of 1095. Personally, I have found it to be a devil of a job to sharpen knives made with S30V with an ordinary stone, whereas VG-10, 01, 1095, Sandvic 12c, and others come up fairly easily. I also had a VG-10 blade that a stone the size of Mt. Rushmore couldn't sharpen. Keep in mind that these are general comments. Your results may vary.

Mostly, I use Norton stones. From the large bench size to pocket-sized stones, I have found them to do a good job. If the bevel on a knife has been worn away, I start with the rough grit then go to fine grit. If there's still a good bevel, I only use the fine grit.

I also use the Spyderco Tri-Angles for quick touch ups. The Tri-Angle is a good tool until you've gone through the bevel and need to reset it. Then you'll have to go to the stone. I also sometimes use a Lansky pocket touch-up device for just that, a quick touch-up in the field.

There are good alternatives. DMT and EZE-LAP both produce diamond sharpeners that I have seen do good work. I look forward to trying them out.

Almost everyone tells you to sharpen a knife using the same method: lay your blade on the stone and, according to the angle of the bevel you want, push your edge into the stone as if you were slicing off a thin slab. This works for most edges most of the time.

If you have a convex edge, or want one, do exactly the opposite. Lay your blade on the stone and, according to the angle of the bevel you want, pull your edge away from the stone, in effect stropping it.

In either case, continue working one side of the blade until you get a wire edge, which you can feel with your fingers. It's a good idea to count your strokes. When you get a wire edge on one side, turn over the blade and repeat on the other side.

Once you get to a working edge, you will need to remove the wire edge. You can do this by stropping the edge carefully along the stone, or stropping on leather; even cardboard will serve.

To use a pocket stone, you reverse the entire process. Hold the blade steady and move the stone along the edge. Since pocket stones are small, you do not want to push into the edge. Doing so will likely result in a cut. Instead stroke away from the edge. This is how swords, machetes, and other large blades are sharpened in the field. Any knife can be sharpened with the same method.

Use some kind of light oil to float steel particles up and out of the stone's pores. Wipe everything clean afterwards.

Flint and obsidian knives are sharpened by using pressure to flake small chips from the edge. A piece of antler is an ideal chipping tool. If you get a chance, do try a flint or obsidian knife. The cutting ability will likely surprise you. A good obsidian blade will cut

▲ A good angle for sharpening a Tops Mil-Spie 5.

▲ Sharpening an obsidian blade with a piece of antler.

as fine as any modern steel blade. The downside, as there's always a downside, is that they break easily.

Maintenance

Taking care of your knife is extremely simple. When it gets dirty, wash it. When it gets wet, dry it. If it's carbon steel with no rust-preventing coating and you're in an area of high humidity, keep a light film of oil on it—it doesn't matter what kind. In the tropics, where rust is ever lurking and ready to pounce, I keep my carbon steel knives rust-free with coconut oil. Olive oil is equally good. So is machine oil if you're not going to use the knife for food preparation. I don't think you need to oil a carbon steel knife if you live in a desert area, but keep an eye on it. I do the same even with stainless steel in the humid tropics. Otherwise, I do what the makers say and don't worry about it. Flint and obsidian do not rust. There is no maintenance requirement.

Chapter 21

Self-Defense with the Knife

nife fighting, or more specifically, self-defense with a knife, is a terrible thing and a bloody mess. It is not like the movies. In theory, you know that movies and television are not real. But their images are so pervasive that they create their own reality. People begin to believe that what they see in films is what happens in real life.

In the movies, when the bad guy gets stuck with a thrown knife, he falls down and dies rather bloodlessly. When the bad guy gets stabbed, he clutches his wound and falls down dead. When the same things happen to the good guy, he shrugs off the wound—just a flesh wound right? As if we're made of something other than flesh—and fights on. Doesn't work that way. Depending on a person's individual nature and the severity of the wound, he or she might become enraged and attack with more determination. Or he or she might freak out at the sight of his or her own blood and faint.

I'm not going to write about knife fighting, the military use of the knife at war, the edged weapons martial arts, and certainly not about lethal knife techniques. However, if you're considering the use of a knife in self-defense, I will outline some basic techniques that I have taught, primarily on a pro bono basis in coordination with a rape crisis center. These methods are designed to allow a small, relatively defenseless person to defend himself or herself from large or multiple attackers.

The object of these methods is to allow a victim to escape from a predator. I will not cover methods designed to take the attack to the aggressor. One of the few things in favor of the knife as a defensive weapon is that you can cut an assailant a little bit, whereas you can't really shoot someone a little bit and be sure you won't hit a vital organ. With some control, which is difficult to have if you're in fear for your life, it is possible to discourage or disable an assailant with the odds being that you won't take a life.

The Method

My method is called cut and run. It's an old phrase, a cliché; you've heard it a hundred times. But in spite

An official disclaimer: I do not recommend that you defend yourself with a knife. I cannot decide when your life is in danger and you need to protect yourself. You must accept full responsibility for your actions. If you do decide to defend yourself with a knife, the methods that follow may work for you. **I am not an attorney, and I offer no legal advice of any kind.**

of how it may sound, cutting and running is an emergency escape method that has been taught to various US government clandestine agents over the years because it works. That's what lapel daggers, sleeve daggers, coin knives, and related weapons were used for: cutting and running when faced with overwhelming force and the possibility of death or severe injury. Those little blades were not designed for standing and fighting. The approach to self-defense with a knife that I teach is based on these methods and concepts.

However, going to the knife, or any weapon, is the last thing to do to escape an assailant. First try to avoid the situation. If you cannot do so, try to talk your way out if you are trapped. If you are not trapped, simply leave out the first part, cut, and initiate the second part, run. If you have no other options, no one comes to your aid, and you think your life is in danger, then you might make the decision to go to the knife.

Critical Points

The only purpose in choosing the knife is to secure your release from an aggressor. Therefore, the only part of the body you should consider cutting is the hand or the arm. The only exception is when you are confronted with more than one assailant. In that instance, you might decide to use a wide slash to free yourself.

If you decide to act, you must act decisively and with speed. If you move slowly, your attacker can intercept your hand and disarm you. You cannot allow your attacker to see your knife before you draw it, or he or she can prepare for it and possibly disarm you. For this reason, once you decide to act, you must not delay. If you initiate self-defense actions, you must not stop until you are free from threat. If you decide to act, act with resolve, determination, and speed. Never threaten with a knife. Do not try intimidating your attacker. Everyone has seen the movie where the bad guy says, "You won't use that." He or she will not believe you will use it and will not be intimidated. An attacker should not see your knife until he or she feels it.

The techniques are simple, basic, and easy to learn. They follow the mind–body's genetic response to danger. Practicing the moves over a weekend, about four hours each day for two days, is enough for most people to get the moves into muscle memory. Once the moves are learned, you will be in a better position to act with speed and determination when threatened.

The accompanying photos demonstrate the method. Note that in each sequence, the action taken by the potential victim is in response to an aggressor having already attacked and gained potentially harmful physical contact. In each sequence the response to a single attacker is always directed to the hand or arm—with

Defensive Response to an Attempt to Seize

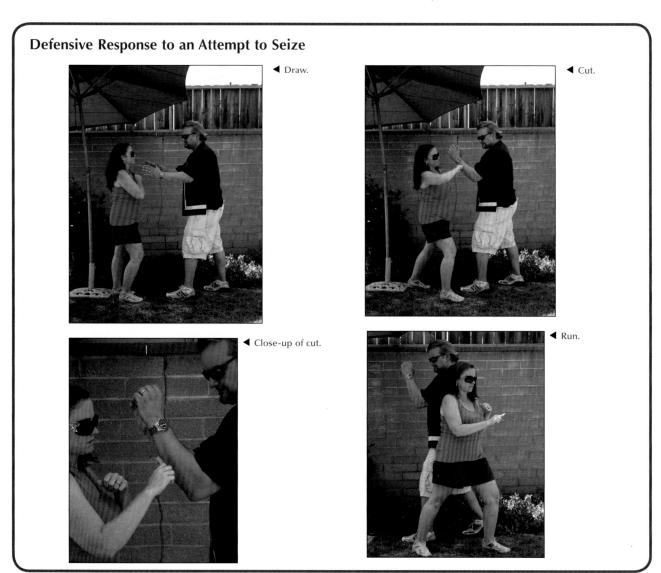

◀ Draw.

◀ Cut.

◀ Close-up of cut.

◀ Run.

the goal being to gain release from the attacker. Note also that after securing release, the potential victim at once runs.

There are only three moves to each sequence. These three moves can be applied in a wide variety of positions.

The moves are:

1. **Draw**
2. **Cut to release**
3. **Run**

First practice slowly, very slowly. Only practice with a training knife or appropriate substitute, such as a marker. Do not practice with live steel. After you have performed the moves to the point that each move is precise and comfortable, speed will come. With proper practice, the three moves eventually become one move: draw–cut–run.

If the assailant does not release after being cut on the hand or the arm, you may have to cut again. If so, try to only cut to the hand or arm. Do not cut other parts of the body if at all possible.

Note that all moves are shown with a small knife, in fact a tiny knife. The knife shown is a Spyderco Cricket. This is an effective self-defense knife. It opens with one hand, locks up solidly, and has a recurved point, which

Defensive Response to Being Seized

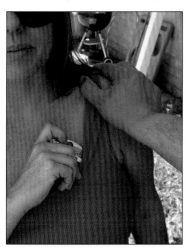 ◄ Draw.

 ◄ Cutting arm.

 ◄ Continuing cut across the chest.

 ◄ Run.

Defensive Response to Being Seized from Behind

▲ Draw.

▲ Cut.

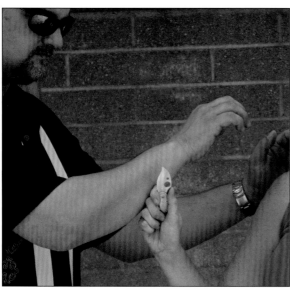

▲ Close-up of cut.

▲ Run.

is excellent for the slashes shown. Once this tiny knife is secure in your hand, it is difficult for an attacker to disarm you. Do not think you need something larger. If your intention is self-defense, you do not.

Note that we are only dealing with the possibility of being attacked by an unarmed person who possesses overwhelming force. Defending from one or more attackers armed with blunt instruments differs a little from the methods covered. The object in this instance is to "pull the fang" by disarming your assailant. The same is true for an untrained attacker with an edged weapon. Cut the hand holding the weapon—pulling the fang—then run.

What if a person skilled in the use of edged weapons attacks you? I hate to sound pessimistic, but it's unlikely an untrained person can defeat a trained one. Notice I said defeat. It might well be possible to escape a trained edged weapons person, which is really all we want.

These are the two possibilities, in order of desirability:

1. **Scram:** Run. Exit. Evacuate the area at once.
2. **Pull the fang:** Concentrate all your efforts to disarm your attacker. If you try this against an experienced person with an edged weapon, you will probably get cut. Probably more than once. Your attacker has seen your defense before. Your main chance is surprise and

Defensive Response to Front Stranglehold

 ◀ Draw.

 ◀ Cut.

 ◀ Run.

extreme aggression. Don't let him or her see your knife until he or she feels it. Then run.

Dealing with firearms is beyond the scope of this material. However, I will note that police officers take edged weapons very seriously, even when they have their weapons deployed. All is not lost if you are faced with an attacker armed with a firearm. People do take knives to gunfights and prevail.

You might surprise yourself if you actually practice these techniques with a partner or partners. Even a little practice can serve you well in a tight spot—if you are fully committed. If you are seriously interested in self-defense with the blade, I recommend you seek out an accomplished teacher of Eskrima in almost any of its variations. Formal Western fencing has, at its roots, very effective techniques. However, most fencing masters focus on competition, which is far removed from the reality of combat, or stage fencing, which has little or no relation to defensive methods.

I hope you never have to defend yourself in any way. If you do, I hope this information will be helpful.

Defensive Response to Stranglehold from Behind

◀ Draw.

◀ Cut.

◀ Run.

Defensive Response to Group Attack

◀ Draw.

◀ Cut 1.

◀ Cut 2.

◀ Cut 3.

◀ Turning from attackers.

◀ Run.

Defensive Response to Right Punch

◀ Draw.

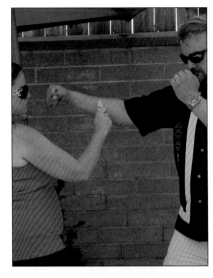

◀ Cut.

◀ Close-up of cut.

◀ Run.

Variation on Punch Response

◀ Draw.

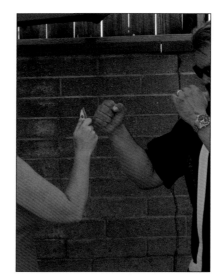

◀ Close-up of draw.

◀ Cut while
avoiding punch.

◀ Close-up of cut while
avoiding punch.

◀ Run.

Defensive Response to Weapon Hand Being Seized

◀ Hand is seized.

◀ Twist wrist to position blade.

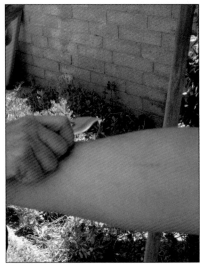

◀ Cut.

◀ Run.

PART FIVE:
FIELD REVIEWS OF A SELECTION OF
CURRENT TACTICAL KNIVES
WITH COMMENTS ON THEIR MAKERS

Chapter 22

Knife Reviews

My field reviews and background comments are based on personal experience and my observations of knives in use over a period of more than a half century, as well as on stories I have collected and verified. I am not a scientist, just a regular guy with a fair amount of irregular experience. I leave scientific studies to those who are qualified to conduct them, including experts at the companies that develop and make steel for cutlery and some makers who use scientific studies and publish their results, such as Fällkniven. I think the makers of knives and all those who stand behind them—foundries, heat treaters, mills, etc.—know more about what they are doing than I do. Therefore, my approach is to trust the maker to do his or her job, then try the knife out and see if it works for me under actual field conditions.

The tasks I undertake to review a particular knife are those that I or others I know have faced in the real world and are reflective of situations others might encounter. I do not set up conditions designed to destroy knives, nor do I continue stressing any knife to destruction. Anyone can destroy almost anything if he or she puts his or her mind to it. Testing to destruction is useful under controlled conditions and the observation of trained scientists or engineers, but that's not what we're up to here.

I know a few things about the use of knives and what does and does not work for certain applications. I review each knife as it comes from the maker for the

▲ Assortment of fixed blades stabbed into the hood of a car © Justin Ayres.

use the maker states it is intended. I use my common sense: I am not going to pound a folding knife, no matter how strong it may be, into a tree and climb onto the lateral surface of the knife, because I know it will break. Such use is beyond the limits of today's folder technology.

What I offer the prospective knife user is more than fifty years and many thousands of man-hours of real-world field use and careful observation. Scientific studies are useful tools, but they are not the real world. The real world is a place with so many variables that scientists have adapted terms, such as chaos theory and fuzzy logic, to account for certain aspects of our universe.

Many knifemakers have little in the way of real world experience in the use of tactical knives, or any realistic understanding of what is required of a knife that will be carried to war or used under survival conditions. Therefore, some knifemakers create and present to the market knives that will not serve in either instance. Fortunately, others have real-world experience or make it their business to work closely with those who do. They produce knives well-suited for extreme use.

I can't count how many times I've heard a knifemaker claim abuse when the knife he or she produced has been broken by a customer. A friend of mine once bought a new survival knife at a knife show. The knife was accidentally dropped when he was showing it

▲ Downward beat with the spine of Sabatier against a Cold Steel Laredo Bowie.

to another friend. The knife fell point down, hit the concrete floor of the convention center, and shattered into three pieces. When my friend took his brand new broken knife back to the maker, he was told that dropping a knife on concrete was abuse. The maker refused to replace it. In my view the knifemaker's response was absurd and inappropriate. The knife was sold as a survival knife, not a crystal wine glass. Any common kitchen knife can be dropped on the floor of a restaurant kitchen with no more damage than a minor ding, if any.

I have also heard knifemakers offer the following admonitions: use the right tool for the job; use a knife for a knife and a hammer for a hammer. Such advice is all well and good if you've got a toolbox to hand. It is patronizing, disingenuous, and totally useless advice for someone whose life is on the line. What if I don't have a Hooligan Tool to get me out of a burning building? I don't walk around with a crowbar in my belt. I do have a small fixed blade knife in my waistband. Can it get me out of a burning building if need be? A similar knife once did. I don't much care if the maker thinks it is abuse if I try and use it to save my life and the lives of others. Such advice is an insult to the intelligence of anyone in life-threatening circumstances. If you are under life-threatening pressure, you *will* use whatever tool comes to hand to save your life. That simple human fact seems to escape the attention of some knifemakers.

In addition to a military person or a civilian in a tough spot, having to use a knife as a pry bar or demolition tool, let's remember that tactical knives are also sometimes used as weapons. In response to a question I asked, a knifemaker who was selling combat and fighting knives told me that using a knife to defend oneself from an attacker in hand-to-hand combat places no more demands on a knife than dressing out a deer. That statement is most certainly and emphatically incorrect and clearly comes from someone who has never had to face an aggressive enemy bent on his destruction with noting more than an edged weapon to defend himself. Butchering a dead game animal and trying to defend your life from a determined foe have about as much in common as ping-pong and NFL football.

The person I often have in mind as I review tactical knives is the someone out there on the front with his heart in his mouth, sweating and praying that it's all going to turn out alright and that the knife he's depending on will do its job. If a knife is advertised as hard use or combat and fighting, the blade must be tough. It must not break under combat or other extreme conditions. A soldier cannot say to his enemy, "Please turn your head because I might miss and stab you in the helmet and break my nice, new knife." There are no niceties in mortal combat. There is only savagery, aggression, skill, and the will to live. Everything else, as they used to say in China, is "Look see never mind."

Here's some advice for knifemakers on a topic about which I know a little bit: if you're selling knives advertised as combat ready, make sure they are. If you're selling knives as survival knives, make sure they're fit to survive with. There's no bureau of standards for combat, survival, tactical—whatever you want to call them—knives. The maker's only standard is his skill and conscience. If you're marketing a knife as a combat knife, ask yourself this: would you want your child to go to war with the knife you made?

Review Methods and Goals

The Edge

Edge-holding looms large for many. It's well down on my list of priorities. First on my list of importance is the ability of the blade to take an edge. Not just any edge, not the kind of edge with which you might cut your Brie, not even a paper slicing edge. No, I want a fierce, wicked, scary dog edge, an edge sharper than a serpent's tooth. What I'm looking for ahead of any other quality is cutting ability, which is a product of the three critical elements discussed in an earlier chapter: geometry, heat treat, and steel.

As late as the eighties, maybe into the nineties, it was common to encounter knives, both factory and custom, with stainless blades that would mush out at the edge. Nothing could be done to get them sharp. It was also common to see knives with shallow, dubbed-on edges that needed to be reprofiled before they would take a proper edge. I haven't seen a knife like that from a major American manufacturer in some time. But I do still see knives that will barely take a paper-cutting edge. I don't use knives like that.

Toughness

I hope you will never be in combat of any kind, and I hope you will never have to use your tactical knife in any kind of extreme situation. But if you do find yourself in that place, your knife must not fail. Of course we expect different standards of toughness from a folder than a fixed blade, but even a tactical folder should be able to handle rough work.

Stainless Steel and Edge Holding

If a knife doesn't rust, that's a good thing, especially in the tropics. If a knife holds an edge during a lot of work, that's also a good thing, especially if you have a lot of work in front of you. But all that's extra. Sharp and tough is what I want first. Everything else is everything else.

Review Methods

There are a few more or less standard things I do to determine functionality in a knife and whether it is suitable for survival use, either wilderness or urban, or combat. To start, I simply use the knife for functions the maker states it is meant for, except for fighting. Based on experience, I simulate combat stress. Then I move on to several benchmarks I use to help my evaluations. From years of using knives, I can get a good idea of what kind of knife I have by actual field use and these benchmarks.

General woodworking, which includes cutting, chopping, and drilling, is basic. We also stab the tips into pine and snap them out laterally, a test all ABS members' knives must pass. I also make fuzz sticks, split kindling, and split and chop though two-by-fours.

▲ Downward beat with Ontario Knife Company's Old Hickory Sticker against Fällkniven A1.

▲ A close-up view of the HEST used as a climbing aid on an ancient stone wall on the island of Gozo.

▲ Justin Ayres hanging from a HEST wedged into ancient stone blocks on the island of Gozo.

Sometimes I make primitive bows, traps, and so on. Meat cutting, game dressing, and general food preparation are basic functions, and I do them all as a matter of daily life. While doing so, I cycle through a range of knives of all kinds. Cardboard not only dulls a knife quickly, it also will cause any knife that doesn't have ideal geometry to drag. I cut quite a bit of cardboard. Cutting hemp rope is something I picked up from the guys at the ABS. Hemp has a hard finish and it takes a sharp knife to cut it. A toothy edge will slice rope, a really sharp smooth edge will allow a push cut. We don't often cut the hanging rope as the ABS does, because this is as much a test of skill as it is of the knife. I consider making a hobo stove and opening canned food to be light field use, and so I often use this as a test.

In addition to general food preparation, slicing veggies and meat and so on, I also use a standard test I think of as the Attack of the Killer Tomatoes test. I once asked a custom knifemaker why his knife as delivered was not sharp enough to slice a ripe tomato. He replied that his knives were used by manly men who cut C4 (composition explosive plastic) with his knives, not wimps who spent their time in kitchens doing women's work. That may sound pretty macho to the inexperienced. But I've cut up enough C4 to blow up . . . well, lots of things. And I've mostly done so with a mess kit knife that had no more edge than a butter knife. We've even used popsicle sticks for that purpose. C4 has a composition similar to Silly Putty, that stuff kids play with. Inspired by the knifemaker's macho posturing, I decided to incorporate the Killer

▲ Preparing a fishing spear with the Mora knife.

▲ Using a baton with a Strider folder.

Tomato test into every knife evaluation. This demanding and highly technical test requires that the knife be able to slice ripe tomatoes without squishing them. Ripe tomatoes will squish if the knife is not sharp. If you have a knife that will accomplish this, you have a sharp knife. Making a knife that will slice tomatoes and also cut through walls and auto bodies without damage to the knife requires an uncommon level of sophistication on the part of a knifemaker.

If a knife is designated for fighting or combat by its maker, I will strike it on the back with another knife, as in a beat—similar to a parry—you might encounter in a blade-on-blade confrontation. I hit both the spine and the lateral surfaces. Usually, I use a Sabatier carbon steel chef's knife or an old Hickory Sticker as the impact knife, sometimes a KA-BAR. If your four-hundred-dollar custom combat and fighting knife will not stand up to this, you need to have a heart-to-heart talk with its maker. Ask him why a ten-buck kitchen knife is stronger than his purpose-designed knife.

Any knife billed as hard use will be used by me and my cohort to partially demo buildings, grind mortar from between concrete blocks, and cut through heavy sheet metal or steel doors and auto bodies. Why? Because today's conflict areas are often urban, and anyone, civilian or military, can find themselves in a building that comes down around them and traps them. You doubt that? Read the news from September 11, 2001. Heck, read the news anytime.

We test for lateral strength by bending the knife or by weight-bearing. The need for a knife that will bear the owner's weight in an emergency is desirable. It may not be always obtainable. We use this test with a large measure of caution and consideration for the owner's weight and the designed function of the knife. I do not think it's reasonable to expect a SAK to support the weight of a 270-pound linebacker. But it's well within reason to expect a survival and hard use knife to support the weight of an active 175-pound person. Limited lateral weight-bearing ability is not, in

my view, a deal killer. It's just that I want to know how much there is if I need it. Fällkniven's approach to this question is exemplary.

When I find knives that do all the things they should do within my understanding of their purpose, I consider them good to go. That's a term from my formative years with the paratroopers and Snake Eaters; it was the highest praise that could be offered, as in, "He's good to go."

I have been told that the things I do in my reviews amount to abuse. I do not abuse knives. If you advertise your creation as a collector's piece, I will treat it kindly and review it appropriately. Present your knife as a tool and weapon for the military, as a tactical knife, a combat or fighting knife, or a survival knife, and I will review it as it could be used and as similar knives have been used. I have also been told that no knives are meant to be used for such extreme functions or extreme conditions, even though many are advertised for exactly that use. Extreme use? I review for people who live in extreme conditions, who live out there on the edge, a place I used to call home.

• • • • • • • • • • • • • • • • • • •

The selection of knives in this book is not a complete listing of all quality tactical knives made today. In this, the second edition, we have been able to expand coverage, and we expect to expand our coverage even more in future editions. The knives selected are simply those I, and others I work with or know, have used in the field and I am comfortable recommending. If you do not see your favorite knife here, it does not necessarily mean it is not a good tactical knife. True, there are knives I have used that failed miserably. Those knives are not recommended. But don't read anything into that statement. There are thousands of knives available that I have not tried. If a knife is not mentioned, most likely it only means that I have not yet used it and so cannot comment on it.

▲ DPx HEST II being batoned into a seasoned oak log.

▲ Using fixed blades to chop wood.

Some of the knives are limited production, others are handmade, still others are from large factories. Not all are finished to the same standard. Many are made with premium materials; others are made to fit a budget. Whether finished to jewel-like quality or made to a basic factory standard, all performed as stated in the reviews.

I have personally worked with knives from all the companies below, some of them over a period of years. I have used at least one of each model I review. Many of my students in survival and Escape and Evasion classes have also used many of these knives. Quite a few knives were sent to active duty military and paramilitary, and those people reported back on their knives. I also solicit feedback from butchers, chefs, combat veterans, survival instructors, and others who use knives professionally. While we have not used all the various models these companies make, as that would amount to many thousands of knives, over time patterns emerge and empirical evidence accrues. We have used enough representative models from each of these companies to recommend their products with confidence. However, I advise you to try each knife you buy under field conditions before you rely on it.

When I was a young paratrooper, my buddies and I bet our lives on the skill and diligence of the riggers who packed our chutes. We trusted the riggers to pack our parachutes so they would not fail in use. But some did. There's no substitute for extensive testing.

Reviews

Al Mar Knives

PO Box 2295
Tualatin, OR 97062
www.almarknives.com

Although company founder Al Mar passed away some years ago, the company that bears his name continues. Many of the same models that Al designed are still being manufactured. The current management also makes variations on those original designs, such as their Lightweight series and an updated SERE folder, as well as some new designs in both folders and fixed blades.

▲ In the top left corner, the Al Mar Lightweight Eagle makes a good addition to your bug-out-bag.

The **Lightweight series** is a line of folders based on the original Eagle and Falcon, but with Micarta handles without bolsters. I used one of the Lightweight Eagles for some years; so has a family member who spends a good deal of time outdoors and has a reputation for being hard on his gear. We also used the Lightweight Eagle in some of my classes. While not designed for hard use, this folder stands up well under field use. It is also relatively inexpensive, considering its design heritage and overall quality. The four-inch blade of AUS-8 steel comes quite sharp from the factory and stays that way for a good length of time.

The **Eagle Talon** has a smooth black Micarta handle, a red chop signature on the blade, and a black spring clip. The design is a classic. It efficiently slices meat in

▲ The Al Mar Eagle with ivory Micarta handle—a truly civilized knife.

the kitchen and is just as capable at whittling a barbed wooden fishhook or a sharpened spear tip. It also crunched through one-inch hemp rope easily.

A newer model, the **Shrike**, seems to be designed for meat-cutting. The angle of the blade connecting to the slightly curved handle lends itself to deep slashing cuts, and the blade offers nearly zero resistance through the large muscle structure of a pork shoulder. It was more than capable at making kindling, rope cutting, and whittling tasks, as well. The handle is textured Micarta for a sure grip with slippery hands.

The updated **SERE 2000** model has stood up to hard use by many of my inexperienced students. The liner lock is solid and remains so even after they have used it to construct shelters with the use of a baton, which qualifies as hard use. The SERE 2000 suffered no damage of any kind during some weeks of use by a variety of students. The 3.6-inch blade is a modified spear

point made of VG-10 and is useful for a wide range of tasks. The scales are textured G-10. The comment most often heard about the SERE 2000 is that it's comfortable in the hand even after hours of work.

We have continued to use the SERE 2000 over the past few years. It has stood up well to continued hard use and rarely needs sharpening. Most importantly, it cuts very, very well. This particular spear point blade has proved its efficiency in use over time in field and shop work, as well as daily use. It sliced through the large muscle of a large pork shoulder roast like it was designed explicitly for that purpose. When used to punch holes through a tin can for a hobo stove, it was more than capable; with a strong, sure grip and a stiff, razor-sharp blade and point, it made short work of the task. The clip is secure and carries the folder in point up configuration. The SERE 2000 carries on the Al Mar tradition in a way that I think Al would be proud of.

▲ Al Mar SERE girdling a limb in preparation for making a bow stave.

Bark River Knives

6911 County 426 M.5 Road
Escanaba, MI 49829
www.barkriverknives.com
(906) 789-1801

Bark River is a family owned business whose stated goal is to produce the finest cutting tools with the emphasis on maximum performance. For Mike Stewart, the company founder, that means using the best steel for a particular knife, the best heat treat, the finest and most careful grinding, fitting, and shop work—and a convex edge. Bark River only produces convex edges; all BRK knives that I have seen have slim, scary-sharp convex edges.

During an extended journey a couple of years ago, due to a series of mishaps, most of our luggage went astray. For some weeks, the only gear I had was my ready bag and its contents and some stuff I picked up at a local bazaar. My only fixed blade was a **Bark River Necker II**, big brother to the Necker. When I first received the little knife, I had been intrigued by its grind, convex from spine to a thin, almost delicate looking edge with no secondary bevel, and had tossed it in my bag thinking I would try it and see how well it performed. The term razor sharp gets bandied about quite a bit, but this small, light, delicate-looking knife actually did have an edge about as sharp as an old-fashioned straight razor. I know that to be so because I when I first took it from its sheath, I had a klutz

▲ Bark River Necker II and Bark River Necker.

moment and shaved a layer of epidermis from the back of my thumb, which gave me an idea. I tried actually shaving with it. Yeah, I'm that kind of knife guy. I lathered up, and without even stropping, shaved—carefully. As the television commercials say, it was a smooth, clean shave. Well, no, actually that's an exaggeration. I did shave with it, but the edge dragged and the shave wasn't Gillette quality. But, hey—it shaved. Amazing really, a knife billed as an outdoorsman's tool, right out of the box with that kind of cutting—well, shaving—ability. Pretty cool, I thought, but it probably can't stand up to hard usage, not with that edge. I was wrong.

For about a month on a small island in the Mediterranean, using the little Necker II, I cut tough scrub for a beach hut and palm fronds to roof the hut. I cleaned fish and rabbits, split melons, and sliced and chopped vegetables. Later, on the Turkish coast, I used it to make a fish spear, to show some kids how to make a quickie bow, and to forage some wild vegetables. In Bulgaria, I sliced a mountain of pork ribs for a barbeque, split kindling and shaved fuzz sticks for fires, drilled holes in wood to make a fireboard for use with a drill, and cut staffs for two walking sticks to fend off village dogs. Along the way, I cut open boxes and packages, and in short, I used the little blade for everything a knife might be used for. During all this the edge held up, never rolled, and remained reasonably sharp, sharper than some knives come from the factory. No, it wouldn't shave after a month's use, but after a touch up on a chunk of sandstone (I didn't have anything else) and stropping on my belt, it was again working sharp.

Everyone in our group was attracted to the little blade, not just because it was a nice-looking knife, which it is, but also because it was so easy to use. That's one of the things about a really sharp edge—it makes cutting things easier and makes the work go faster. Everyone who tried it found the handle to be comfortable, although those of us with large hands found it to be a little on the slim side. It comes with a Kydex sheath, can be had with or without your choice of scales, and at two and a half ounces with scales is so light you don't notice you're carrying it, whether on a dog tag chain around your neck, in a pocket, or tucked away somewhere.

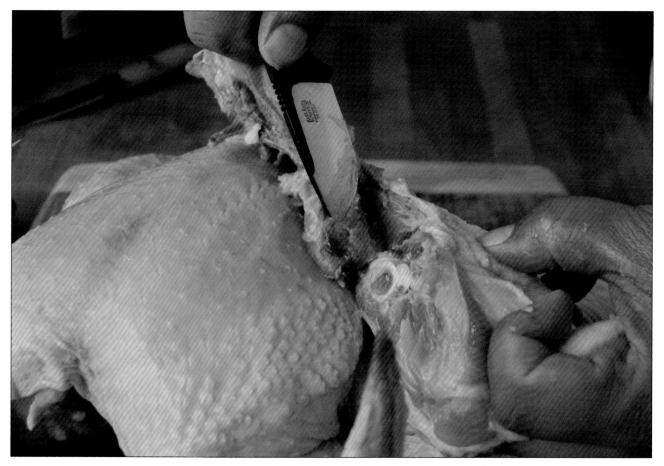

▲ Bark River Necker slicing cleanly through bone joints.

▲ Bark River Necker II deboning a whole chicken with ease.

The **Aurora** is Mike Stewart's personal design for an all-around bushcraft knife. It displays excellence in design and, like all the Bark Rivers I've seen, excellence in build quality. Its convex blade enables easy and controllable push cuts, supports the edge for batoning, gets into a cut aggressively, and has a centerline point allowing precise control. The handle is ergonomically contoured, does not slip, and is comfortable in hard use. Its balance is good, and it feels light and quick in hand. The pouch-type leather sheath provided is handsome, secures the knife well, carries comfortably, and has a loop for a firesteel. On a recent weekend, we used it to build a shelter, split kindling, make fuzz sticks, and ignite a fire with the firesteel. Then we split and quartered four chickens for grilling. Back home, we sliced up a pile of cardboard and cut hemp rope and an old rubber hose into one-inch sections. Through this, the Aurora held its edge as well as the Necker II. Although not billed as a survival knife, I think the Aurora is an excellent choice for a survival knife or a traveler's knife.

I look forward to using some of Bark River's larger knives. The small- and medium-sized ones have proven themselves in hard use over three or four years. I expect the bigger blades would also. The combination

▲ Bark River Aurora cutting a sapling.

▲ Bark River Aurora with a quickie bow.

of thin convex grind and all the other elements Mike Stewart has brought together in the Bark River brand produce excellent quality knives—ones I'd be confident using anywhere, anytime.

▲ Bravo Necker II batoning through a log.

Becker Knife & Tool Co.

KA-BAR
200 Homer St.
Olean, NY 14760
(716) 372-5952
www.kabar.com

The BK&T range of knives is well designed. All are made from 1095 Cro-Van steel. We have only had the opportunity to try out two knives from their range: the **Companion**, a stout utility knife, and the **Becker Necker**, an exceptionally well-designed little knife billed as a neck knife.

As I wrote in an earlier chapter, I think of the category commonly called neck knives as tiny tacticals, largely because I don't think the term neck knife, which only refers to a carry method, does much to define this type of knife. The **Becker Necker** is an excellent little utility knife and emergency weapon and tough enough to stand up to hard use; it's tactical in every sense of the word. We have batoned the Necker through hardwood and sheet metal and used it for everyday tasks. It took no damage from the hard use and, with its good blade design, was efficient in the kitchen.

With its 3.25-inch blade, overall 6.75-inch length, and three-ounce weight, the Necker is hardly notice-

▲ Becker Necker knife.

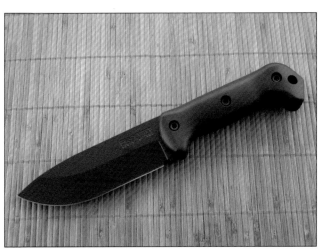

▲ Becker Companion BK2.

▲ Becker Model BK3.

able when worn. It has a functional skeleton handle and a flat ground blade with some useful belly and a strong point. The handle can be cord wrapped or, for the impatient, wrapped in duct tape. If you are handy, it would be fairly easy to put some thin scales on it. As a bonus extra, there is a bottle opener built into the heel, a feature some of the younger fellows in our group much appreciated. There's also a wire cutter, but it didn't get the same amount of use as the bottle opener. I like this little knife. There is another version offered in laminated steel that I look forward to trying.

The Necker comes with a plastic sheath designed to work with a metal clip, which I have not seen, or suspended from the neck, thus the name. Don't use the cord that comes with it to hang it around your neck. A nylon cord worn around the neck is an accident waiting to happen. Instead use a ball chain—as per Buck and Bud Nealy—which will break before injuring the wearer. Or wear it in the waistband, tucked into a sock, or in some other discreet place. But do wear it. It's a keeper.

◄ Becker Companion prying open a doorframe © Justin Ayres.

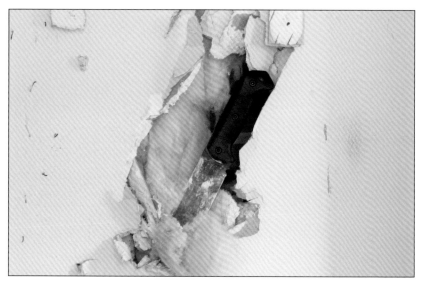

◄ Becker Companion BK2 cutting through Sheetrock wall and insulation © Justin Ayres.

▲ Side view of the Becker Tac Tool prying open the lock in a steel door © Justin Ayres.

▲ Becker Necker comes in handy for slicing limes.

The **Companion** is a pretty good chopper for having a relatively short blade of five-and-a-half inches. At a full pound in weight, it's a hefty little bulldog, but one that handles well. The point is fine enough for good work, the belly cuts smoothly, and the handle is comfortable—even when stabbing it into a heavy gauge steel door, which one of my companions did repeatedly; during this use it suffered no damage. BK&T bills the Companion as a sportsman's knife, useful for splitting kindling, dressing game, and slicing onions. It is good for all that. It's also as good a SERE knife as many that are advertised for that purpose.

Benchmade Knife Company, Inc.

300 Beavercreek Rd.
Oregon City, OR 97045
(800) 800-7427
www.benchmade.com

Les de Asis, CEO and founder of the Benchmade Knife Company in 1988, started his company as a result of his quest for a high quality butterfly knife. Butterfly knives, also known as balisongs, are folders distinguished by two handles that rotate around the tang, enclosing the blade when closed and locking up solidly when open. Anyone who has seen a martial arts movie will recognize the butterfly knife by the twirling, swirling, showy opening methods used, mainly in the movies.

Actually, there is a simple method of getting a butterfly open fast. Butterfly knives are actually an ingenious solution to the problem of constructing a folder that won't close on your hand. If you keep a firm grip on the opposing handles, the knife blade cannot close. Aside from all the martial arts tricks riding on the butterfly, it is a perfectly good everyday tool, one in daily use in the Philippines.

Like many American soldiers from World War II to today, I saw quite a few butterfly knives when I was knocking around South East Asia and the Philippines. None that I saw even approached the quality of those produced by Benchmade. In fact, Benchmade's **Bali-songs** are made so well that they redefine the design.

Of Philippine decent, de Asis was intrigued by the butterfly knife's roots in Philippine martial arts. De Asis turned to custom knifemakers to produce his Bali-song, and eventually started his own company, which was at first dedicated to the production of high-quality Bali-song knives. Later Benchmade branched out and developed a wide array of folders and fixed blades, many of them designed by talented custom knifemakers.

◄ Benchmade's trademark knife, the Bali-song.

◄ Another example of Benchmark's trademark knife, the Bali-song.

Benchmade is now an industry leader, well-known for innovation and quality and for producing a wide range of tactical folders, as well as some excellent fixed blades. And yes, you can still get an excellent Bali-song from the company. Benchmade's knives are produced to the highest standard of factory production and the company's warranty is second to none.

Some years ago, a young woman showed up at one of my wilderness survival classes without a knife. I loaned her a Benchmade **Walter Brend** design, a liner-lock folder with a slightly recurved blade that already had quite a few years of hard use on it. I touched up the edge for her, and she used it for the three-day course, batoning it through a small stand of saplings to make a shelter, cutting up a number ten can to make a hobo stove, splitting kindling, and preparing wild food we gathered.

After the course was over, she asked me if she could buy the knife. She was a college student on a scholarship majoring in wildlife biology and didn't have two nickels to rub together. Of course, I gave her the knife with my blessings. But first I sent it off to Benchmade to have the edge reset and generally cleaned up, fully expecting to receive a bill for the work. Instead, I received a refurbished folder with a new blade, and no bill for service. Over the years, I have found that this kind of exemplary service is business as usual for Benchmade. We have used a dozen or so different Benchmade designs over the years, and have never once had a problem with any of them.

The AXIS lock is a Benchmade innovation and generally considered to be one of the strongest folder locks yet developed. The AXIS has been in use for many years now and is employed on many different models. I have yet to see one fail.

The **Rukus**, a relatively new model, is a big beefy folder with a 4.25-inch blade and the AXIS lock. I used the Rukus for several months and asked some of my students to try it out. We all found it to be as useful as a daily carry folder as it is in the woods, albeit at 7.8 ounces, it's a tad heavy for anything but pants pocket carry or mounting on web gear. The Rukus has good blade geometry and S30V steel. The handle consists of black G-10 and olive Micarta scales and is comfortable in hand, even after hours of hard use. The Rukus is an exceptionally strong and useful tactical folder and

also available in a mini-version with a 3.4-inch blade, weighing only 5.9 ounces.

The **Nagara** is a slim, elegant folder with what Benchmade calls their Nak-Lok. It's classic 3.25-inch blade design and smooth anodized blue aluminum handle qualify the Nagara as a gentlemen's knife. Its performance on everything from meat to rope qualifies it as tactical. Two of my fellow knife testers wanted to

▲ Benchmade Rukus showing the AXIS lock.

▲ Benchmade Rukus being batoned.

keep it after they tested it. It's a beauty. If James Bond carried a folding knife, it would be the Nagara.

I'm currently experimenting with a Benchmade **940 Osborne**, a slim, handsome AXIS-lock folder with a 3.4-inch blade of S30V steel and what Benchmade calls a reverse tanto point. Its attractive green handles are of anodized aluminum with a bead-blasted finish. Its weight is a modest 2.9 ounces, which makes for an easy pocket carry. As I write, it is clipped to my shirt pocket—a place you wouldn't want to carry a heavier folder, such as the Rukus.

▲ Not only a gentlemen's knife, but a gentlewomen's knife, too—the Benchmade Nagara.

▲ Benchmade 940 Osborne with AXIS lock feels good in your hand.

▲ Not only pretty, but also quite adept at cutting through this hemp rope—Benchmade Nagara.

◄ Clip side of the Benchmade 940 Osborne.

▲ Benchmade 940 Osborne—excellent at handling this pesky hemp rope.

With its green handle, slim profile, and moderate size, Benchmade's 940 Osborne presents as a gentlemen's folder. Its has some nice metalwork along the spine, and it also doesn't appear to be particularly fierce. Actually, with its AXIS lock and S30V steel blade with a razor-sharp factory edge, it is a wolf in sheep's clothing. It probably won't alarm the clueless, yet will do a good bit of heavy work. In fact, the 940 Osborne fits my definition of a gentlemen's tactical folder and is deceptively tough and capable. I haven't spared the 940 in any of the field reviews, and it is still sharp, tight, and every bit as attractive as when it came out of the box. It cut hemp rope, which is notoriously hard to cut, with an easy push cut. After three years of daily use by one of my associates, the 940 Osborne still locks up solidly and only requires occasional sharpening. It shows signs of use but looks and works as good as new.

The **Griptilian** collection is a group of Benchmade folders all using the AXIS lock, a nonslip handle, and one fixed blade. More than one organization devoted to wilderness and emergency survival has designated one or another of Griptilians as its preferred folder for survival use. We have used one of the Griptilian folders and agree that it's a good choice as a survival folder, as well as being a handy everyday folder at an affordable price. The **151 Griptilian** fixed blade is a well-thought-out design, sturdy, and useful for just about anything a four-inch bladed straight knife could be used for.

The **140 Nimravus** is a fixed-blade with a 4.5-inch blade of 154CM or D2 tool steel, which is chosen by the buyer. I have used both and have found the D2 to be somewhat tougher when scraping through a cinder-block wall or field dressing a Honda. Both work well. The overall length of 9.45 inches makes for a compact package, and its weight of only 6.2 ounces brings it in at a lighter weight class than many folders. The Nim, as some of its users call it, is a full tang design made from one piece of steel with anodized aluminum scales. You can get it with a Molle compatible sheath, as many service people do, or the standard sheath.

I like the Nimravus a good deal. If I wanted to carry it concealed, I would get a simple sheath made up with a

▲ Benchmade Nimravus stabbed into the hood of a car © Justin Ayres.

◀ Benchmade Nimravus dealing with those tough mushrooms.

clip for carry inside the waistband. It would also be nice if Benchmade would consider making the Nim up with a plain, non-coated blade. Without the black finish, it would look like any ordinary belt knife. This is a compact, tough, handy little fixed blade and perfectly fits my definition of a traveler's knife and a survival knife. The blade geometry is quite good and works well for kitchen work, dressing game, wood carving, and the above mentioned extreme tasks, as well as others, such as pounding into a tree and using it as a weight-bearing device. You could probably rip open the door of a stuck elevator with it. The Nimravus is also available in a smaller version, the **Cub**, or with a tanto point.

As you can see in accompanying photographs, we used the Benchmade **158 CSKII**, along with some other knives, to help tear down a construction shack scheduled for demolition with permission from the owners. We cut through sheet metal walls, ripped through wallboard, stabbed and chopped into steel fire doors, and chopped through two-by-fours. Through all of this, the edge of the 1095 carbon steel six-inch clip point blade did not chip out and only rolled over a small amount without any serious deformation. The blade did lose much of its black coating, but that's merely cosmetic. The synthetic handle was comfortable, even without gloves and with my keyboard soft hands. A couple swipes across an India stone, and the blade was ready to go again. Although I must admit that our chef was a little taken aback at the appearance of the knife we gave him to prepare dinner. Never the

less, the CSK sliced tomatoes just fine. This is a good, solid fixed blade at a relatively low cost. It can be obtained with a plain blade or one with serrations at the hilt. Personally, I prefer the plain blade. The serrations did not work as well as the plain edge on sheet metal or on anything else, for that matter.

Benchmade also produces a line of top quality automatics. The **Infidel** model is an out-the-front automatic that looks delicate with its slender blade. Having had a good bit of experience with out-the-front switchblades and gravity knives, I had little confidence in the Infidel's lock strength when I received one for field-testing a few years ago. All of the out the front switchblades or gravity knives I had ever used were subject to lock failure with little pressure, including the famous World War II German paratrooper gravity knife, which is a hefty piece of work that happens to have a weak lock.

So, predictably, the first thing I did with the Infidel was to stab it forcefully into a tree, thinking the lock would fail, and that would be the end of a short field review. The lock held. Not only did the lock hold, the stab did not loosen the lock. Never one to give up, I stepped back from the long-suffering tree and executed a fencing thrust at about half speed and power. Skinned my hand a little, but no problem with the Infidel lock. Just to be difficult, I snapped the blade sideways; out popped a divot of pine with no damage to the blade. I have seen many knife tips break clean off when snapped out of wood, including some on expensive custom fixed blades.

◀ Close-up of Benchmade CSKII deconstructing a wall © Justin Ayres.

▲ Benchmade CSKII, a handy all-around tool to have in your bag.

▲ Benchmade Infidel—clean lines, easy open, and very sharp.

▲ Close-up of Benchmade Infidel slicing rib meat.

▲ Benchmade Infidel being tested against a pine log.

Okay, I thought, solid lock, strong blade, guess I'll have to revise my opinion of out-the-front folders. But how does it cut? One evening we had company and my wife tossed a few racks of ribs on the grill, a perfect opportunity to check out the Infidel's abilities. While cutting up a few dozen ribs into manageable size, I learned that the Infidel makes a dandy rib slicer. It also did fine on various vegetables. Over a period of some weeks, we used the Infidel to make a hobo stove, get up kindling, and whittle a rabbit stick. I'm pretty sure the knife's designer envisioned none of these tasks. I'm pleased to report that the Infidel is not delicate, works fine for general fieldwork, and cuts well indeed.

I have also found that this level of strength and quality is typical of Benchmade's other automatics, such as the **Presidio** series. The mentioned knives are only a small selection of the many excellent tactical folders and fixed blades offered by Benchmade, but they are models I can recommend from personal use. I'm confident that the rest of the Benchmade lineup is of the same quality.

Boker USA, Inc.

1550 Balsam Street
Lakewood, CO 80214
(800) 835-6433
www.boker.de/us

Boker is an old-line Solingen, Germany, knife company that was founded under a chestnut tree in the seventeenth century—thus the name. Since then, the company has made everything from scissors to sabers. Although Boker has changed hands since it was founded, the tradition of making fine knives continues. The company makes a wide range of just about every kind of knife.

Recently, I reviewed two of their models, the **Trance**, a Chad Los Banos designed frame-lock folder with a 2.75-inch AUS-8 blade, and a **Chad Los Banos fixed blade**. Both had a nice feel in the hand and performed well on light cutting jobs. The handles are comfortable and snug tight and secure in your hand. They're nice little knives at modest prices.

New for this edition, we've used the Fred Perrin Shark, distributed by Boker in the United States. This is yet another exceptional design from Fred Perrin. A tiny knife, so small it disappears in a wallet or pocket and

▲ The Fred Perrin–designed Shark, ready to travel.

little heavier than a simple chain when worn around the neck, the **Shark** will dress out small game, carve fuzz sticks, and in general serve as a tiny tactical. It was so easy to cut heavy cardboard with the Shark that it got away from me and cut a two-foot long slash with slight effort. An innocuous sliver of steel, the Shark is amazingly effective and useful.

Browning

One Browning Place
Arnold, MO 63010
(800) 322-4626
www.browning.com

In addition to their ranges of sporting and tactical knives, Browning makes the **Crowell/Barker Competition Knife**, so billed because it was designed by James Crowell and Reggie Barker, two men famous in the knife world as ABS Mastersmiths, and for winning many cutting competitions. I have no plans to enter a cutting competition, but I do pay attention to them to watch developments. This is a big knife, fifteen inches overall with a ten-inch blade, but it is not clunky or heavy. It has a tapered full tang handle and a distal tapered blade, is well balanced, and handles easily. Really, this is an affordable factory version of an ABS Mastersmith's blade, which would set you back the price of a good used car. The Crowell/Barker Competition Knife can be purchased for fewer than two hundred fifty dollars, and at that price, it's an incredible bargain.

▲ Browning Crowell/Barker Competition Knife Model 580 slicing through a seasoned oak log with ease.

▲ Clean cut while limbing a pine tree with the Browning Crowell/Barker Competition Knife Model 580.

This is a camp knife in the ABS style first put forth by the famous Bill Moran, a field knife that will handle anything with aplomb and ease. The Micara handle is comfortable, and it comes with a traditional leather sheath. But the best thing about this big blade is its cutting ability. It makes short work of any cutting or chopping job. We split a pile of seasoned oak chunks into barbeque-sized pieces with little effort and no baton. River cane, pine, wood crates and heavy fiberboard, fiberglass shed roofing, and sheet metal all fell before the Crowell/Barker. It's hefty compared to a ten-inch chef's knife; nevertheless, it sliced through a pork roast like it was designed for that purpose. Big knives come into their own when there's work to be done, especially in the field when there's no ax, machete, or other tools available, and this is a grand example of the big knife.

Buck Knives

660 South Lochsa Street
Post Falls, ID 83854-52000
(800) 326-2825
www.buckknives.com

Buck Knives is an American institution. Buck has been a family company since it was founded in 1902 by Hoyt Buck, a young blacksmith searching for a better way to temper steel. Hoyt made knives for the military during World War II, but the company has always been best known for making sportsmen's knives. It was Al Buck, Hoyt's son, who designed the Buck 110 Folding Hunter, which became famous and widely accepted by sportsmen across the country with its lockback and exceptional edge-holding. In fact, with more than forty years of production behind it, the Buck 110 has become a modern icon. Buck has also, over the past century, made a secure place for its fixed blades with hunters and outdoorsmen. More recently, Buck has entered the tactical knife field. The current range of tactical knives is about a dozen or so models, which includes folders and fixed blades, premium priced knives, and affordable knives.

The **Buck/Mayo Kaala**, with its 3.125-inch blade of S30V and weight of 1.9 ounces, is sized like and marketed as a neck knife, and with its lightweight nylon sheath, which is no bigger than needed, and beaded chain carry system, it carries well around the neck. It spite of the neck knife tag, I think of this knife as one of the tiny tacticals. The chain Buck uses is like the dog tag chains worn in the military. This is a good thing, because the neck chain on dog tags is designed to be reasonably strong but to break under a hard pull, thereby avoiding the possibility of neck sprain or an even more severe injury, such as death. It bothers me a great deal when I see people wearing neck knives suspended with parachute cord, which has a breaking strength of five hundred and fifty pounds. Paracord is strong enough to strangle a person or break a neck;

▲ Buck/Mayo Kaala cleanly slices through a lime.

▲ Buck/Mayo Kaala neck knife cutting hemp rope.

in fact, it has been used for that purpose in combat. The cord can get caught on anything during a fall with unpleasant results. The dog tag chain is the best idea I've yet seen for suspending a neck knife.

The Kaala itself performs well out of its weight class. Like a select few tiny tacticals mentioned elsewhere, it is a useful working tool rather than an emergency only device. It's able to stand up to being batoned through hardwood and retain its edge afterward to slice a pile of meat and veggies. It's little; it's shiny; it's cute. It is not a toy.

Buck's **Nighthawk** has been around for a few years and is a good knife. Its 6.5-inch blade of 420 HC has been well-thought-out, as has the whole package, and will serve a military person as a weapon and tool and the sportsman as an outdoor knife. The nonslip nylon handle is comfortable, even after an hour or so of woodworking. This is a well-designed, well-made knife at a reasonable price and a good value.

We used the **Bravo Rescue** as its name implies, as a rescue tool. It worked as advertised, which I consider high praise in today's world of hyperbole. The chisel ground 3.5-inch blade of 420HC penetrated a heavy-duty steel fire door with little tip deformation, which is surprising since this particular door was of heavier

gauge steel than others we have used. (All the knives we tested on this door required some solid baton work to penetrate.) The blade was also useful for general tasks and the handle was comfortable in hand. The seatbelt cutter in the heel of the handle cuts like it was designed for the job. The tester slid the seatbelt of a junked car in the slot and put very little pressure on it and before he realized it he had cut through the seatbelt. Zip, and the job was done—a good tool for an EMT or anyone who likes to be prepared.

Everyone knows that Buck warrantees all their knives with a warranty that's second to none. Right? Well, if you didn't know, now you do.

Bud Nealy Knifemaker
125 Raccoon Way
Stroudsburg, PA 18360
(570) 402-1018
www.budnealyknifemaker.com

Bud Nealy is widely recognized as being in the top rank of knifemakers in the world, and his work is sought by many collectors of note. Bud is also famous in certain circles for making some of the finest fixed blades available for covert operators, clandestine

▲ Buck Bravo cutting through sheet metal in field testing © Justin Ayres.

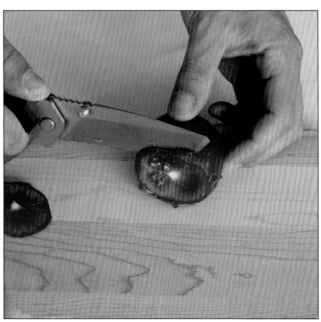

▲ After the sheet metal test, Buck Bravo takes on the tomato.

agents, and military and law enforcement personal. His patented and unique sheath system, the MCS (Multi-Concealment Sheath) is in use, along with his knives, by people in the previously mentioned occupations, as well as SWAT and RAID teams, US Embassy guards, EMT personnel, reporters, NGO workers, and other international travelers who work in dangerous environments.

Bud's knives are tough, effective, and purpose-designed. They are also little gems made with such craft, grace, and style that on first viewing you might think they're too nice to actually use; I thought that the first time I handled a Bud Nealy knife, his **Pesh-Kabz**. But the jewel-like appearance is deceptive. All of Bud's knives are tough beyond expectations, and they come with an edge that bites. That Pesh-Kabz still looked as nice as new after being batoned through a car body and used to rip out a plaster wall. After it pulled down Sheetrock, solid plaster, and lath, it was still sharp. You

▲ Bud Nealy Amoebas, which are hollow ground © Bud Nealy.

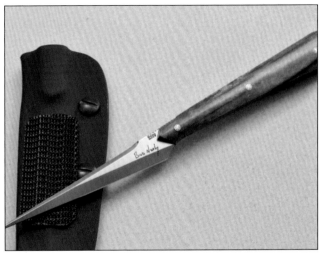

▲ Bud Nealy Vendetta with a giraffe bone handle © Bud Nealy.

▲ Bud Nealy Beladau with a purpleheart wood handle © Bud Nealy.

▲ Hollow ground Bud Nealy Battle Blade with a dyed maple burl handle © Bud Nealy.

can count on all of Bud Nealy's knives performing like that, at the top of the tough use knife category.

Nealy uses premium materials in all of his knives: CPM 154, S30V, and textured G10 on his basic line, if you can call anything Bud Nealy does basic. In his custom work, he also uses Mike Norris's stainless clad Damascus, mastodon ivory, and various luxury materials to make everything from carving sets and steak knives to one-of-a-kind camp knives and daggers.

Generally speaking, Bud prefers CPM 154. He wrote that CPM 154 is "a dream. It's tough. It holds an edge and finishes out beautifully." He thinks S30V is "overkill for a self-defense knife, but if you make a living cutting up barbed wire and get paid by the minute, then maybe it's worthwhile." Given that Bud is known for using high-tech steels, I was a little surprised to see him write that in his view, "a clad damascus steel blade, with a homogenous edge and some high and low carbon layers on the outside, is the way to go." There are quite a few other makers who agree with Bud on this point. These days, Bud is doing more flat grinding because "it makes a much better cutting edge, stronger too." Many experts will agree on this point, as well.

The **Aikuchi** was the first knife Bud designed for the MCS System. It began what was to become a pattern with his tactical designs—looking back at ancient knives used for tactical purposes and adapting those designs for modern usage and materials. Knives of similar design were used for piercing leather armor in fifteenth century Japan. The spine of the knife retains the same width from hilt to tip, which is a chisel grind, offering maximum strength and piercing ability. Available in 3.5- or 5-inch blade lengths, the Aikuchi is an effective and handsome interpretation of an ancient classic.

The same is true of the **Kinzhal**, an Eastern European and Turkish design that has been in use for centuries. If you spend some time in the Balkans, especially in rural areas and if you befriend the right people, you will find that many men still carry versions of the ancient Kinzhal somewhere about their persons. But probably

▲ Bud Nealy Aikuchi with earthtone Grip-Skin © Bud Nealy.

▲ Bud Nealy Aikuchi clad in Mike Norris Damascus © Bud Nealy.

not a Bud Nealy model unless they're part of the special operations community.

Without any hesitation, Bud donated one of his tough little knives to my Knives for Soldiers program. It wound up in the hands of an officer in Special Forces who was working in nonuniformed service in Bosnia and needed a covert knife. This officer told me he preferred small fixed blades to any folder because if he needed a knife as a weapon, that meant things had gone wrong, and he wanted to be able to get his knife out fast, and he didn't want to depend on any opening or locking system. If memory serves, he used the term, "grab and stab." He said his Nealy was the best knife of any kind he had ever owned. He liked the Nealy knife so much, he bought another one. He carries them both in deep cover and is never without them.

The Kinzhal spear point, which is almost needle point, is a little more versatile than the Aikuchi's chisel grind for general tasks and provides overall service as an excellent utility knife, as well as an effective small combat knife. It's available with a 3.5- or 5-inch blade. I'm not the only person who has cut through a car body with a Bud Nealy knife. An undercover agent in Norway was carrying a five-inch bladed Kinzhal when his Toyota van went off a bridge and into an icy river during a chase. Trapped, he used the Nealy Kinzhal to cut an opening in the roof and escape.

The **Pesh-Kabz** design, which introduced me to Bud Nealy's knives, has an armor-piercing point adapted from an ancient Persian design and a spine that is the same width from hilt to point. The slightly dropped edge serves as a guard and provides some extra utility. As noted above, the Pesh-Kabz I used pierced an auto body with no damage. I would suspect that it could also pierce body armor, ancient or modern, with equal ease. Like all the knives I review, I also tried out the

▲ Bud Nealy Pesh-Kabz slicing zucchini.

Pesh-Kabz in the kitchen. The results were surprising, as I thought the armor-piercing point might get in the way of slicing and dicing on a cutting board. But the Pesh-Kabz sliced through zucchini and assorted steaks, chops, and ribs as easily as it went through that Honda.

The **Cave Bear** is a little more muscular than the others in the Nealy MCS collection, but hardly what you could call overweight. Made with the same materials as the rest of the series, it's just as handy, just as tough, and just as nice in appearance.

▲ Bud Nealy Cave Bear slicing hemp rope.

Bud has continued to refine his **MCS System**—now **MCS II**—over the years. A complete description of the system is available on his website, but in short, the system uses Kydex and Dual-Lock an industrial grade, adhesive-backed material that can be stuck securely to almost any surface on one side. On the other side is an interlocking material stronger than Velcro and, to my eye, thinner. There are also attachments that provide a wide variety of carrying positions. They include a breast pocket flap for the inside pocket of a sport coat and a special clip for the inside of a waistband, boot, or armhole of a jacket.

Also included is a thirty-pound test ball chain for neck carry, which is a particularly intelligent way to wear a neck knife. The chain is strong enough to secure the knife but not so strong it can serve as an inadvertent noose in the event of a fall or an impromptu garrote for an assailant. There seem to be a hundred or so ways to carry the knife with the MCS System, including: inverted, horizontal, multi-angled waistband, and others. Bud says that a number of undercover law enforcement officers have gone through pat downs without having their Nealy knife in its MCS sheath discovered. I believe him.

Even without the ingenious MCS System, Nealy's MCS knives can slip into any place you can think of and some you might not. While on undercover duty, the Special Forces officer I mentioned earlier uses

▲ Bud Nealy Cave Bear II with a hollow ground © Bud Nealy.

▲ Bud Nealy Kwaito with Mike Norris ladder pattern Damascus © Bud Nealy.

▲ Bud Nealy Mini-Kwaito with a Kydex neck sheath © Bud Nealy.

▲ Bud Nealy Kwaito II © Bud Nealy.

only the sheaths, without the MCS attachments, so he can conceal and secure them completely inside his underwear. First he tried the sheaths with just clips, but they stuck out. Then he simply taped the sheaths to his body.

Bud also produces a collection of knives he calls **Multi-Adventure Knives**. In the same general size and weight range and made from the same materials as his MCS collection, these knives are a little more focused on outdoor use. The names of the knives in this collection—**Appenzell**, **Pocono**, **Appalachian Trail**, and so on—certainly suggest the outdoors, and I'm sure any backpacker, fisherman, hunter, or trail runner would be well served by any of them. They have all the virtues of their somewhat more martial cousins, and the blade

▲ Bud Nealy PK-21 with a gemsbok handle © Bud Nealy.

designs do indeed look a little more utilitarian. These knives are as good to go as the MCS System knives.

Virtually all of Bud's knives fit into the category I call traveler's knives, which I defined in an earlier chapter. In fact, both the MCS and the Multi-Adventure series help define the category: unobtrusive to the point of virtual invisibility, tough enough to use for anything you'd use a knife for, and useful as an all-around tool. Clip one to your trunks and it's a diver's knife, step up to a cutting board and you're ready to prepare dinner, baton it through a log to get up some kindling, or rip your way out of a burning building. Nealy's knives definitely prove that a knife doesn't have to be a thick pry bar to be tough.

Since the first edition of this book, I've been working with a Bud Nealy **X-Cel**, a perfectly proportioned small knife with a four-inch blade and four-inch handle that nestles comfortably into the heel of my hand. Everything I've written so far of Bud's knives applies to this deceptively simple blade. It's so light you forget you're carrying it, the MCS System sheath provides comfortable carry, and the little wonder cuts and rips through resistant materials with little effort. The X-Cel surprised one my co-testers when he slashed a double thickness of heavy cardboard and the blade penetrated both layers; it slipped through and created a clean two-foot long gash with little effort. Shawn, the butcher who helps us evaluate knives, used it to bone out a

▲ Bud Nealy X-Cels with a cocobolo handle, Grip Guard G-10 handle, and silver G-10 handle © Bud Nealy.

chicken. He said, "This blade just cuts right down to the bone."

In addition to their features as utility knives, these are ideal knives for clandestine agents or anyone out there on the edge. If Bud's knives had been available back in the day, as my sons refer to my past, I would have carried a couple of them in place of the boot knives I carried then. That's the best possible recommendation I can offer.

Busse Combat Knife Co.

11651 County Rd. 12
Wauseon, OH 43567
(419) 923-6471
www.bussecombat.com

Busse uses a proprietary steel, INFI, as well as a proprietary heat-treat method. The company attributes many virtues to this steel, including the ability to bend to 35 degrees and spring back to true, along with exceptional edge retention and an absence of edge damage in hard use. We have substantiated these claims in actual field use.

The first Busse knife I used, the **Steel Heart**, cut through a couple of auto bodies like they were tinfoil; there was no damage to the edge or blade after doing so. Over a few weeks, we used the Steel Heart for about anything you would use a big knife for, including chopping a stack of seasoned oak for the fire. It

▲ (left to right) Wayne Goddard Custom, Puma interchangeable blade, Ontario Bagwell Gambler, Chris Reeve Nakona, Becker Bowie, Busse Steel Heart, and Cold Steel Trailmaster © Justin Ayres.

was tough. It stayed sharp. With a nine-inch blade, the balance forward, and quite a bit of belly, it was an excellent chopper. And—unusual for such a big knife—it would also slice ham so thin you could see light through it.

All Busse knives come from the factory with a sharp convex grind, which supports the edge, stays sharp for a long time, and enables them to cut through resistant mediums with ease. A convex edge also gets into a deep cut with less resistance than some other grinds.

In recent testing we have used: **Busse's BOSS Jack LE** with a 6.25-inch blade, **Choiless Anorexic BOSS Street** with a 4.25-inch blade, **Nuclear Meltdown Fusion Battle Mistress** with an 11-inch blade, and the **Nuclear Meltdown Special Forces Natural Outlaw** with an 8.25-inch blade. In addition to my work with them, all were field tested by three experienced outdoorsmen, one of them a former butcher who commented, "The bigger Busse knives go through bone like a cleaver, and both the big and small ones cut meat as well as my professional knives. This is unusual. Most of the knives you give me to try have edges too thick for meat cutting. They're still sharp, too, no touch up." One of the others, a combat veteran, said he "wished he had a Busse BOSS Jack LE during his last deployment."

Both of the big knives were used for cutting a variety of materials. They performed as well as any big knife we've used, and far better than most. The **Battle Mistress** chops better than the **Outlaw** simply because it's a bigger blade. Both were exceptional knives in every respect. I would have no trouble with walking into the wilderness with only the Battle Mistress as my big blade, although I would prefer one without a choil.

The smaller Busse knives cut as well as the big knives—that is, very well. We've cut everything from old rubber hose to sheet metal with these knives, and they keep on performing. We batoned the 6.25-inch bladed **BOSS Jack LE** into a pine tree, and one of the guys, who weighs 235 pounds, stood on it. No bend, no break, no problem. We also pried open a military issue ammo box without damaging the blade.

▲ Busse BOSS Jack fixed blade.

I've been using the Busse 4.25-inch bladed **Choiless Anorexic BOSS Street** daily. It is, as you might have figured out from the name, the only Busse without a choil. The absence of a choil allowed me to use this knife effectively for press and shear cuts when building a field expedient shelter for a survival class I was teaching and to demonstrate notching. It has a smooth convex grind from spine to edge and no secondary grind, which helps it to cut deep into most materials with only slight resistance. Like all Busse knives, this has a full tang. It also has comfortable, textured Micarta scales.

During the past couple of months, I've cut about ten feet of two-inch hemp rope into one-inch sections, sliced up a mountain of cardboard, used it in the kitchen to cut meat and vegetables, and in the field for woodworking, splitting kindling with a baton, and so on. I haven't touched it to a stone, and have only stropped it on a leather strap once, and it will still

▲ Busse Choiless Anorexic BOSS Street fixed blade.

▲ Busse Choiless Anorexic BOSS Street after cutting a mountain of cardboard.

slice tissue paper. I drove this one point first into a tree and asked our large friend to stand on it. He did. No problem. This is a tough knife that performs at the top of its class. It is an excellent traveler's knife and small survival knife. Another inch of blade and it might well be the fabled "one knife," but with a four-inch blade and a five-inch full tang handle, it's a tad handle heavy. I'd like it better if it lost an inch of handle or added an inch of blade. Still, if I had a sheath for it, I might well take it with me on my next trip. Busse makes high performing, tough blades, and all are good to go.

NOTE: Busse knives do NOT come with sheaths. These knives deserve a good sheath, which the customer will have to supply.

Chris Reeve Knives

2949 S. Victory View Way
Boise, Idaho 83709
(208) 375-0367
www.chrisreeve.com

Over the past decade, I've put in many hours using Chris Reeve knives to demonstrate survival techniques, and I've loaned Chris Reeve knives to many of my students. We've worked with almost every model the company makes. During all that time, I have never once seen a poorly made Chris Reeve knife or one that failed to perform as advertised. The Chris Reeve reputation for quality is second to none. Every detail of every knife made by this company is carefully thought

of and attended to. Even a seemingly minor thing, such as the adhesive used to cement the inlays in the Sebenza—a folder Chris Reeve is famous for designing—is given deep and thoughtful consideration.

At a trade show a couple of years ago, Chris explained to me how he had searched technical journals from a dozen industries and carried out a series of controlled experiments to come up with the perfect adhesive to secure the inlays on his Sebenzas. This adhesive is used to cement racks of lights onto scaffolding on airport runways and has a holding strength of thousands of pounds in all kinds of weather conditions. That the company owner was willing to invest days in searching out such a seemingly minor item, and take the time to explain it to a journalist, is indicative of the quality of the man and the company. If he

▲ Chris Reeve Sebenza—minimalist industrial chic.

▲ Field expedient baton being used on a Chris Reeve Nakona to baton through the hood of the car. © Justin Ayres.

puts that much thought into glue, how much thought and care do you think he invests in steel, design, heat treating, grinding, and finishing?

Chris Reeve may be best known for his iconic **Sebenza**, a folder that embodies minimalist industrial chic and is as much a work of modern art as it is a functional knife. Nothing needs to be added. Nothing can be taken away. I get the feeling that Reeve read the story about Michelangelo. When asked how he visualized a statue in a block of marble, he said that he just took away everything that wasn't the statue. The Sebenza is nothing but knife, one of the very best.

Chris Reeve upped the strength ante in tactical folder lock strength with his development of the integral lock for the Sebenza, which was first offered to the public in 1987. The integral lock is a piece of the frame that snaps into place when the blade is opened and makes a solid lock. In addition, the lock is also secured by the grip of the person holding the knife. The lock is not dependent on grip; the mechanics of it are plenty solid. However, as an added security measure, if a firm grip is maintained, the blade cannot close.

The Sebenza has evolved a bit over the past couple of decades. New versions are only a little different from the original. Trends and fashions have been ignored in favor of steady, incremental improvement. The steel has been changed as new steels have been introduced to the industry—after Reeve applied his usual rigorous research and testing to determine if the new steels were really an improvement. But the core design is basically the same, as is the concept behind it. Sebenza is a Zulu word meaning "work." And work is what it does—day after day, year after year, the Sebenza just keeps on working.

The current classic iteration, the **Sebenza 21**, has the same 3.7-inch blade, only now the steel is S30V. The blades are tumbled, or stonewashed, to give them a smooth, understated finish. The titanium handles are sandblasted. Phosphor bronze thrust washers ride against the oversized pivot bearings, which ensures long life, smooth opening, and extra strength at the blade handle joint. The whole package, which weighs 4.7 ounces, is put together with nifty screws made of 303 stainless.

Before I could correct his technique, I saw a new student swing his baton at a Sebenza like he was

▲ Sebenza Classic being batoned through a sapling, like passing through butter.

▲ Chris Reeve Sebenza being batoned into a two-by-two.

▲ Chris Reeve Sebenza with wood inlay handle being batoned into a two-by-two.

trying for a home run. No damage. One kid used a Sebenza and a baton to cut enough saplings for a four-person shelter in about twenty minutes of non-stop cutting and tapping. The knife just went through saplings like they were butter. I've used Sebenzas for everything a folding knife could be used for, and for some it shouldn't, off and on for a decade or so. You can rely on a Sebenza.

There's also a small Sebenza with a 2.9-inch blade that weighs in at only three ounces. It's as tough as the larger knife and easier to fit in a suit pocket. I think of the small Sebenza as a gentlemen's tactical. If you have it in your pocket and the party gets boring, you could just wander outside and keep on walking, right up into the hills, where you could put up a shelter using your little folder, maybe make a few traps to catch breakfast, and just relax, watch the moon, and think about what a good idea it was to leave that party and have your little knife with you.

Also available are a series of decorated and engraved Sebenzas in both sizes and some other models of folders. Some are offered with Damascus blades. They're all very nice.

Since the first edition of this book, Chris Reeve has discontinued his One Piece Range. However, he does still make fixed blades, including the official knife awarded to those who graduate today's Q Course at the Special Warfare Center. It is known to the US Army Special Forces as the Yarborough and to everyone else as the **Green Beret Knife**. As you might imagine of a knife that was selected by active duty serving SF soldiers, the Green Beret Knife and its smaller brother will do anything a special warfare operator could expect of a knife. Available with either a 7-inch or 5.5-inch blade of KG Gun-Koted CPMS30V, the knives were designed by well-known knifemaker and designer Bill Harsey with function and manufacturing input from Chris Reeve. A civilian version without a serial number, is available to the public. My students and I tried out the seven-inch version over an extended period. This is an excellent knife.

The **Professional Soldier** is a relative newcomer to the Chris Reeve lineup. Designed in collaboration with Bill Harsey for a group of SF soldiers, it is a small, solid, deceptively simple looking one-piece, flat frame fixed blade. With its 3.3-inch blade and an overall length of 7.5 inches, it is small and light enough, at 3 ounces, to tuck into a pocket, sock, or just about anywhere. Like the Green Beret Knife, it's made of Gun-Koted CPM S30V. Mine arrived sharp enough to

▲ Chris Reeve Green Beret cutting a two-by-four.

▲ Chris Reeve Green Beret splitting a two-by-two with ease.

easily shave hair and stayed that way through about a month of daily use, which included some woodwork on hardwoods, as well as the usual stuff—you know, cutting Sheetrock to size, slicing tomatoes, and so on. Even then, it wasn't really what you would call dull. It's just that I like my knives sharp. A quick touch up on the Spyderco Tri-Angle sharpener brought the edge back.

▲ Chris Reeve Professional Soldier.

▲ Chris Reeve Professional Soldier doing double duty making a hobo stove.

This is a well-conceived, well-designed, and well-made little knife. During manufacturing, it was tumbled or polished and has no sharp edges, making it comfortable in hand. The frame cutout works as a shackle wrench and contributes to its light weight and good balance. Balance is something I find conspicuously lacking in many neck knives, although I think of this knife as a tiny tactical. The Professional Soldier is an actual working blade, as opposed to a use-it-only-in-an-emergency knife. It's also a slick hideout. I like this little tough guy very much.

Cold Steel, Inc.

6060 Nicolle St.
Ventura, CA 93003
(800) 255-4716
www.coldsteel.com

Cold Steel first came to public recognition about twenty years ago with its Tanto, a fixed blade with a tanto point and a nonslip handle. Building on that success, Lynn C. Thompson, the president and founder of the company, expanded his product range, and now Cold Steel has one of the largest selections of tactically oriented knives on the market. From affordable to premium prices and from daggers to kukris, there seems to be something for everyone in the Cold Steel shop.

When asked to donate knives to troops serving in war zones, Cold Steel was one of the companies that responded with no delay. Some of the knives they donated were **Survival Rescue Knives** (SRKs). We've worked with a number of the SRKs over the years and have found them to be good solid working blades. We have also sent quite a few of them to troops serving overseas, both donated by Cold Steel and from private purchase—something we would not have done if we didn't think they were functional, reliable knives. The SRK's six-inch AUS-8A blade is .1875-inch thick and has a black Teflon coat. It has a clip point, and the overall blade design is useful for everything from dressing game to levering open an ammo box. The handle is non-slip Kraton and nicely sized at 4.75 inches, which brings the knife in at 10.75 inches overall, a good handy size. There is a lower guard that serves to keep the hand safe if it should slip, which is unlikely given the nature of the handle material. I have noticed that many sportsmen also chose the SRK, which is understandable given its overall balance of useful features and lack of anything that would impede performance. The SRK is a good all-around fixed blade available at a price most military people can afford.

▲ Cold Steel Trail Master ready for outdoor adventures.

▲ Cold Steel SRK slicing cucumbers.

Some years ago, we tested a **Trail Master Bowie** in Cold Steel's O-1 High Carbon steel. It came with a .3125-inch thick, 9.5-inch long blade and a Kraton handle, and it weighed in at about a pound. One of the Trail Master's key features is a convex edge, which allowed it to chop through the hood of a wrecked Honda with little effort and then, with no touch up, slice various vegetables for soup. We also chopped our way through a stack of downed wood and in general used it as you would a survival knife.

In the Bowie knife chapter I wrote that a good Bowie makes an efficient wilderness bush knife. This is a knife that proves that point. Although shorter than a machete and lighter than a hatchet, it chops so well that a baton becomes redundant. This allows for faster work when, for example, you need to get up some kindling for a fire and construct a shelter before a storm comes in. Due to its pronounced belly, you might want to have along a smaller knife to clean small game more efficiently, but the Trail Master will also take care of

that job if needed. The Trail Master is a good Bowie. Actually, considering that it's a factory-produced knife, it's an excellent Bowie.

With its 10.5-inch blade and sharpened clip, Cold Steel bills the **Laredo Bowie** as being more weapon-oriented than the Trail Master. Well, maybe so. I can see that it is a better weapon. But the Laredo works fine for me as an outdoor knife, and in some ways I like it better than the Trail Master for wilderness work.

There are two things that make it the better choice for me. First, it has a sharper point with less belly, which I find better for all-around use. Second, it weighs an ounce or so less then the Trail Master, but it has a longer blade. These two things give it a balance I like better. It has more whip, which translates to being faster in the hand and chopping better. I have no doubt the Laredo would make a fearsome weapon, fully capable of disarming an enemy in the right hands.

I tried out the laminated **Laredo San Mai** model. San Mai is a Cold Steel trademarked steel that I found to be tough and, at least in this configuration, to have excellent cutting abilities. I went to work with it along a stream while clearing out some undergrowth. Then I gave it to a young friend and asked him to try his hand with it. He used it pretty hard during three days we spent together in the nearby mountains. He also used a dozen or so other knives I had brought along to review. When we were on our way home, I asked

▲ Cold Steel Laredo Bowie.

▲ Cold Steel Laredo Bowie slashed through a limb with one swing.

▲ Cold Steel Laredo Bowie crossing blades with a Sabatier chef's knife.

him, "Which knife would you choose, out of all these knives, if you could only have one knife if you're in the mountains for a month and will have to provide everything for yourself?" After a long thoughtful pause he said, "It would have to be that [Laredo] Bowie. It would save time. I could make a shelter and get firewood in like . . . 10 percent of the time it would take with a little knife. And the point is good enough to skin a squirrel. Besides, no one who sees me in the mountains would freak out at its size like they would in town."

Cold Steel's Laredo is an excellent example of the Bowie knife and clearly demonstrates the value of the Bowie. Either of the Cold Steel Bowies will do the job and clearly demonstrate that a nine-to ten-inch blade, if properly set up, will outperform medium-sized blades of six to seven inches.

The **Bushmaster** is a great value. It's a survival knife that actually works and only costs about the price of a case of beer or a few bottles of wine. We used it in the bush to chop and clear some underbrush, and we then stripped bark from a sapling for a quickie bow and split kindling. Then, using a pole we cut with the Bushmaster, we fitted the hollow handle onto the pole and were able to easily cut fruit from branches that grew about ten feet from the ground. The Bushmaster is lightweight, has a thin seven-inch carbon steel blade, and has good edge geometry. I would be willing to bet that if Cold Steel offered a version with a nine-inch blade, it would sell well.

▲ Cold Steel Bushman—a handy knife to have in the bush.

Columbia River Knife & Tool

18348 SW 126th Place
Tualatin, OR 97062
(800) 891-3100
www.crkt.com

CRKT, with Douglas B. Flagg at the helm, makes a wide range of knives for sport and work, but here we are mainly concerned with their professional knives, which are designed and made with the needs of the serving military and related occupations in mind. The Professional Collection draws on the expertise of veterans and knife designers who have expertise in tactical knives. That expertise shows in the collection. These are knives that would be of use to those on the ground in hard places.

A few years ago, when I started my Knives for Soldiers donation program, I called Doug and asked him if he would consider donating a knife to a needy serving solider in Iraq or another combat zone. Three days later, the UPS guy dropped off a large box. When I opened it, I found a box full of knives from CRKT's Professional Collection—not one or two knives, a large box full of knives. Some people step back when asked to do something that costs them; others step up. Douglas B. Flagg stepped up and gave to men and women who truly needed professional knives.

Their **M16** folding tactical series, designed by former paratrooper Kit Carson (yes, that's his real name), is famous among the troops. They are some of the most popular knives sold at the PX, and for good reason. Well-designed and well-executed to be everyday tools and emergency weapons, every model in this series is exactly that. The troops use them for everything from opening boxes, packages, and MREs (Meals Ready to

▲ CRKT Desert Tact Group (top to bottom): M16-14ZSF, M16-13ZM, M16-1-4D © CRKT.

▲ CRKT M21 slicing cardboard.

◄ CRKT M21-04G folder with an extra safety lock.

Eat—three lies in one name, according to the troops) to cutting rope and nylon strapping. Since they carry them all the time, they are available as emergency weapons.

I am sometimes asked by active duty service people to recommend a knife that fits the following criteria: a folder, so it's convenient to have on their person at all times; tough enough to stand up to generally harsh field use; designed so that it can be used as a weapon if needed; and affordable on an enlisted person's salary. The M16 series is the one I most often recommend.

The two M16 models have Zytel handles and a rigid InterFrame build with 420J2 stainless liners and back spacers. Blades are AUS 4 stainless with a bead blasted finish.

The **13ZM Military** has a 3.5-inch spear point blade and weighs only 3.5 ounces. The **14ZSF Special Forces** has a 3.8-inch blade and features two Carson Flippers, which make a hilt when the blade is open. The **14D Desert Big Dog** has a textured aluminum frame and a 3.8-inch blade. All models come with two clips and extra screws, allowing four different positions for carry, and CRKT's patented AutoLAWKS safety, which locks the folders up solid when open.

Columbia River Knife & Tool also makes good solid fixed blades at a price our guys in uniform can afford. Although first conceived and designed as a weapon with its 4.5-inch blade and fierce tapered tip, take a look at the photos to see the **C/K Dragon** model in action as a field tool. From hobo stoves to woodwork and food prep, the Dragon did fine.

The **Elishewitz F.T.W.S.** (For Those Who Serve) was designed by noted custom knife designer Allen Elishewitz. With a background in martial arts and service in the military, Elishewitz knows what works in the field. The 6.3-inch fixed blade of SK 5 carbon steel

▲ CRKT Dragon ready for a job.

▲ CRKT Dragon easily cutting through a can for a hobo stove.

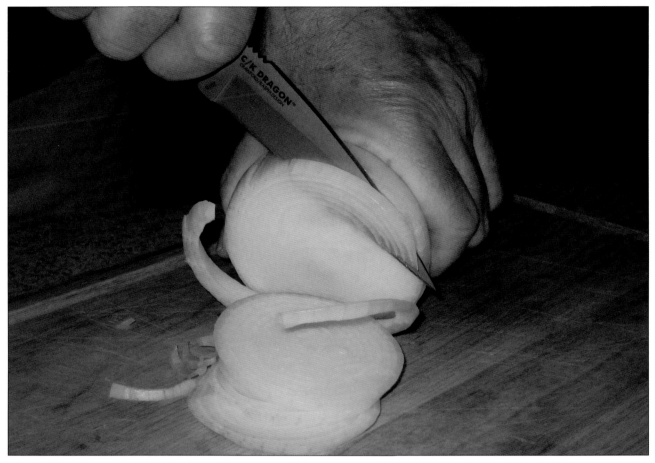

▲ CRKT Dragon doing kitchen duty.

has a spear point and a 4-inch chisel grind on the back for chopping. We used the F.T.W.S. to help take apart a building, cutting through Sheetrock, studs, and a steel door. We didn't need to use the back chisel grind. There was no noticeable damage to the blade or the handle, in spite of some enthusiastic but unschooled baton work by one young fellow who assisted.

The **Hissatsu** and Hissatsu Folder are designed by James Williams, a former US Army officer and martial arts instructor who has trained tactical law enforcement and military personal in close quarter combat methods using the system of military tactical strategy, which Williams himself developed. The Hissatsu is a fixed blade single-purpose knife for use in close combat, a purpose for which it is totally functional. The Hissatsu's seven-inch blade of 440A came be-careful-ouch sharp from the factory. At 7.9 ounces, it is light-

▲ CRKT Elishewitz F.T.W.S.

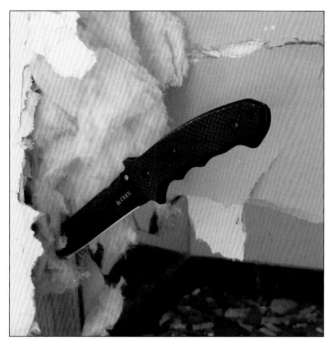

▲ CRKT Elishewitz cutting through Sheetrock and studs © Justin Ayres.

▲ The CRKT Hissatsu sliced through an entire chicken, bones and all, with one stroke.

weight, well-balanced, and fast handling. The Japanese styled blade penetrates and cuts roasts and ribs like it is going through whipped cream. The handle emulates the traditional Japanese ray skin with a non-slip Kraton surface. I've used some fairly expensive Japanese blades over the years, and I'd say the Hissatsu is a bargain in that it emulates the performance of expensive hard-to-get blades.

The **Hissatsu Folder's** ability to penetrate both hard and soft material has to be seen to be believed. I watched Williams's DVD, which shows him stabbing the folder into what appears to be plywood with full force. The blade penetrated up to the hilt. Frankly, I was more than a little apprehensive about trying to duplicate this feat with a folder. I need not have been. The blade locks up solid and didn't loosen a bit during a series of hard stabs into a tree. The Hissatsu Folder

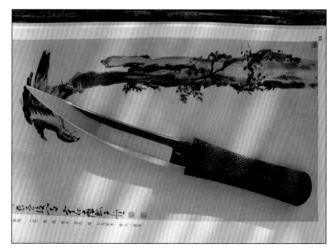

▲ CRKT Hissatsu—well-balanced and pleasing to the eye.

▲ CRKT Hissatsu Folder.

is a good companion to the fixed blade and both will well serve their purpose.

Bearing the same DNA as the Hissatsu and also designed by James Williams are two new CRKT models, the **Shinbu** with a 9.25-inch blade, and the **Sakimori,** with a 5.75-inch blade; both are beautifully executed renditions of classic Japanese blades. These are weapons—deadly efficient weapons. They are not meant for wood chopping or kitchen or general usage. These are single-purpose blades that I evalu-

▲ CRKT Shinbu Wakizachi.

▲ CRKT Sakimori Tanto.

ated as edged weapons. I can tell you this: I am not an expert in the use of Japanese blades, but I do have some experience with edged weapons, and I wouldn't want to face a capable user of one of these blades with anything less. They both come nicely boxed in wood and velvet, fitting the tradition from which they spring.

CRKT is also now making the **Sting**, a model designed by A.G. Russell some years ago and named for Frodo's famous blade in the *Lord of the Rings* books. The Sting is a dandy little dagger and comes with a forearm sheath secured with Velcro.

We've been using the **Eros** and the **Eros II** for the past year or so. Both are terrific little framelock folders with needle-sharp points, good sharp edges, and utility that defies their size and elegant appearance. The Eros II is an excellent tiny tactical, and the Eros, somewhat larger, is a solid tactical in gentlemen's folder dress.

▲ CRKT Eros II on KP duty.

Condor Tool & Knife

7557 West Sand Lake Rd #106
Orlando, FL 32819
(407) 354-3488
www.condortk.com

Condor Tool & Knife's roots go deep. First started in 1787 in Solingen, Germany, as Gebr. Weyersberg Company, they made swords, knives, agricultural tools, and household cutlery. In 1964, the company formed IMACASA with a new factory in Santa Ana, El Salvador.

Today, IMACASA is one of the largest machete and shovel manufacturers in the world. In 2004, IMACASA developed a top quality line of tools and knives for the North American and European markets: Condor Tool & Knife. This history shows in their products.

As a result of working and traveling for many years in Mexico and Central America, I'm familiar with the importance of the machete for the Latin American *campesino*, a farmer or country person. The machete is an all-purpose tool that is used daily and harder than any such tool is likely to be used in the United States. (It is also sometimes a weapon—one that is brutally effective and can cause fearsome, deadly wounds.) The machete is not only the farmer's all-purpose tool, it is the indispensable tool of the tropic jungle traveler and is used by everyone who ventures far from a road in Latin America. The *campesino* is careful with his hard-earned money and will not buy a machete that is not top quality or overpriced. To say that Condor's knives and tools are made in the same factory as that which produces machetes popular in Latin America is high praise.

The Condor products we have used, from bushcraft knives to barongs and goloks—designs of which were derived from Asian jungle knives—have been of uniformly excellent quality and value. Made from well-tempered, 1075 high-carbon steel that has served generations of soldiers, explorers, outdoorsmen, and farmers, and with comfortable wood or synthetic handles, I would be hard-pressed to tell readers where they could find a better bargain for outdoor hard use blades. Condor's steel won't hold an edge like today's high-tech steels and alloys, but it also doesn't require a diamond hone to an maintain the edge.

I've seen workers in sugarcane fields carry a stone in one hand and a machete in the other, and they give their edge a quick stoke on the stone every half hour or so to keep the edge toothy sharp, which makes cutting easier and reduces their workload. All the Condor blades we have used hold their edge for a good length of time and come up to an aggressive sharp with no more than a few quick strokes on a stone.

Condor's **Bushcraft Basic Knife** has a comfy wood handle, a blade with a lot of belly, and a full tang. When driven into a tree, it was strong enough for a two-hundred-pound guy to do a pull-up on; we tried it, no problem. The belly of the blade proved its worth in general usage. A little more point would have been welcome, but in knife design everything is a compromise, and this is a good one. The leather sheath holds the knife securely and is unusually nice for a knife in this price range. Condor's offering would be a good option for the bushcrafter or woodsperson looking for a handy and robust camp tool at a bargain price.

The **Barong Machete** has a leaf-shaped fourteen-inch blade with a wicked point and a well-beveled and sharp edge. It performs well, chopping through thick brush, reeds, and saplings with ease. Barongs are the favorite jungle tool of the Philippines, and with good reason. During my time in those islands, I saw the barong used by seamen, as well as by every rural man, to kill and dress large fish, one about as big as our twenty-foot boat. Condor's iteration of the barong is of higher quality than all but a few hand-forged blades I used while in the Philippines. Its leather sheath is sturdy but requires the user to push the blade firmly and deeply to secure it.

With its eleven-inch weight-forward blade, the **Pack Golok Knife** is small enough to be carried in a daypack until needed. Its double snapped leather sheath carries it comfortably and securely on the belt while in use. This hefty little chopper will make short work of hardwood, as well as tropical vegetation; it's a lot of chopping ability in a relatively small package with comfortable hardwood scales.

▲ Condor Matagai ready for action.

▲ Condor Golok with leather sheath.

The **Matagi Knife** is an interesting variation on the hollow-handle survival knife concept. Made from one piece of steel with no weak spots, a person so inclined could stash a fair amount of small items in the cord-wrapped handle, then secure them quickly with duct tape. This is perhaps not an elegant approach, but a functional one. The eleven-inch straight blade has a good belly and a sharp enough point to do small work. This is a good design—uncluttered, versatile, sturdy, and at the modest price, truly a bargain.

▲ Condor Barong hollow-handle knife.

Condor's recreation of the **Hudson Bay Knife**, which was originally used by fur trappers and traded to Native Americans for more than a century, is a faithful and functional, even handsome, take on a design that was held in high regard in the not too distant past by those who spent most of their lives in the North American forest. Its 8.5-inch blade works well for a wide range of outdoor work, and its smooth hardwood scales make for a comfortable grip whether chopping, slicing, scrapping, or whittling—a classic blade as good today as in the past.

Condor produces classic blades in honest and well-proven carbon steel at affordable prices. With a little care, carbon steel blades are easy to maintain—I never see rusted machetes in the humid tropics—and easily sharpened. They have served as field knives and working blades for many, many years, and I see no reason why they shouldn't continue to do so. I would have no hesitation in taking to the field with a Condor blade.

▲ Condor Hudson Bay Knife with an eight-and-a-half inch blade—an all-around useful tool.

Crawford Knives, LLC

205 N. Center Drive
West Memphis, AR 72301
(870) 732-2452
www.crawfordknives.com

Pat Crawford has been making knives for more than thirty years—very good ones. Many of his tactical

▲ The Point Guard © SharpbyCoop.com.

▲ Pat Crawford Dragon fixed blade designed by Bob Kasper © PointSeven Studio.

◄ Pat Crawford Perfigo Folder with a four-and-a-half inch Damascus steel blade, and mammoth tooth handle, which was designed by Bob Kasper © PointSeven Studio.

folders are in use by the military and law enforcement, mostly the plain ones with bead-blasted finishes that are known for their quality, durability, and all-around good design. However, Pat may be best known for his tactical gentlemen's folders, which are every bit as functional as their workday cousins. There are gentlemen's tacticals and then there are Pat Crawford gentlemen's tacticals, which occupy a place of their own in the tactical world.

The average gentlemen's knife is one you would feel okay taking out in polite company, say at a garden party to slice the cake. Pat's are dressed for the presidential ball, or to appear with Daniel Craig when he shows up at the Academy Awards. Take out a Pat Crawford tactical folder to slice the cake at that garden party, and you'll likely be mobbed by the ladies who will want to take it, home with them. Anyway, the guys are going to lust after it, too. Pat's folders are just drop-dead gorgeous. But under all the fancy dress beats

▲ Crawford Marauder Folder © PointSeven Studio.

the heart of a back alley fighter. There is something inherently attractive about the combination, as if Beau Brummel, the best-dressed man at court, were also the deadliest duelist.

In some recent correspondence, Pat wrote, "We started doing fancy decoration on our combat knives as our customers requested it. It started with people wanting a little decoration. Then it grew to the point where we are making combat knives that are works of art. But underneath, they are still combat knives."

Daniel Winkler Knives

P.O. Box 2166
Blowing Rock, NC 28605
(828) 295-9156
www.winklerknives.com

Daniel Winkler occupies a unique place in tactical cutlery today. He is the only ABS Mastersmith I know of who has for years specialized in knives and toma-

▲ Mini Triumph Raider Folder © PointSeven Studio.

▲ Two matching Kasper 21 folders, one with a four-inch blade and one with a three-inch blade, stainless steel Damascus blade and bolsters, mammoth ivory handle, and titanium liners© Pat Crawford.

▲ Pat Crawford Kasper folders, four-inch blades with titanium handles © Pat Crawford.

hawks of the colonial period, and now he brings that expertise and coconsciousness to the creation of war-ready knives for the special operations community.

Daniel Winkler is perhaps best known for his creation of period correct knives and tomahawks for the film *The Last Of the Mohicans*. In an earlier chapter, I wrote that the long knives of early America were our

country's first tactical fixed blades. Daniel has done even more research on this topic than I and agrees with that statement. "Nothing could be more tactical than the fight to settle our country," he said in a recent interview.

▲ Daniel Winkler Hawkeye Belt Knife, forged 1080 blade of seven inches, overall length of eleven-and-a-half inches, bone handle with rawhide thong wrap, color bands, and sheath by Karen Shook © Daniel Winkler.

▲ Daniel Winkler Uncas Belt Knife, forged 1080 blade of seven inches, overall length of eleven-and-a-half inches, bone handle with braintan deer hide thong, and a wrap sheath by Karen Shook © Daniel Winkler.

Daniel draws inspiration from knives used by Rogers' Rangers and other ranger units—which were, in effect, our country's first special operations units—and creates knives for today's special operations units at Fort Bragg and Virginia Beach. The creations from Winkler's forge are made one at a time to custom order. Knives bearing the logo Winkler II are made with considerable handwork, but also with the use of modern production methods.

To get a better understanding of the man and his methods, here is an excerpt from recent correspondence from him:

> I have great respect for many of today's "tactical cutlery" manufacturers. The designs and innovations developed by these companies are to be commended. However . . . my direction is a little different. The designs I produce are directed by history and the currents needs of our nation's most elite warriors. I have no desire to reinvent the wheel, just adjust it a little.

The genesis of Winkler II knives was only a few years ago when Daniel was contacted by a military Special Operations team to design and make a specialized tomahawk to be used as a combination combat or breaching tool. The special operations community had been using Winkler hawks and knives since the First Gulf War. But now, satisfied that Winkler's concepts and cutting instruments worked, they wanted more production and they wanted knives for issue to special warfare units. To meet the demand, Winkler went to computer-controlled water-jet-cutting of his tapered tang blanks. Doing so enabled him to produce a product with the virtues of his hand-forged blades but in larger quantities.

The two most popular models with the special operations community so far are the **WK II Belt Knife** and the **WK II Field Knife**. Both designs were developed with input and requests from active duty SOF operators and Naval Special Warfare Units. There was also input from an operator with an extensive background in Sayat, a martial art similar to Eskrima. Both knives are made of 1080 and both are .1875-inch thick. Heat treat brings the 1080 in at 58 Rockwell.

The Field Knife has a 5.75-inch blade and measures 10.5 inches overall. The Belt Knife comes in a little shorter with a 4.5-inch blade and 8.75 inches overall. Optional handle materials include: G10, Micarta, wood, or recycled rubber. The Belt Knife I reviewed had scales of recycled rubber, the Field Knife scales of G10.

Sheaths are leather-covered Kydex with a simple, flat, compact, idiot-proof, virtually unbreakable, ingenious attachment that allows for a vertical or horizontal carry. Or they can be used with a Molle adaptor. Individuals and units choose one or the other of the two knives based on personal preference. Some prefer the larger knife, which is a little better adapted to field chores, as well as combat usage. Others prefer a more compact knife that is easier to carry and access. The blade finish is Caswell blackener that looks similar to a parkerized finish. The finish will wear with use, but will still protect the blade and leave it a medium gray color.

▲ Daniel Winkler Field Knife with leather sheath and 1080 steel © Daniel Winkler.

▲ Daniel Winkler Hawkeye Belt Knife with a seven-inch forged 1080 blade, overall length of eleven-and-a-half inches, bone handle with a rawhide thong wrap, color bands, and sheath by Karen Shook © Daniel Winkler.

▲ Daniel Winkler Belt Knife about to cut hemp rope.

I recently posed the "if you only had one knife" question to two people whom I called on to help with evaluations. A Recon Marine about to leave for his third tour of Iraq said, "Dude. It's that little knife with the funky handle. That blade is the bomb." He was referring to Daniel Winkler's Belt Knife with recycled tire scales.

A professional butcher—a guy who spends eight hours a day taking apart beef carcasses—said, "No question. That little black knife." He too was referring to Winkler's Belt Knife. "It cuts so much more efficiently than anything else I've tried here that it would make my work easier . . . it cuts as well as my work knives."

I like both of these knives very much. If I were in service today, I might well choose one of these knives as my everyday carry. The designs are sensible and useful. The execution is top notch. The flat ground blades do not hang up in wood or other dense materials. They cut through meat, as well as any thin-bladed kitchen knife. They are seriously tough and will serve as survival and Escape and Evasion tools just as well as any commercially available knives I am aware of and far better than most. They are well-balanced for use as weapons. The nonslip grips do not in fact slip, even when hands are wet or greasy. In short, they are excellent all-around knives for special operators or anyone else who lives life on the edge and might need a knife to keep him or her from going over.

To the inexperienced eye, the Winkler II knives might look a little tame with their dropped edges

▲ Daniel Winkler Field Knife testing its hemp rope cutting ability.

they resemble chef's knives. What few realize is that the dropped edge has been in use from ancient times on many weapons. The slightly dropped edge provides a built-in guard, and if the maker knows what he is about, it can be balanced for both utility and weapon usage. In these two deceptively simple knives, we see no saw teeth, no tanto points, no swooping curves or deep hollow grinds. Instead we see classic designs that a Roman centurion, a Viking raider, or a Rogers' Ranger would recognize. Those who have used knives as tools, emergency devices, and weapons, and who have observed carefully and thought deeply will recognize these knives for what they are: a unique fusion of modern materials and time proven design. Both the Field Knife and the

Belt Knife are part of a small group of exceptional performers, as are the men who have chosen to use them in harm's way.

The **WK II S.A.R.** was designed for search and rescue teams. With an overall length of slightly more than nine inches, this is a handy-sized fixed blade that will unobtrusively ride on a belt in the sheath that comes with it and be easily accessible for emergencies. The steel is 154CM; the handles are Micarta or rubber, customer's choice; the blade coating is Caswell or camo. Toughness is Winkler II, which is fast becoming a standard for hard use knives. Serrations on the spine are designed for cutting fiber, as in seatbelts, with ease, and there is an effective glass breaker pommel. This is such an efficient and potentially life saving tool that I'd like to see the Winkler II S.A.R. became standard issue for S.A.R. teams.

The **WK II Spike** has a 5.25-inch blade and an overall length of 10 inches. This knife was designed in response to reports from the field with requests for a knife that will do things other than cut, such as breaking, pounding, and prying. The spike of the name is at the butt and is meant to do all of those things, saving the blade and edge for cutting. Handles and blade coating are the usual Winkler II options.

Both the S.A.R. and the Spike possess all the Winkler II virtues: inspired, classic, and effective design; extraordinary toughness without thickness, weight, and bulk; edges beveled to allow cutting highly resistant materials without deformation; and a total package—heat treat, geometry, steel—that makes a superior blade. Another feature that stands out with all Winkler II knives is their overall balance, the relationship between blade and handle, and the well-proportioned handles. All tangs are tapered, which helps to place the balance of the knife where it belongs. Some makers seem to think that oversized handles are required for a field knife. This is not so. If you look carefully at Randall knives, which are some of the best balanced and easy-to-handle knives being made, you will find that their handles are, on average, about half an inch shorter than many similar knives made today; for example on the Randalls Model 1, handles are adjusted for blade size. This

results in a handle and knife that better lends itself to manipulation and balances better for all use. This is also true of many knives made before the current era. Some other makers use the same size handle for all their knives regardless of blade length, resulting in handle heavy or otherwise out of balance knives. I don't know if Dan has studied Randalls, or if he draws the inspiration for his handles from the colonial era that he has studied in depth, or if he's working from his own innate sense of proportion and balance; but he has hit the sweet spot in knife balance and handling with all the Winkler II knives I have used.

The Belt Knife is a particular favorite of mine, it demonstrates this balance well. Its proportions are to knives what the golden mean is to art: a standard of harmony and function. Its 4.75-inch blade is balanced by a tapered tang and an overall length of 9.5 inches. This places the balance point right at the index finger, which is where it should be for this type of knife. The Belt Knife's weight of six to seven ounces, depending on handle material, is less than that of some tactical folders; its strength and overall utility is light-years beyond any folder. At present, I'm working with a Belt Knife with maple scales and the Caswell finish. With its flat, leather-covered Kydex sheath, it rides out of the way on my belt. As this Belt Knife—and most other Winkler II knives—is set up, it is optimized for extreme use, mostly, I would think, by special ops team mem-

▲ Variations of Daniel Winkler Belt Knives with leather sheaths and 1080 steel © Daniel Winkler.

▲ Variations of Daniel Winkler Field Knives with leather sheaths and 1080 steel © Daniel Winkler.

bers. If you would like a version more suited for, say, civilian wilderness use, I would suggest asking Dan to make you one without blade coating; this is better for dressing game, cutting meat, and so on. The Winkler II range continues to develop and expand, and I look forward to what Dan will come up with next.

DPx Gear

(888) 233-3924
www.dpxgear.com

Robert Young Pelton, the well-known adventurer, filmmaker, and author of several bestselling books—including *Licensed to Kill*, *The World's Most Dangerous Places*, and *Come Back Alive*—has spent a good bit of his life in places most people wouldn't visit with a free round-trip first class ticket and an 82nd Airborne Division fire team as bodyguards. War zones, low intensity conflict areas, failed states, developing nation dictatorships, pestilent swamps, parched deserts, and places where guys with AKs and bad attitudes hang out are home to RYP, as he prefers to be addressed.

His first design, the **DPx HEST** (Hostile Environment Survival Tool) reflects that experience, as do all of his later designs. The original DPx HEST is made from 1095 carbon steel. We tried one out over a period of about two years. The DPx HEST has a number of features that I was initially not so sure about: a wire beaker, a bottle opener, and a mini-pry bar on the butt. Generally speaking, I'm not a fan of multipurpose knives, except for the SAK, which I view as a small toolbox rather than a knife. Also, I was concerned that the bottle opener, which is a notch on top of the blade, would make for a stress riser and lead to blade failure. To test that hypothesis, one of my younger students obliged me by trying out the DPx HEST as a climbing device. After stabbing the point into a pine tree he levered himself upwards into the lower branches. No problem. Wanting to try something a little harder, he batoned the blade into the tree truck about two inches, then put all of his 175 pounds on the lateral plane and walked up the side of the tree. No problem. The blade did flex at the bottle opener notch but went back to true as soon as his weight was removed.

I couldn't figure out what to pry with the little pry bar, so I decided to use it as a scraper. Five minutes of working on the mortar between two concrete blocks resulted in no damage to the knife and demonstrated that the little lip could serve as an effective escape tool. If we had scraped away the mortar around one edge of the steel door of the shack we were taking apart, instead of a concrete block, any reasonably fit person could wedge in their fingers, get a good grip, and rip the doorframe and door out of its mounting. The hollow space under the removable scales has

▲ DPx Gear HEST folder and HEST fixed blade, tool, and luggage tag.

▲ A close-up view of DPx HEST wedged into ancient stone blocks on the island of Gozo.

▲ Justin Ayres supporting his weight using the DPx HEST fixed blade in ancient stone blocks on the island of Gozo.

▲ Mortar scraped away using the built-in pry bar of DPx HEST © Justin Ayres.

room for a couple of Ben Franklins, a few hundred Euro notes, and a small sparker, good things to have in an emergency. Cash can solve quite a few survival problems, and you can always use it as tinder to get a fire started.

You might think that such a short, thick blade would be a poor slicer, but not so. The little blade did just fine at helping to prepare dinner, and that was after a hard day at demolition duty and no touch up on a stone. We didn't have occasion to break any wire, but many bottles of beer were opened successfully at day's end with the DPx HEST. The DPx HEST is an excellent example of a traveler's knife.

Since that beginning, DPx Gear has expanded their product line. The **DPx HEST II** is now available in Niolox tool steel and a variety of finishes. This version has a slightly slimmer blade profile, cuts resistant materials better, and holds its edge longer. Overall, a subtly more sophisticated version of the original DPx HEST with better performance.

The **DPx HEFT 6**, Hostile Environment Field Tool 6, has a 5.75-inch blade of Uddeholm **Sleipner tool steel** and a combination striker and pry bar at the butt. A 4-inch HEFT 4 also available. We gave the DPx HEFT 6 a heavy, month-long workout during which we split a stack of two-by-fours, chopped through a stand of saplings, cut sheet metal, and pried open a locked steel gate. After all that, and with only a quick touch up to the edge, I loaned it to a professional butcher, Shawn Carlson. Shawn used it for a week, during which he broke down a beef carcass, dressed out a couple dozen slabs of ribs, a stack of pork roasts, bacon, and assorted other meat products. He also sliced up twenty slabs of ribs and split fifteen chickens for a barbeque. Shawn reported, "This is a well-designed knife with a comfortable handle. It's easy to work with and doesn't fatigue your hand during a full day's work. Unlike some sharpened pry bars you've given me, this knife has a fine point that allowed me to easily get into muscle and separate it from connective tissue. I didn't need to touch it to a sharpening steel even after chopping through joints and cartilage."

▲ DPx HEST beer test.

▲ Cleanly sliced tomato using the DPx HEST.

The **DPx HEST/F 2.0** was designed to be a folder suitable for those same hostile environments. It has a frame lock that secures the 3.1-inch blade like a Swiss bank vault and a patented RotoBlock that locks the framelock in place. This folder will not close on your fingers. Its textured G10 scales, mil-spec phosphate-coated blade, and overall length of 7.6 inches make a well-proportioned design and a handsome package at just more than five ounces. The DPx HEST/F 2.0 features a glass breaker, wire stripper, quarter-inch hex hole for a driver, and bottle opener and comes with an adjustment tool that looks like a steel skull. We used the DPx HEST/F 2.0 for about two weeks for all the usual things. This sturdy little bulldog of a folder established itself as a go-to knife—the one you grab when you have to rip open a thick box or really any tough cutting job. Giving in to frustration, one of the folks who helped to evaluate knives, twisted, pried, and tore open a stubborn wooden box with it, no damage. Its grip is comfortable, and its D2 blade required no sharpening. We haven't had a chance to test the window breaker, but based on prior experience, I see no reason why it shouldn't work as advertised.

The DPx HEST/F 2.0 is an innovative folder with twelve patented features that combines hard use func- tions, features, and materials in a handy size. Its build quality is excellent, and it has exceptional strength in a folder of manageable size. This is as close as anyone has yet come to my knowledge to creating a pocket-able folder with strength approaching that of a fixed blade. It is a worthy addition to the DPx line and holds its own with its stable mates.

Elsa Fantino

20 route de Ponneau
71390 Jully les Buxy
France
+33 (0)3 85 92 04 17
elsaforge@yahoo.fr
www.elsaforge.fr

As a professional, I've seen and worked with thousands of blades over the years, and few attract my attention these days. Elsa Fantino's stunning pieces create their own aesthetic, a unique fusion of feminine art, power, and purpose. Medieval, otherworldly, or from a dream world, I've never before seen their like.

If your imagination is captured by Elsa's work, as was mine, be assured that these brilliantly designed and crafted blades are functional tools and weap-

▲ One piece hammer-forged with a curled self-grip and beads.

▲ DPx HEST being batoned through a seasoned oak log.

▲ Fantino forging a new blade.

▲ Forged from files is this very high carbon steel.

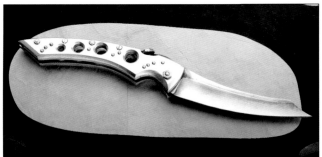

▲ Friction folder made of steel with brass.

▲ Elsa with a hammer, anvil, and knife-to-be.

ons, not only creative craft. Hand-forged, well-tempered, strong, and sharp, they would serve anyone well. Contact her to see what she has in stock or to order a custom blade. You won't regret it. Elsa is a rising star.

▲ A hand-forged, bejeweled piece of Elsa's otherworldly craft—as functional as it is gorgeous (Photos courtesy of maker).

Emerson Knives, Inc.

1234 254th t.
Harbor City, CA 90710
(310) 539-5633
www.emersonknives.com

Before starting his company, Ernest Emerson was a journeyman custom knifemaker, one of the first to adapt the liner lock. As a custom knifemaker, Emerson focused on imbuing his knives with the highest quality he could produce, which was high indeed. He brought that same focus to his later work. Bringing together the chisel grind, which was first introduced to the modern American knife world by Phil Hartsfield, the tanto point, and the liner lock, Emerson designed a folder that went on to achieve legendary status: the **CQC-7**. Featured by the famous author and distinguished veteran SEAL officer Commander Richard Marcinko in his book, *Rogue Warrior*, the CQC-7 shot to fame, resulting in a contract with Benchmade Knives to produce the design in volume. Other models followed, as did the creation of Emerson's own knife factory. Emerson Knives has become a producer of a wide range of tactical folders that are popular with both the public and the military community.

The CQC-7 I tried out many years ago was well-made, tough, and in general lived up to its billing. I haven't used a knife from current production, but from their appearance and reputation, and from comments from my trusted testers, I would think they are as good as ever.

ESEE Knives

P.O. Box 99
Gallant, AL 35972
(256) 613-0372
www.eseeknives.com

Mike Perrin and Jeff Randall, the head honchos of ESEE Knives (formerly RAT Cutlery) appear to be having fun while making some good knives at affordable prices. If you take a look at the photos on their website, you'll see guys thrashing around in the Peruvian jungle having a great time and using their knives. An outgrowth of Randall's Adventure Training, ESEE Knives has been designing affordable field knives targeted toward the military and law enforcement since 1997. Based on my work with their knives, I would say they have hit their target and their on-the-ground experience has helped them to do so.

ESEE uses 1095 for most of their knives, with some models available in Damascus or 440c stainless. With the heat treat they are using, they get strong blades that will flex under fairly hard stress without breaking and spring back to true. The textured power coat staves off rust and, so far, hasn't chipped off on any of the knives we have reviewed, even though we've worked them very hard. There are a number of sheath systems, blade colors, and handle colors for each knife, all of them well-thought-out and designed for field use. Blades are available with or without serrations.

Military SERE instructors designed the **ESEE-5**, and it shows. The 5.25-inch blade's cutting edge is brought back to the guard, thereby eliminating the choil and adding an inch of cutting edge where it is needed for sheer cuts, notching, and other survival-related work. The handle is comfortable, even after long, hard use. The balance in hand is good, even if a little heavy at sixteen ounces. At .25-inch thick, the blade is sturdy enough to serve as a demolition tool while the grind retains cutting efficiency. In fact, the blade geometry is nearly perfect for SERE usage, or really for general use.

▲ A demo job well done using DPx HEST and the ESEE SERE © Justin Ayres.

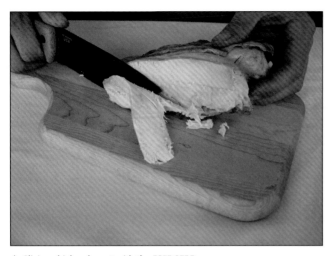

▲ Slicing chicken breast with the ESEE SERE—easy.

5.2 ounces without the Molle compatible sheath, it's light enough to tuck in a sock and easy to carry almost anywhere on your person. ESEE also offers lightweight Kydex sheaths with a clip attachment, which I think is just right for this type of knife. The ESEE-3 is a good traveler's knife, a small, handy, lightweight fixed blade that an international traveler can pack knowing that it will serve as an everyday and emergency tool.

The **ESEE-4**, with its 4.5-inch blade and overall length of 9 inches, also fits into the traveler's knife category. Like the ESEE-3, it loses 0.5-inch of cutting edge to a choil. But then, some people must like choils; there sure are a lot of knives sold with them. Either the ESEE-3 or ESEE-4 will serve today's international traveler well.

At the end of a long day of knife work and photography, I asked one of my students to use the ESEE-5 to slice tomatoes and onions for some pico de gallo salsa. At first he balked. He thought the blade would be much too thick to cut and chop thinly and finely. He also thought, understandably, that it would be too dull for kitchen use after we had ripped out a wall and batoned it into a steel door. He gave it a try anyway without sharpening but after washing it well to remove residue from Sheetrock, insulation, and assorted debris. After a few minutes, he held up the knife and called out to get my attention. "Hey," he said, "this slices good. How do they do that?" The answer to that question is likely in the blade geometry. There are some extras built into the ESEE-5, including a glass breaker and bow drill pivot, design elements that indicate considerable field experience with primitive tools. Overall, the ESEE-5 is a model of working efficiency.

The **ESEE-3** is kind of a little brother to the ESEE-5. At .125-inch, the blade is half as thick and with an overall blade length of 3.875 inches, a little more than 1.5 inches shorter. The blade does have a choil, which shortens the cutting edge to 3.375 inches. Four of us used the ESEE-3 for the usual variety of tasks, and everyone liked this knife very much.

Like all the ESEE knives I've handled, the balance and ergonomics are good. In many ways, this is an excellent all-around, daily carry fixed blade for the person who wants a serious survival tool on hand. At

▲ ESEE Izula slicing the limes for Margaritas.

▲ ESEE Izula cutting hemp rope.

▲ ESEE Izula II making a fuzz stick.

The **Izula** is ESEE's entry in the neck knife or tiny tactical category, and a good one it is. At 6.25 inches overall and two ounces, it's certainly light enough for neck carry. Its 2.88-inch flat ground blade is a good cutter. Its hollow frame handle provides room for a few goodies for anyone willing to cord wrap the handle or, for the impatient, slap a couple of layers of duct tape on it. If you carry it around your neck, use a ball chain with a breaking strength of no more than thirty pounds or a light cord with about the same breaking strength.

The ESEE guys are making good knives from time-tested tool steel to functional designs at prices a military person or international backpacker can afford. I have no reservations in recommending ESEE knives.

▲ ESEE Izula with quiver from Borneo.

Fällkniven AB

Granatvägen 8
96143 BODEN
Sweden
www.fallkniven.se

US Distributor:
Blue Ridge Knives
166 Adwolfe Road
Marion, VA 24354
(276) 783-6143
www.blueridgeknives.com

Fällkniven designers appear to be tapping into a deep reservoir of Scandinavian aesthetic consciousness. The product lineup at Fällkniven has a unique design sensibility and integrity—restrained, subtle, understated—that extends to all their knives. The Fällkniven knives simply look terrific. They also work very well. Over the years, I have found Fällkniven knives to be not only functional for a wide variety of knife work but also exceptional in performance.

▲ Fällkniven H1 & F1 with travel accoutrements.

They all have convex grinds, excellent ergonomics, and blade geometry. All are available with nonslip grips. They all do their primary job—cutting—well. The Fällkniven lineup is quite large and includes everything from a small but comfortable neck knife to large Bowies. Every model in the product range has the same design sensibility and commitment to function; here you will see no knives designed by a marketing department. The quality of manufacturing is top level.

I have used many Fällkniven knives, but most of my experience has been with the F1 and the A1. The **F1** is billed as a survival knife. I haven't handled a newer model Fällkniven in some years or the ones made with laminated steel, which is marketed as stronger than the VG-10 that the standard model uses. I do have a model F1 that's about ten years old, which has seen considerable use. Everyone likes this knife. With a cleanly designed blade just under four inches and a nonslip handle, it is handy and versatile. The full tang protrudes slightly from the back of the handle, which makes it easy to baton. And we have batoned it, both

▲ Fällkniven F1 resting after its labors with a walking stick.

▲ Fällkniven F1, cutting hemp rope.

lengthwise and horizontally, through green wood, lumber, and sheet metal. The convexly ground blade slips through both soft and hard materials easily, and the edge shows no damage.

The F1 is often the knife I loan to students who have no knife-handling skills. The nonslip grip is secure and comfortable in the hand. The blade design is easily adaptable to every form of work. It is also tough. No one has yet damaged it significantly. The only damage we have seen in about ten years of hard use is a small chip from the point from working through a concrete block wall. The chip was barely noticeable, and a little bit of stonework blended the point into the blade as if nothing had happened.

I tossed my old F1 into my bag for a month-long walk through the mountains in Italy last year. I had no adventures, no burning buildings, no attackers in the night, just a lengthy stroll with a good bit of camping along the way. I used the F1 for almost everything requiring a knife, including digging up wild roots, foraging other fresh wild food, and cleaning a couple of high country trout. I also used it in the kitchens of friends; none of them had sharp knives. One of them, a British expat living in Italy, called the F1 my ouch knife, because it bit him when he was peeling cucumbers. He was not accustomed to sharp knives. My F1 takes a sharp edge and holds it. I did not have to touch it to a stone in well more than a month of daily use. Its plain—as in not black—blade and general nonthreatening appearance were a definite plus. I chose to bring this particular knife on this journey because I like it as a daily use knife, it has a reserve in strength, and it causes no alarm among the general public.

I know how much reserve strength it has because Fällkniven has its knives tested for breaking strength by the Division of Solid Mechanics at Luleå University of Technology, and they publish the results on their website. This is a good thing. By doing this, they eliminate much of the guesswork that goes into evaluating any new knife. In addition to breaking data, they provide the rationale for the testing and the methods used. A testing process such as this might be beyond the reach of individual makers and small companies, but for large companies in the business of selling tactical knives, independent testing under controlled conditions would go a long way toward establishing industry standards and providing products with quantifiable properties.

Since Fällkniven has published the breaking strength of the VG-10 F1—195 pounds—we haven't tried to stress it beyond those limits. There is no reason to do so because we know what it will handle. In an emergency, I know that the F1 will, on its lateral surface, support the static weight of a person up to around 185 pounds, leaving some margin for error. If that same 185-pound person or a heavier one (me for example) were to bounce or otherwise apply velocity to the blade on its lateral surface, such as in a fall, the blade would likely break since velocity increases force quickly. This is according to Fällkniven's published data, which I trust. Suppose you weigh two hundred fifty pounds, does that mean you shouldn't buy this knife?

Not at all. To the contrary, it means you can make a more informed decision regarding the selection of this knife. This information is data that informs my use of this tool. For example, if I were to fall and slide down a cliff and needed to use the F1 as an arresting device, I would stab the blade into the surface of the cliff so my weight was brought to bear on the vertical plane, which is much stronger than the lateral plane.

The F1 was not designed as an arresting device for a large person. However, since we know its breaking strength, we know that under certain emergency conditions, it could be used for that purpose. The most important things about the F1 is that it is a well-designed and well-made knife, it is useful for just about everything, and it has a quantified margin of strength that makes it reliable for some emergency situations. Ten years of use by survival escape and evasion students is testament to its utility. If you need a stronger knife, the A1 would be a good choice.

The **A1** is the knife I loan to students who look like they have a tendency to break things. According to the data published by Fällkniven, the A1 has a breaking strength of 556 pounds, more than double that of the F1. The A1 has a blade a little more than six inches in length and about a quarter inch thick. Like the F1, and all the Fällknivens, it has a convex grind. This ten-year-old A1 has been hammered into trees and used as a climbing aid dozens of times, and it has

been pounded through car bodies and walls. It was also used for general knife things: splitting kindling, cutting saplings for shelter, dressing game, and so on. It's an excellent knife and still good to go after ten years of hard use.

▲ Fällkniven A1 cutting up red peppers for salad.

I've tested other Fällkniven models while with the Yurok nomads in the Taurus Mountains of Turkey and in the Stara Planina Mountains in Bulgaria. In rural Bulgaria, I recruited a local friend, Ivan Petrov Ivanov, to help with fieldwork. With the exception of the Bowie, all knives were used as everyday kitchen and utility knives. We also cut about a hundred feet of quarter-inch hemp rope, the only size we could find in small town Bulgaria, and sacks of plastic bottles and cans. During the cold months, we split a small mountain of seasoned oak firewood for kindling.

Fällkniven's entry to the tactical folder field, the **PXL**, is a gorgeous piece that has the appearance of a gentlemen's folder. When taken in hand, it reveals its true nature as a hefty, solid, hardworking tool. It is offered with ivory or maroon Micarta scales, or in a workday version with black synthetic scales.

I elected to focus on the **PXLim** with ivory Micarta scales. The fit and finish are excellent, equal to many custom folders. The grinds on the semi-spear-point blade are true. The folder was so handsome I was reluctant to try it in the field. For a week or so I pussyfooted around with it, slicing tomatoes and the like. Then I decided to get down to work. I started

▲ PXL ivory Micarta handle after cutting 1/4" hemp, 200 cuts without dulling.

◀ PXL ivory Micarta handle.clean press cut through 1" sapling.

with rope cutting. An easy push cut crunched the blade cleanly through two hundred cuts of the narrow hemp; I could have cut more, but I was tired of counting. With moderate pressure, the blade sliced through one-inch saplings cleanly. Thicker saplings, two to three inches, required two or three cuts and some rocking back and forth in the cut, again with moderate pressure, no batoning required. After all the above, the 3G blade would still shave hair from my arm. The handle is sculpted with smooth edges and is comfortable during heavy use over extended periods. The clip looks a little short, but it worked well, never slipped, and held the folder in a low waistband position. Personally, I prefer a somewhat slimmer configuration for a folder and would like to see Fällkniven release a similar model about one-third thinner and lighter. But the PXLim fits into the current heavy-duty tactical folder concept with excellence and at the top of its class.

The **Professional Hunter's Knife (PHK)**, combines a curved sweeping edge with a dropped point to make a blade design both handsome and efficient. It is well balanced, with an ergonomic handle that is comfortable even after an hour or so of work. We used it for preparing a goat to be roasted for a local holiday; the blade skinned, sliced, and disjointed as if it were a light saber. The long, sweeping edge served well for all cuts, and the point was placed just where it needed to be.

Since it is billed as a hunter's knife, and reasoning that a hunter could get caught out overnight, I decided to see how well it worked as an all-around field knife. The knife is balanced well, which, along with the blade design, enabled it to snap cut poles for a survival tepee with a flick of the wrist—for the skin of the teepee I used an Adventure Medical Kits Survival Blanket. Then I split kindling and cut a foot-thick pile of weeds for ground insulation. Splitting

▲ Fällkniven PHK after a snap cut.

kindling didn't require a baton. Cutting bunches and weeds was almost as easy as if I'd been using a sickle. The entire process resulted in an emergency shelter in about thirty minutes. We also used the PHK for rope cutting, slicing plastic and cardboard, and daily food preparation. After two weeks of usage, the edge would still shave, though not as cleanly as when fresh. I liked this design very much.

NL1, Fällkniven's interpretation of the Bowie, is billed as a chopper, and it chops well indeed. It is a good-looking, well-made, well-balanced knife with a stacked ox hide handle. I spent an hour or so chopping small trees up to about three inches in diameter.

The handle was comfortable; the blade bit deep and did not stick in the cuts. Wanting to see how the edge would fare in heavier work I loaned it to Ivan, who used it for a long day's work clearing saplinging, averaging about two to three inches thick, and brush from the grounds of the estate where we were staying. At day's end, Ivan had three piles of saplings and miscellaneous brush. Each pile was over waist high and about four feet wide by seven feet long. It's true that smaller knives can be used for heavy work, but this big boy changes the game and makes short work of heavy chores. It did not require sharpening during a total of three days of brush clearing.

▲ Fällkniven NL1 Bowie making short work of cutting saplings.

If you take a look at Fällkniven's website, you will find a good deal of related useful information, such as the relationship between blade length and thickness and breaking strength. I think it would be a good thing for other companies who can afford the expense to do similar research. Or better yet, if an independent agency could establish testing standards for the industry. Such standards would not eliminate the need for field-testing; rather, it would give us a starting place.

Peter Hjortberger, the founder and president of Fällkniven, creates top quality products and has run his business with integrity since 1984. A family business, Peter's son Eric has joined the company and will no doubt continue meeting the standards set by his father. Fällkniven has come to stand for outstanding functional modern design and excellent working knives in both sporting and tactical. I use them and recommend them without reservation.

Fred Perrin

20 route de Ponneau
71390 Jully les Buxy
France
Workshop: +33 (0)3 85 92 04 17
Mobile: +33 (0)6 74 99 50 02
fredperrinconcept@yahoo.fr

Fred Perrin is a French knifemaker, a former French Army commando, and a world-ranked martial artist. Fred's background is apparent in his highly functional knives. His aesthetic sense shines through in all of his graceful and elegant designs. He has designed a number of knives for Spyderco, including his Street Bowie and Street Beat, which are reviewed in the Spyderco listing.

The Street Beat and the Street Bowie are favorites with us, and so we were pleased to receive a **Neck Bowie** direct from Fred's production. A small knife at two ounces with a 2.75-inch blade, the Neck Bowie, like all of Fred's designs, is graceful and elegant, well-made and tough. Its flat grind, useful belly, and sharp point combine to make a terrific utility knife. The handle is ergonomic and comfortable, the deep finger guard is at the balance point, and the knife feels right in hand. I used the Neck Bowie extensively while traveling with ML, my intrepid wife, along the South coast

▲ Fred Perrin at the grinding wheel.

▲ Splitting wood with the Spyderco Street Beat.

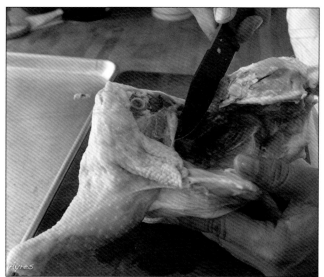

▲ Spyderco's Fred Perrin Street Bowie boning a chicken with ease.

▲ Fred Perrin Neck Bowie.

▲ Fred Perrin Neck Bowie ready to travel.

of Turkey. Some areas there are as wild as they must have been during ancient times. Along the coast, small fish swim in tide pools and are easy to catch without fishing gear.

One day, as part of an experiment in which we used only small knives—we had two tiny folders and another tiny fixed blade—I used the Neck Bowie to help make a fish trap from a discarded plastic water bottle by cutting off the tapered part of the top, slicing off the lid, and placing the resulting cone inside the bottle. Tuna scraps served as bait, and I wedged the bottle in place with rocks, opening facing the outgoing tide. While waiting for our fish trap to produce, we went foraging. The hills above the Mediterranean are covered with edible plants. Some require local knowledge to identify; others include familiar dandelion greens, rose hips, wild peppers, and prickly pear cactus. Prickly pear pads can be eaten raw in a salad, grilled, or cooked with tomatoes to make a delicious Mexican dish.

While foraging, I used the Neck Bowie to cut shelter poles to make a tripod, secured a space blanket as a covering, then used it to cut tall grass to cover the ground under our shelter with a foot-deep grass bed. When we returned to the water, we found two small fish in our trap. While anticipating the tasty dinner to come, we set up the results of our foraging for photos.

▲ Fred Perrin Neck Bowie trimming a shelter pole.

▲ Fred Perrin Shark filleting a chicken thigh.

However, as we fiddled with cameras, a feral cat crept up, snatched one of the fish, and made off with it. I almost fell from a slippery rock into the water laughing. Rather than chase the hungry cat away, we made a short video of the bold adventurer stealing the other fish. (The video can be seen on my website: www. jamesmorganayres.com.) Deprived of our fish dinner, we fell back on emergency rations—a block of goat cheese and a bottle of white wine, which we had with the wild green salad at our little shelter while watching the sun sink into the sea.

I continued to use the little Neck Bowie in the kitchen for a few weeks. Then, wondering just how strong this little knife really was, I gave into temptation and punched it into oak tree, hard. The blade penetrated well. The butt of the Neck Bowie's handle is nicely curved and fits comfortably into the base of my palm. It is so well-formed that there was no discomfort on impact.

For the past couple of years, I've also been using a Fred Perrin **Shark,** a tiny sliver of steel that fits in my wallet, card case, watch pocket, or on my key ring. I ground off the secondary bevel on a diamond stone, leaving a fierce edge that I use mostly for the mundane function of opening packages. However, each time I use it, I'm reminded of the lapel knives used by the Office of Strategic Service (OSS) intelligencers in World War II and other organizations during the Cold War Era. The large finger ring provides a sure grip, and

▲ The Shark ready for traveling.

the little slicer can be quickly drawn from discrete carry and used to cut and run.

What words and the accompanying photos do not fully convey is the elegant tactility and balance of Fred Perrin's knives. You'll have to actually handle and use them to fully appreciate the combination of art and uncompromising function realized in every Perrin knife.

Gerber Legendary Blades

Gerber Gear
14200 SW 72nd Ave.
Portland, OR 97224
(800) 950-6161
www.gerbergear.com

Joseph Gerber launched Gerber Legendary Blades in 1939. Since then, the company has been through many changes. Previously known for sporting and kitchen cutlery, Gerber got into the tactical knife arena with its single purpose **Mark II** double-edged dagger in the late sixties. A version of that knife is today still sold by the Military Gear division of Gerber, serial numbered for collectors and with serrated edges.

The **LMF II ASEK** is a fixed blade with an overall length of 10.59 inches, a blade length of 4.84 inches, and a nylon handle a with nonslip grip. The blade is constructed of Sandvik 12C27 steel and showed no damage after some rough use. As I have previously written, I do not in general try to evaluate steel, as opposed to evaluating knives. However, I will note that have noticed a variety of exceptional knives from a range of makers constructed with Sandvik 12C27. Many years ago, one of my personal knives, a boot knife made of Sandvik 12C27, outperformed a number of knives made by ABS Masters, both in cutting and toughness testing.

Gerber bills this knife as highly adaptable, good for cutting through the fuselage of an aircraft, sever-

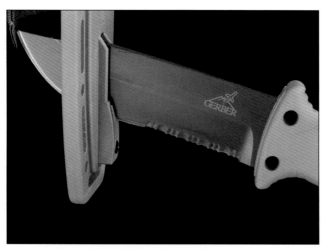

▲ Gerber LMF II ASEK with a knife sharpener © Justin Ayres.

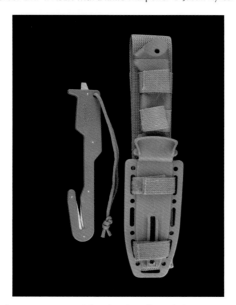

▲ Gerber LMF II ASEK with a sheath and seat belt cutter © Justin Ayres.

▲ Gerber LMF II cutting through Sheetrock.

▲ Gerber LMF II cutting tomatoes after field-testing.

▲ Gerber 06 Auto Drop Point after having cut Hemp rope.

ing seat belts, cutting firewood, and building shelters. With that kind of billing, we tested some of its functions by using it as an improvised demolitions tool on a building scheduled to be taken down. We ripped out Sheetrock walls, cut through studs, slashed through sheet metal, and finally pounded it into a heavy gauge steel door. Not only was there no damage to the LMF, the edge wasn't rolled over or dinged. Later on we subjected the LMF to our famous Attack of the Killer Tomatoes test, wherein we slice, ripe tomatoes. This is actually a good test of sharpness; if an edge isn't just right, it will squish the tomato rather than slice it. With no touch-up, the LMF sliced and diced with the best.

The handle was comfortable during all this cutting and pounding and has a pointy kind of skull-crusher-looking pommel, which worked pretty well to crush some bricks. The handle is also nonconductive to electricity, a significant safety feature for some.

The LMF is a tough knife. It is available in a number of finish options and comes with a sheath suitable for MOLLE mounting or belt wear. This knife is purpose-designed for general military use and, based on our testing, is well-suited to it. It's also available at a price a military person can afford.

KA-BAR Knives, Inc.

200 Homer St.
Olean, NY 14760
(716) 372-5952
www.kabar.com

The KA-BAR company started life as Union Cutlery in the early days of the twentieth century. The company name was changed to KA-BAR in 1952 due to the fame and name recognition of the USMC KA-BAR knife. Originally KA-BAR was a division of Union Cutlery and was named for a letter received from a trapper in the twenties who had used one of the company's knives to kill a bear that was attacking him; he had killed a bear or, in the trapper's rough short hand, KA BAR.

The company presented the original KA-BAR design to the US Marine Corps in 1942. After some revisions, it was adapted as an issue item. The KA-BAR Company produced about a million of their KA-BAR knives during World War II. Due to overwhelming demand, millions more were produced by contractors, such as Ontario, Camillus, Case, and others. Within a short time, the knife became emblematic of the Marines

▲ KA-BAR TDI Knife.

▲ KA-BAR 02-1212.

fighting in the Pacific. Soldiers in the Army also managed to get their hands on the sought after KA-BAR, often by trading. Military histories of the time record many bloody hand-to-hand battles where the KA-BAR was used to devastating effect. In addition to use as a weapon, the KA-BAR was the favored everyday tool for everything from pounding tent stakes to cutting open C-ration cans. In the Pacific Theatre, the KA-BAR was the tactical knife of World War II.

Today this old-line company still produces their USMC Fighting and Utility Knife of World War II fame. Today's knives are of high quality. None we have used over the past few years have broken, as did some old World War II surplus KA-BARs back in the sixties. Those knives were made by many different government contractors under wartime conditions and should not be confused with the modern products.

KA-BAR catalogs a half-dozen or so variations on its classic fighting and utility knife, some of carbon steel, some of stainless. The classic leather stacked handles are still available, as are Kraton handles. The leather handles are of excellent quality, far beyond any I ever saw in the World War II versions.

Today the basic KA-BAR, like its ancestors, has a seven–inch Bowie-inspired clip point blade of 1095 carbon steel and a 4.75-inch handle of leather-stacked washers. The blade has a flat, or saber (depending on terminology), grind and the same high degree of utility that it has always had.

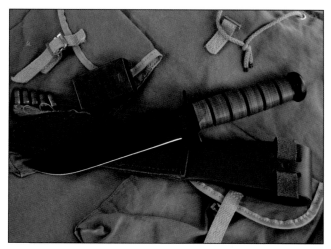

▲ KA-BAR USMC Fighting Knife with firestarter, bullets, sinew, and ready bag.

▲ KA-BAR 02-1212 with bullets and firestarter.

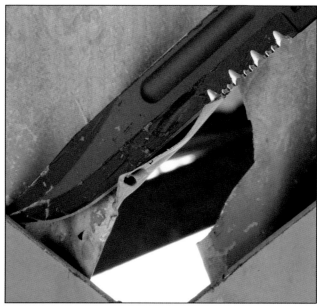

▲ Closeup of KA-BAR cutting corrugated sheet metal © Justin Ayres.

▲ Sheet metal testing (clockwise): KA-BAR 02-1212, Benchmade CSK II, SOG Seal Pup, and Buck Bravo Rescue © Justin Ayres.

Many of our students have shown up for class with a new KA-BAR, understandably, since in many ways the KA-BAR is one of the most famous tactical knives ever manufactured. None of our students' KA-BARs have failed, and they've seen some pretty hard use. During a recent review, we used a KA-BAR with a black finish alongside some more modern knives to partially tear down a building, cut through sheet steel, plus all the daily functions a field knife would be used for, food prep, etc. The KA-BAR is still good to go.

Today KA-BAR also produces a wide range of tactical knives, both fixed blades and folders, at affordable prices. The ones we are most familiar with are those designed by Ethan Becker, who at one time manufactured and marketed his own brand, Becker Knife & Tool Co. Now the Becker knives are manufactured by KA-BAR and marketed under the BK&T/KA-BAR brand. See Becker.

Kellam Knives Worldwide, Inc.

PO Box 3438
Lantana, FL 33465
(800) 390-6918
www.kellamknives.com

Kellam Knives is owned and operated by husband and wife team Jouni **and** Harriet Kellokoski. They have been in business for more than two decades and import carefully selected, handmade knives from Finland, some of which are tactical by any measure. Harking back to the Winter War of 1939–1940, Harriet reminded me of some history, when these kinds of knives were used to devastating effect by the Finnish soldiers who infiltrated the invading Russians' camps at night and silently killed Russian soldiers. Like other Finns I have met, Harriet and Jouni are in touch with their country's history, their heritage, and with the long tradition in Finland that recognizes the importance of knives and their centrality to life.

Jouni is an outdoorsman, and he and Harriet have a small farm and some forested land in Finland where, for part of each year, they live close to the earth and use their own products daily.

With its high-carbon seven-inch blade, the **Slasher** is the largest of a line called the Wolf Pack. There are many kinds of sharp: paper-cutting sharp, hair-shaving sharp, wood-cutting sharp, and so on. Out of the box, the Slasher came with a different kind of sharp—scary sharp, hair-splitting, tissue-paper-cutting sharp. Any sharp knife will slice paper. The Slasher filleted sheets of computer paper into thin sections. It slipped through tissue paper with no drag and shaved thin curls of tough inner oak effortlessly. With care, it sliced through a section of epidermis to get at an embedded splinter without cutting into the dermis. It also kept that scary edge after being batoned through chunks of live oak, cutting up a half-dozen cardboard boxes, and crunching though three feet of two-inch hemp rope. While batoning it through seasoned oak, we snapped it sideways, splitting the oak; we also forcefully stabbed it into a chuck of wood and snapped it out sideways—no damage to edge or point in either case. We took it to the kitchen after all this, and it effortlessly sliced a pork shoulder roast into paper thin slices.

This level of cutting and overall performance is due to steel, heat treat, and geometry. The blade is ground on one plane from about the middle of the blade to the cutting edge with no secondary bevel, thus eliminating drag. The blade is polished from the middle to the edge. The upper part of the blade is left black from the heat treat. This shows the differential heat treat; the edge is hard for better cutting and edge holding, the spine a bit softer for shock absorption.

▲ Kellam Slasher.

The Kellam knife was not only an excellent cutting tool, it proved itself as an all-around outdoorsman's knife. We slashed through a stand of river cane while clearing some mountain property with ease, and with little effort cut, slashed, and chopped a waist-high pile of brushwood—enough to make a functional shelter. The 4.75-inch birchwood handle is handsome, ergonomic, and contoured; it provides a secure grip without a guard and is exceptionally comfortable during heavy work and extended projects.

There is much to be said for the medium-sized knife (six to seven inches) as an all-around outdoor knife. The extra blade length provides enough leverage to quickly slash through saplings, and in some cases thicker wood that would require a baton with a

▲ Kellam Slasher and Wayne Goddard's camp knife cutting one-inch hemp with ease.

▲ Kellam Slasher slicing roast wafer thin.

four-inch blade, while being more convenient to carry than a big knife. In the case of the Kellam Slasher, the slight difference in weight due to the seven-inch blade of eighth-inch steel was negligible. This blade length and design also is quite good for small work, if not as convenient as a shorter blade. Like others, I've transitioned from big blades to little blades and back again. These days I'm tending towards medium-sized blades for all-around use.

▲ The Kellam Slasher always cuts clean.

Another point in the Kellam Slasher's favor—the plastic-lined leather sheath enabled comfortable and convenient belt carry. Unlike some sheaths that are designed for use with military load-bearing equipment or for security during parachute jumps and related acticivities, the light pouch sheath supplied with the Kellam knives is optimal for civilian use. It makes carrying the longer blade hassle-free. All in all, the Kellam Slasher and sheath make an excellent purpose-designed package and a handsome one. Is it tactical? Yes, it is. Tactical knives are not defined by appearance, but by function. A handsome, traditional knife with a leather sheath can be just as functional as a black-coated, Kydex-sheathed knife or, as in this case, more functional than many such knives.

I would have no hesitation in choosing the Kellam Slasher as my only knife for extended wilderness use, and with further testing might well choose it for urban, hard use survival, as well. It has a rattail full tang as opposed to a full slab tang that most hard use knives have; but all of my Model 1 Randalls have had the same kind of tang, and they have never failed me. In addition, the well-designed and well-shaped handle combines with the blade to make a well-balanced, quick, lightweight knife. I'll continue to use and evaluate this Kellam knife; it's exceptional in every way.

Knives by Mace Vitale

Laurel Rock Forge
(203) 457-5591
www.laurelrockforge.com

Mace Vitale makes beautiful collector-grade Bowies and camp knives, as well as a variety of smaller blades, that perform as well as they look. Mace has been an ABS Journeyman Smith since 2006, and it shows in his work. I recently reviewed one of his camp knives that balanced well in the hand and cut through hardwood branches on a tree in my son's yard like . . . well, like a knife from an ABS smith.

You can see from the accompanying photo that the blade snicked through the branch smoothly and cleanly. It also did so with hardly any effort. My son made the cut, and he was surprised by how quickly and cleanly the knife cut. We had planned to get a shot of the knife as the cut was being made, but the blade

◄ Mace Vitale Forged Camper.

▲ This orange tree limb didn't stand a chance against Mace Vitale's Forged Camper.

went through so easily the shot turned into one that showed what had happened, not what was happening.

Reviews of knives made by ABS Journeymen or Master Smiths can get kind of predictable. Not boring, but predictable. Mace's Camper knife cut and sliced a stack of tri-tip roasts effortlessly. It cut rope like it was string. Old leather and denim hanging from a rafter parted before the blade like the Red Sea parted before the Israelites. If you want a knife that works, call Mace. If you want a pretty knife, he's also a good guy to call.

▲ Mace Vitale coffin-handle Bowie: 11.5-inch blade, 17.0625-inch overall length, 0.25-inch spine at the guard; 1095 steel blade heat treated with clay; wrought iron fittings; curly maple handle with a nickel silver pin.

Mora of Sweden

Box 407, 792 27 MORA
Sweden
+46-250 59 50 00
www.moraofsweden.se

North American distributor:
Industrial Revolution
5835 Segale Park C Dr.
Tukwila, WA 98188
(425) 285-1111
www.industrialrev.com

Okay, here's what you do. Get one, or even two or three, of these seriously cool knives for about twenty bucks each. Do that, and you'll be good to go for cutting about anything you can think of: meat, melons, wood, cloth, rope, rattan, deerskin, snakeskin, maybe even dragonskin. They'll cut through a heavy leather motorcycle jacket like the winter wind off the Great Lakes cuts through a summer suit.

The Scandi edge serves as both a sharpening guide and a guide for whittling fuzz sticks or any other kind of whittling. You can easily keep a jump up and cut you edge with very little stonework, which is a good thing because you will need to sharpen your Mora fairly frequently compared to knives made with some of the more high-tech materials. I do not regard the need for more frequent sharpening as important; I only mention it for readers who have not yet learned how to sharpen a knife. Use the bevel as a sharpening guide on, say, a Norton stone, and you will soon have one of the sharpest edges you have seen.

▲ Mora Bushcraft Survival knife making a spear.

▲ Close-up of using a Mora knife to cut a hardwood limb.

I know of a bunch of guys and gals who live year round under what a city person would consider wilderness survival conditions. They use Moras for all their knife needs unless they require a chopper, which these knives are not. For choppers, they use machetes or hatchets. I even know a wilderness survival instructor who cuts his hair with a Mora; he likes to keep things simple.

Forget about ripping your way through a steel door with one of these slender slicers, because they aren't up to that job. You could grind away the mortar to take down a concrete block wall and take it apart. But it would wreck the knife in the process, which would be no big deal if you really needed to get out of a building. If a Mora is your only knife and you want to be able to pry a door open, get yourself a titanium pry bar (seven ounces, twenty-five bucks) and put it in your bug-out bag. Although the Moras are light knives, you can baton them through wood without fear of breakage.

Moras come in stainless steel, carbon steel, and laminated steel, and they're all good. The Swedes know a thing or two about steel, and they've been producing these knives all in the town of Mora.

Cody Lundin, a well-known wilderness survival and primitive skills instructor, carries the **Mora Classic 2**, which has a carbon steel blade and a wood handle, on a buckskin thong around his neck all day every day and probably sleeps with it, too. (That's a thin buckskin thong, not a rawhide cord that could cause neck injury.) I know Cody and can tell you he's for real, one of the guys who can wander off into the desert or mountains with just the clothes on his back and his Mora and fire starter, and set up house: build a shelter, trap a rabbit for dinner, make a bow, track a deer, and bring home venison.

There are good reasons why Cody chose the Mora, and it wasn't because he could buy it for the price of dinner for two at Taco Bell. The little Mora excels at woodworking, which is what quite a bit of wilderness survival entails. It's lightweight and handily sized, so he will always have it with him. He can sharpen it on a river rock if need be. The blade is tough and will bend before it breaks. Actually, I've never seen a Mora blade break; although in hard use, I did bend one to ninety degrees, but it did not break and could be brought back to true.

▲ Traditional Mora with custom buckskin sheath by R. Figueroa and fire-starting materials.

▲ Using the spine of the Mora 840 Carbon to strike a spark.

Cody recommends the **Mora 840** for his students. The 840 also has a carbon steel blade, but it has a cushioned handle with a nonslip surface. The cushioning is a good thing for urban folks with soft city hands, and the nonslip surface is a safety measure. Both models work equally well.

The instructors at the Boulder Outdoor Survival School (BOSS) use the same knives as Cody, or the **780 Triflex**, which has a laminated blade. Cody is an alumnus of BOSS, as are many other wilderness survival and primitive skills instructors. As a group, the BOSS folks have probably got more dirt time living in primitive conditions than any other group I can think of, with the exception of some people in developing countries who still live close to nature. When it comes to knives for this purpose, these people know what works for them.

◀ Close-up on using a Mora knife to make a fuzz stick.

◀ Mora with a hunting bag and rabbit stick.

That said, you also need to understand that the Mora knives are not designed for, nor suitable for, the demands of modern warfare. I've been trying out the **Mora 2000**, which has a stainless steel blade and is billed as a Swedish army survival knife. If we're talking wilderness survival with all that entails, I would agree this is a good tool for that purpose. But if we're talking urban survival, which is where many conflicts are happening today, this is not the right tool for the job. Try to pry open a locked door, and you'll either ruin the knife or still be stuck inside, or both. Try to baton it through a steel fire door and you'll be severely disappointed in the results. The blades are tough, but they are thin. Thin makes for good cutting, but not for prying, twisting, and other hard use. Every Mora I've tried will easily pass the blade on blade test I described in my review procedures.

A new model, the **Mora Bushcraft Survival** knife comes with a firesteel and diamond sharpener in its composition sheath, both valuable tools. This version of the standard Mora has a thicker blade but gives up nothing in its justly famous slicing and wood shaving ability, and it is still strong enough for batoning. As

with other Moras, the handle is comfortable. However, the sheath provided is not secure and needs some work. The knife popped out of the sheath, which was worn on a belt, while jumping over a log. This is potentially dangerous, since a cut or loss of the knife could result. The sheath we had may have had a defect, and this could have been a one-time problem. But check the sheath if you order one of these knives, which you should if you want a good wilderness survival knife at a modest price.

Mora knives are excellent knives for their purpose, and a heck of a bargain. They are tactical in their own way. But they are not war knives, nor were they meant to be. Rose-Marie Gontowski, a well-informed person who knows knives and can direct you to a local dealer, runs the business.

Mykel Hawke Knives

www.mykelhawkeknives.com
www.hawkebrand.com

Mykel Hawke is well-known for his role in the reality survival show *Lost Survivors* on The Travel Channel and many other television series. But Mykel is a lot more than a television star. When he's demonstrating survival techniques, Mykel isn't acting; he's doing what he's done for most of his life—surviving. A retired Captain in the Special Forces (Green Beret) with deployments in Afghanistan, Africa, Latin America, and other places and a list of qualifications the size of a Chinese menu, Mykel has acquired deep, hard-won experience on how to stay alive in the world's harshest environments. He's written a book on the topic, *Hawke's Green Beret Survival Manual*. I recommend Mykel's book without reservation.

Working from life experience rather than theory, Mykel knows what personal abilities and qualities it takes to survive—and what tools are critical. Which brings us to knives.

Like most survival experts, Mykel believes the knife is the single most important survival tool. However, based on his years of field experience, he felt that none of the commercially available knives were optimal for him. So he designed first one knife, then

▲ Moras (top to bottom): 2010 Survival, 2000, 780 Tri-Flex, 840 Clipper Carbon, and 840 Carbon.

a series of knives to best serve his needs and the needs of other survivors. Mykel's designs are radically different from mainstream survival knives. They are designs that he has worked out over the years to serve his specific survival needs and to be reliable and versatile tools for all survival situations—tropical, arctic, alpine, desert, urban—anyplace, anytime. His range of knives includes neck knives, folders, and fixed blades from small to machete-size. All incorporate design features similar to those of his signature knife, the knife he chooses when he can have only one knife: **the Peregrine**, a medium-sized, fixed blade.

The Peregrine's five-inch blade of AUS-8 steel is one of intersecting planes, each with a specific function and a tanto point. There are no curves on any of the Mykel Hawke knives. In a recent interview, Mykel said that he preferred straight edges to curves for strength and functionality and medium-sized knives for all-around use because they are more efficient than small utility or bushcraft knives and more convenient to carry than large knives. He also said that, in his view, while bushcraft knives have their place and are good for woodworking, they are not optimal for survival, because they lack the size and strength required for many survival functions.

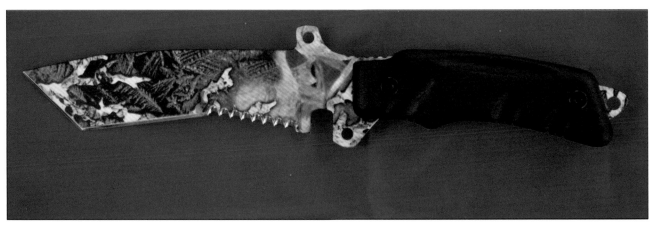

▲ Mykel Hawke's unique survival knife, the Peregrine.

▲ Mykel Hawke's unique pattern on the blade of the Peregrine blends in quite well with the local terrain.

The geometry, the bevels, the handles—each feature of the Peregrine and other knives in the range was derived from his years of fieldwork. The full tang construction is critical for strength; the edge closest to the handle is optimal for notching and whittling, unless serrated, in which case the serrations are most efficient for cutting rope, ripping cable, and other resistant mediums; although no medium sixed knife is a great chopper, the forward edge is at a seventeen-degree angle to maximize what chopping ability is available; the tanto point will drill hardwood without bending or deforming and can be batoned into coconuts or a tree to take it down, or through an auto body or steel door without snapping; the soft silicone handle is comfortable for long work periods and grippy when the user's hand is wet or slippery; there are multiple lashing points.

The standard Peregrine comes with a proprietary gunmetal gray Blackstone coating, which looks as businesslike as a Browning .50 caliber. The knife we reviewed in the field had a limited edition IceKon coating, which seems to shift and fade into the background, making it a challenge to photograph. The Peregrine's radical angles and striking design, combined with the IceKon coating, conjured up images of a Klingon war knife. In fact, the Peregrine is different in almost every way from any other knife I've ever worked with. All of my cohort were amazed at the appearance of this knife. The question everyone had was, how does the Peregrine, and the other Hawke knives, work in the field?

We answered that question over a period of weeks, during which time we worked with the Peregrine and **Harrier Hawke**, a hefty folder with a 5.25-inch blade, doing all the things we do in reviews. Shawn, the professional butcher who works with me on knife reviews, broke down a section of beef, and cut it into steaks and roasts, which is similar to dressing game. We chopped and sliced vegetables, as you would with foraged food. We made kindling and fuzz sticks, digging sticks, spears, and other tools. We pried open a stuck garage door, pounded through sheet metal, and batoned through live oak—all things a survival knife needs to be able to do. We also sliced a pile of cardboard into slivers and cut hemp rope.

If, like me, you're accustomed to traditional blades, the Hawke designs take some getting used to before you start to see their virtues. The notion of having each

▲ Mykel Hawke's Harrier Hawke folder.

▲ Mykel Hawke's Peregrine taking its turn at cutting up cardboard.

▲ Mykel Hawke's Peregrine splitting a seasoned oak using a baton.

section of the blade serve a specialized function was new to me, but after working with them for a while, I found that the various features worked as intended. I've seen the points of dozens of knives bend or break when twisting, drilling, or prying hardwood—the Peregrine's point did not bend in tough seasoned oak, nor did that of the Harrier. Nor did they deform when driven through sheet metal. My review Peregrine has serrations near the hilt; they stripped heavy cardboard with ease and ripped through rubber hose and heavy denim. The polished bevels of the AUS-8 blades aided the edges in slipping through resistant mediums. We did not chop wood with either knife because batoning is more efficient with small- and medium-sized knives. The blade grind on both knives worked like wedges when batoning wood, enabling thick chunks to be easily split for kindling. We also found the handle to be comfortable for long periods of hard work.

Mykel Hawke knives are unusual in appearance and concept, but they fulfill their functions as survival tools with élan. And they're priced so that they're within the reach of anyone. Mykel Hawke knives are good to go.

Ontario Knife Company

P.O. Box 145
Franklinville, NY 14737
(800) 222-5233
www.ontarioknife.com

Ontario has been in business since 1889 and is perhaps best known as a supplier of knives to the American military. Over the years, they have produced the M7 bayonet, the Air Force Survival Knife, and many others. They are currently making the Aircrew Survival Egress Knife for aircrew. In addition, Ontario makes a wide variety of knives and edged tools ranging from machetes and swords to tactical folders and their Spec Plus brand, which is military oriented. Ontario has also been a contractor for the USMC fighting knife, or KA-BAR, and for RAT knives.

In addition to all that, Ontario also makes a terrific line of tactical knives under the Old Hickory brand, most of which are designed as kitchen knives. No, I'm not kidding. I haven't seen a new Old Hickory in years. But I have a **Sticker** that I bought from a friend,

a Native American survival instructor who did the beadwork on the sheath in the photo, and I have found it to be a tough performer that takes a fierce edge and is easy to sharpen. The Sticker is double-edged, which means you need to have some edge awareness when handling it.

I often use the Sticker to test other knives advertised as combat or fighting knives by striking them on the

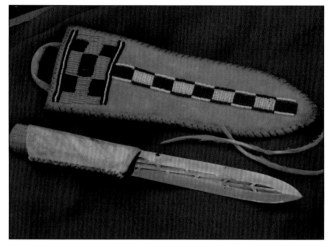

▲ Old Hickory Sticker with a rawhide-wrapped handle and beaded buckskin sheath by Albert Avril.

spine as I would in a beat, which is similar to a parry, during a blade-to-blade encounter. If a combat or survival knife won't stand up to a beat or parry from a simple kitchen knife, I toss it in the junk pile and forget about it. The Old Hickory brand consists of a range of kitchen knives in carbon steel that are much favored by people who work with knives professionally, and I don't mean just chefs and butchers.

A guy who became a good friend showed up for duty with the 82nd Airborne Division headquarters with an Old Hickory Sticker and a .22 Remington Nylon 66 rifle in his duffle bag. Mike was an Inuit from Alaska who helped feed his family by hunting moose and walrus with his .22. He told me he used to have to fight off three-hundred-pound walruses that stole his fish and wrecked his nets with only a spear before he got his .22. Mike was a tough guy and had spent his entire life living close to the ground. The only knife he had was that Old Hickory and a four-bladed scout knife. He said that his father had carried a Sticker, or something like it, when he went off to fight in World War II. Mike figured it would work for him, too. It did.

Ontario also made some of the best Bowies I have seen produced by a factory in modern times: the Bagwell series. I use the past tense, because the factory discontinued this series. I guess big Bowies marketed as weapons just weren't selling. Maybe Ontario should try marketing them as all-around tacticals.

▲ Bagwell Bowie, The Gambler © Justin Ayres.

I tried the **Gambler** model; with its nine-inch blade, it was the smallest in the line and the least complicated. It was tempered soft and absorbed shock well. I ignored the marketing and used it as a bush knife and general outdoor knife. With its pronounced distal taper, convex edge, and well-thought-out geometry, I found it to be exceptional.

It split kindling with little force. A quick snap of the wrist would take down a two-inch sapling. The point was fine enough to dress squirrels. It would break down a beef carcass as fast as a Forschner ten-inch Breaker. I took it to a few Eskrima classes and did a little blade work with it. I liked its balance and speed; it had a lot of whip. I also used it to cut up a Honda. The edge rolled, but it was nothing that a few minutes on the stone didn't fix. The Gambler didn't hold an edge well when used on hardwoods. But I didn't much care. It was easy to sharpen and tough enough to not break when hit hard with well-tested carbon steel knives and even a machete.

The Gambler did pretty much everything well. It was also lightweight for a Bowie. I found that I could carry it with no more difficulty than, say, a KA-BAR. At the bottom end of the big knife range in terms of weight and size, it was not at the bottom end of performance. I've owned two Bagwell handmade Damascus Bowies, both of which were exceptional in every way. This wasn't in the same class, but it was from the some school. I gave it to a young friend who works in a civilian action group and was headed for Afghanistan and expected to be spending time in tribal areas. I figured he needed it more than I did. If Ontario ever puts this knife back into production, I'll be getting another one.

▲ Bagwell Bowie razored right through veggies.

The Spec Plus line is still in production, and that's a good thing, because they're good blades. The line includes almost everything: combat knives, aircrew survival knives, machetes, military-oriented hand axes, Navy diver's knives, and bayonets. The Spec Plus line uses old reliable 1095 carbon, which is steel epoxy powder-coated for rust resistance. Handles are Kraton, and all knives are full tang.

We have extensively used the **SP1 Marine Combat**, **SP2 Air Force Survival**, and the **SP5** ten-inch bladed Bowie. Our students like them. We like them. They cut everything from meat to sheet metal. I often use a Spec Plus SP1 to test impact resistance on other knives, as explained previously. These are good knives at a reasonable price. No high-tech steel, no magic heat-treat, just solid craftsmanship and well-developed technology. Spec Plus knives take a sharp edge, absorb shock, and do what they're meant to do with little fuss or fanfare. They're good to go.

Pohl Force USA

1744 Golf View Drive
Belleair, FL 33756
(727) 468-2002
www.pohlforceusa.com

Pohl Force USA is the US arm of Pohl Force GmbH (www.pohlforce.de), a German company that is the brainchild of Dietmar Pohl. A visit to the Pohl Force website will reveal that Pohl Force's knives, especially their tactical folders, are in use with active duty German forces. After reviewing a Pohl Force **Alpha Two**, I understand why.

The all-black Alpha Two arrived in a nicely made zippered case, along with a detailed instruction booklet and a thumb stud to be affixed by the end user. Pohl Force is an international company, and there are regulations in some jurisdictions that prohibit thumb studs or easy opening devices. However, the blade opens easily even without the thumb stud.

My first impression of the Alpha Two was, "This is a big folder!" It is also a sturdy, well-made folder with a backlock that opens smoothly over polished surfaces and closes like a bank vault. The scales cover solid 2mm thick stainless steel liners and are grooved and scalloped to ensure a solid, slip-free grip with or without gloves—which in fact they do. The blade has a clip point, a scalloped spine, and a slightly recurved 440c Rockwell 58–59 edge, designed to cut cleanly with little effort—which in fact it does. The clip holds the hefty folder securely in place with a point up orientation and can be moved for left or right hand. There are smoothly machined grooves in the spine for secure thumb placement. The release for the lock is indented to guard against inadvertent release. Sturdy machine screws are nested within recesses in the grips so the knife can be disassembled with an ordinary screwdriver. The blade and other steel parts are finished with a black and gray titanium and aluminum nitride coating. All surfaces are smoothly polished, and the blade is centered. The more you handle this tactical folder, the more detail emerges. All in all, this is a well-

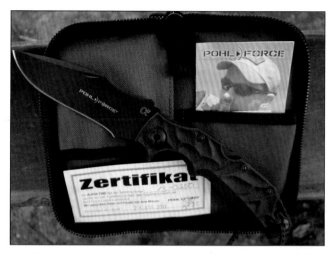

▲ Pohl Force Alpha Two folder in a carrying case—a burly tactical folder much favored by German Spec Ops.

▲ Pohl Force Alpha Two held its edge after cutting a mound of cardboard.

thought-out, handsome, precision-engineered instrument that would be at home in a Porsche showroom.

And, like a Porsche, although its appearance is arresting, the truth of the tool is in its performance. The Alpha Two not only opens and closes smoothly, it cuts well, and it does so with ease and a sense of solidity that engenders confidence in the user. Since this folder was clearly designed for uniform use, we decided to try it on coated wire, plastic—as in flex cuffs—sheet metal, and heavy denim, as well as wood, paper, and other materials. We even did a little light prying. The blade cut all materials well. The point penetrated sheet metal and other materials with ease. There were no nicks in the blade from the sheet metal, although it did dull the edge. There was no loosening of the pivot pin when we carefully batoned it into oak, nor any chipping of the edge when we snapped it free. We did not overstress the lock, as I know well the limits of backlocks and have seen many fail under hard use, no matter how well-made. But then, so will any lock. This is a good, solid, well-made tactical folder, well-suited for uniformed use, if a bit robust and heavy for daily carry in your jeans.

Randall Made Knives

4857 South Orange Blossom Trail
Orlando, FL 32839
(407) 855-8075
www.randallknives.com

▲ Randall Model 1 modified and a Green Beret.

Walter Doane "Bo" Randall Jr. founded Randall Made Knives in 1938. In doing so, he in essence started the entire benchmade knife industry that we have today. It was not until the late sixties that the handmade knife industry as we know it started to develop. Before that there were, of course, handmade knives from the workshops and forges of various craftsmen, but their work was mostly for local people.

As previously noted, Randall Made Knives first gained fame among fighting men during World War II. A number of prominent military men owned Randalls, including General James M. "Jumpin' Jim" Gavin, who led the 82nd Airborne on their combat jump into Normandy on D-Day. Randall Knives also became famous among civilians when photographs of General Gavin with his Randall, as well as photos and articles of other soldiers with Randalls, appeared in newspapers across America

Randall Knives' renown continued after World War II and into the early sixties when, as I wrote in a previous chapter, I joined the legion of military men who came to rely on their Randalls. By that time, new models had been developed, including the **Model 14 Attack** and the **Model 15 Airman**, both of which were extremely popular during the Vietnam era and remain popular today.

Bo Randall passed on some years ago. Gary Randall, his son, worked with his father for many years and is carrying on the family business. The shop is relatively small, and the quality is maintained along with the traditions.

Unfortunately for the knife user, Randall knives have become collector's items today and are much prized by devotees of various cargo cults, various collectors' clubs, and many serious historians and students of the knife, which makes them hard to come by and expensive. Collector enthusiasm is understandable, given all the mojo the Randall name conjures up, although it does make it more difficult today for a fighting man to afford a Randall. If collecting Randalls trips your trigger, then go for it; the field is rich in history. Some Randall collectors focus on knives from the Vietnam era, others from the sixties, and others on particular models.

Collectors' mania aside, Randalls are still made of time-proven designs by men who care about their work and take pride in producing one of the most famous knives in the world. Randall has a backorder of many months, sometimes years, depending on current demand. If you want a usable Randall, and you need it right away, probably your best bet is to buy a new one. It seems like the available used ones get snapped up by collectors and often cost more than a new one.

Check out some of the dealers you can find on the Internet. The current prices of new Randalls are within the range of top quality factory knives and the output of many highly skilled custom makers. Although some say that technology has moved on and that Randalls are old school, the knives still work as well as they did forty years ago when I was a skinny kid at Smoke Bomb Hill.

Today's Randalls are still forged in either 01 tool steel or 440B stainless. The tool steel blades are tempered to a Rockwell hardness of about 54–55. This is a little softer than many contemporary knives. Bo Randall wrote that the softer blades were easier for a customer to sharpen than a harder blade. This is true. However, a softer blade will need to be sharpened more often. I haven't seen it mentioned in Randall literature, but in my experience, all other things being equal, softer blades are more resistant to breakage than harder blades. This is, in my view, much more important for a tactical knife than ease of sharpening and edge-holding.

▲ Randall Model 1—an old friend taking some sun.

The stainless blades run a little harder at about 57–59, so in theory they should hold an edge somewhat longer. But, according to the Randall catalogue, the tool steel blades actually hold an edge longer. It is true that stainless blades don't lose some of their edge from simply sitting around and being exposed to oxidation as carbon steel does. Stainless blades are probably the best choice for tropical use for most people.

I'm going expand a bit about the **Model 1 All Purpose Fighting Knife**, because I think it's one of the best knives of its type ever designed, maybe *the* best, and in many ways, it is the first modern tactical knife. The Model 1 has changed in general silhouette over the years, but it's as well-designed, well-made, and as reliable a tactical knife for the military serviceperson, covert operator, or civilian as it ever was. It is available in five-, six-, seven-, or eight-inch blade lengths, with a variety of handle materials and options and in tool

steel or stainless. I find the six- or seven-inch to be the best for an all-around use knife.

The blade grind is subtler than it looks at first glance, with a slight hollow grind near the hilt and a convex grind towards the tip for added strength. The top clip comes sharpened from the factory. If you're using the knife mainly for utility work, it's a simple matter to drag the edge of the clip across a sharpening stone to dull it for safety. It's equally simple to get that edge back with a few strokes of the stone. The handle is mostly oval in profile with flattened areas on each side at the guard. The handle shape allows for accurate hand index, even in full dark, and a secure grip.

The handsome leather sheath comes with a small sharpening stone in an attached pouch. I have heard complaints that this stone is too small to be of use. Actually, if you know what you're doing, the little stone works well to quickly touch up an edge in the field. The trick is to hold the knife solidly and move the stone along the edge.

On my Model 1 knives, I have made a practice of removing the top guard and shortening the bottom guard. Doing so accomplishes three things. First, it makes the knife generally more handy for ordinary tasks: cutting rope, cleaning fish and game, slicing bread, mangos, and ugly fruit, cutting labels out of clothing, and chopping through fire doors. That sort of thing. Second, it lightens the knife overall and makes it less obtrusive in a slip sheath with a spring clip under a shirt and inside the waistbands of pants, shorts, or trunks. In other words, it makes it easier to conceal. I always get a second sheath made for these knives. Third, in my opinion, removing the top guard and shortening the bottom guard improves the balance. The shorter bottom guard will protect your hand from the edge as well as the larger one. Fourth, I do not need a guard to deflect an opponent's blade. These modifications are simply a personal idiosyncrasy, and I do not recommend them if you are concerned about the resale value of your Randall.

It had been pointed out to me that I could achieve much the same thing by simply ordering a **Model 5 Camp and Trail**. But my first Randall was a Model 1, and I eventually cut off the guards on that one, so I have just stuck with what works for me. Besides, I like the look of the Model 1 better than the Model 5, and the Model 5 is usually seen in .1875-inch stock, rather than the .25-inch stock of the Model 1. I prefer the thicker steel.

▲ Randall Model 1, modified and ready to go.

I have been asked if the Model 1 is just too big and heavy to carry in a clip sheath, rather than in a standard sheath and a belt rig. No. It is not. The knife only weighs about eight ounces, much less than, say, a 9mm automatic. Not that I'm suggesting that anyone take a knife to a gunfight. I'm just pointing out that many people carry a 9mm auto—many of which weigh about thirty-two ounces—all day, every day and think little of the weight. The Model 1, in the right configuration, is light enough and compact enough to always keep with you. With the guards cut back and with the proper sheath, you forget it's even there. Until you need it. Then you have six or seven inches of razor sharp steel to help solve the problem of the moment.

The **Model 14** weighs in at fourteen ounces in standard trim, quite a bit heavier than the Model 1, but still lighter than a 9mm. The Model 14 is also bulkier than the Model 1. This consideration was part of my decision to equip myself with a Model 1 rather than the more popular Model 14 back at SBH so many years ago. The Model 14 was just too bulky to tuck away under civilian clothing, and I was pretty sure I was going to need to do that. Turned out I was right.

My first Model 1 had a seven-inch carbon steel blade with a wood handle of some kind. My others have been set up the same way, although some have had a six-inch blade. Either the six-inch or the seven-inch works fine. For a while a few years ago, I decided the six-inch was a little better, because the handle is a also bit shorter, making it easier to wear under a tropical shirt without drawing attention. Today, I'm not so sure the one-inch difference in blade length matters much, and I am tending back towards the seven-inch. I like the feel of wood, and I still prefer carbon steel. A little oil of some kind—coconut oil, olive oil, gun oil, it doesn't matter what kind—will preserve the tool steel blade just fine, even in the tropics. In the tropics, the leather sheaths can get pretty green if left sitting for a few days. But with a good cleaning, they're good to go again; just wipe them down with some vinegar, nothing high-tech needed.

Since I bought my first Model 1, I've owned, oh probably, three hundred personal knives or so. Some have been larger, some smaller, some had ivory scales and Damascus blades, and some cut better or kept an edge longer. There were tantos, Bowies, and everything between. Most of those are gone now, sold to collectors or given to friends. I held on to my last Model 1 for many years. Then I passed it on to my son. There is something about Randall, some indefinable quality, something special, something in the balance, something that just works.

In the **Model 14 Attack**, I much prefer the variation with the Number One guard and the Border Patrol–style handle. For me, the standard guard on the Model 14 was, and is, far too heavy for its size. It throws the knife out of balance and makes it slow in the hand. Also, I've never been a fan of handles with finger groves. That said, the Model 14, in the right configuration, will do everything the Model 1 will do and more. It is a stronger knife due to its thicker tang construction.

Some years ago, one of my sons went off to an advanced three-month survival school, where he had to make his own shelter on arrival and got nothing to eat he didn't kill, catch, dig up, or scrounge, except for a small sack of cornmeal and a few ounces of nuts provided on the first day. No guns allowed, not even when brother bear came snooping around at night. He lost a few pounds, but he learned to make bows and arrows, fishhooks from bone, all manner of traps, and to kill, cook, and eat everything from deer to tadpoles, cattails, possums, and grubs. The graduation exercise was a weeklong float trip down the Green River—without the luxury of a canoe or a raft or a boat of any kind. My son tells me he became quite fond of his log during that week, and enjoyed the fish he caught on the line he trailed behind his log.

My seventeen-year-old son departed for this survival school with a leather hunting pouch over his shoulder containing some line and hooks, snare wire, flint and steel, a flat three-by-five-inch aluminum box to be used as a cook pot, and a few other odds and ends. The day before he left, I gave him an old Randall Model 1 that I had modified and the Randall shop had refurbished for me. If I had not previously made clear how I feel about Randalls, that little story might put things into perspective.

If you have a legacy knife—one bloodied in combat and passed on—then store it in a place of honor. But if you buy a new Randall or a used working one, then for the sake of all the good men who have carried them in harm's way, don't behave like a squirrel gathering nuts for the winter and stash it in a hollow tree or a safe. Use the knife. Don't let it lay around gathering dust. Good knives want to be used. Failing to do so might cause them to get irritable and bite you the next time you pick them up.

SOG Specialty Knives & Tools, LLC

6521 212th Street Southwest
Lynnwood, WA 98036
(425) 771-6230
www.sogknives.com

The Studies and Operations Group was a covert action unit during the Vietnam War. In 1986, inspired by one of the original knives issued to SOG members and by the legend of the unit, Spencer Frazer founded SOG Knives. Their first product was a recreation of the **SOG** knife. Since then, the company's product line has expanded to hundreds of knives and tools. However, the original DNA can be seen in many of their current knives. The **Seal Pup**, for example, resembles a shrunken SOG knife.

▲ SOG Seal Pup.

▲ SOG Aegis Tanto.

▲ SOG Trident.

The resemblance of the Seal Pup to its progenitor is more than skin deep. We used the Seal Pup to cut through sheet metal walls, rip out plaster, and hack through builder's studs. No damage to the AUS-6 blade or the Zytel handle. Radical blade grinds suggested it would not be a terrific performer on kitchen duty, but it did well, piling up thin slices of veggies for lunch. It even retained its edge from the demolition duty well enough to pass the Attack of the Killer Tomatoes test. The edge of the 4.75-inch blade loses about an inch of working length due to the choil, but in spite of that, there is a good working edge. The point is needle-sharp and stayed that way through all the metal piercing. It would make a good traveler's knife. This pup has as much bite as bark.

▲ Close-up of the sheet metal section cut by the SOG Seal Pup © Justin Ayres.

▲ SOG Seal Pup doing its duty in the kitchen after the sheet metal test.

Spartan Blades USA

P.O. Box 620,
Aberdeen, NC 28315
(910) 757-0035

The motto of Spartan Blades is "Knives with intent." The intention of the company founders is in every line, contour, and edge of their knives. These are weapons meant for men at war. Spartan blades are also excellent utility and survival knives. Curtis Iovito and Mark Carey, cofounders of Spartan Blades, are Special Forces (Green Berets) veterans with more than forty years of combined military and related experience. They have used knives in the field for everything a solider might need to use a knife, and they know from real world experience what's needed in a tactical knife. Their extraordinary experience shows in their knives.

Taking their company name from the famed Spartan warriors—the three hundred Spartans who stood against Xerxes' hundreds of thousands at the Battle of Thermopylae—they also name each of their knives after ancient Greek gods, goddesses, oaths, or warriors.

We have worked with three Spartan designs: the **Enyo**, a small scalpel-sharp but tough neck knife; the **Phrike**, an equally sharp self-defense and utility knife; and the **Spartan Harsey Model II**, a collaboration with the well-known knifemaker and designer William Harsey.

▲ Enyo making a fireboard.

A professional butcher, Shawn Carlson, who works with us to help evaluate knives, used the Enyo, the Phrike, and the Spartan Harsey II to bone out twenty pounds of chicken. He said, "Amazingly sharp, perfectly designed point and edge on all three of these knives. They just want to get into a cut. Actually they work as well as or better than my pro knives." We had sliced up a half-dozen large cardboard boxes, turning them into a three-foot deep mound of scrap, and cut a few feet of hemp rope before giving these knives to Shawn.

Over a period of weeks, I used all three Spartan blades for everything from slicing tomatoes to ripping out a plaster wall. All worked well for these disparate tasks and anything else that came up, albeit with consideration for their size. Each had its own personality.

The **Enyo** is small enough to tuck away anywhere, even under a pair of swim trunks, yet has enough edge and strength to work way above its size. With the Enyo, we made a hobo stove from a thick commercial can, whittled fuzz sticks, and with a baton split kindling, all with no loss of edge. Not just a hide out blade, the

◀ Spartan Phrike.

◀ Spartan Enyo boning out a chicken thigh with ease.

Enyo is also a good field performer and is comfortable in hand.

The **Phrike** doesn't take up much more room than the Enyo. The longer blade provides more utility, and the handle is a bit more comfortable. Neither the Enyo nor the Phrike has a choil, so their blades have as much working edge as possible. Curtis recently told me that both the Enyo and Phrike were designed for a government agency that worked in war zones and needed knives that could be concealed yet could provide a margin of self-defense. The Enyo comes with a dog tag neck chain instead of 550 paracord for neck carry. Five-fifty paracord has a breaking strength of 550 pounds and is an accident waiting to happen when worn around the neck. There is also a length of 550 included, the idea being that you run the chain through the hollow core 550 to silence the slight noise of the chain as it moves through the holes

in the Kydex sheath. This level of attention to detail is evident in all Spartan Blades knives and accessories, and is a result of Curtis and Mark's background. Paratroopers and SF soldiers learn that no detail is too small to attend to, and that tiny equipment errors can cost a life.

Obviously, the **Harsey II**, with its 6.125-inch blade, is a better destructor tool and weapon than the smaller knives, but either the Enyo or Phrike would serve as an expedient Escape and Evasion tool to rip through sheet metal or other building materials. All three blades are made of .1875 inch CPM S35V steel, which is tough stuff. The Harsey has an exceptionally comfortable handle and a well-designed blade that's equally good for slicing, whittling, slashing, and piercing. It became one of the group's favorites when using it in the field. After Shawn used the Spartan Harsey on the chicken, I reached for it and started to slice some tri-tip. I just

▲ Spartan Harsey II.

touched the edge right at the point to the roast and pressed a bit; it plunged hilt-deep into the meat, just went in like the meat was water. Spartan blades are exceptional performers and good to go.

Spyderco, Inc.
820 Spyderco Way
Golden, CO 80403
(800) 525-7770
www.spyderco.com

I don't know if Sal Glesser is the sole genius behind Spyderco's development of new knives, or if he keeps a bunch of designers chained to drafting tables and only feeds them raw meat and Red Bull. However he does it, Spyderco has kept to the forefront of the revolution they helped ignite.

Spyderco has so many excellent tactical designs I cannot cover them all in the available space. So, let's start with one of my favorites: the **Military**. The Military is so slender it appears delicate. It is not delicate. With its nested liner lock and attention to geometry, the Military belies its appearance. It looks like a dancer but performs like a linebacker. I've loaned my Military to my survival students and watched them baton their way through dozens of wrist-thick saplings to make shelters with no damage to the knife, using correct technique of course.

I've done the same thing, and I've used the Military for all manner of rough outdoor work. With its flat ground four-inch blade, it's also a fine everyday tool, in the kitchen or elsewhere. The blade slips through ribs and roasts like cutting whipped cream. Spyderco obviously has its heat treat for S30V worked out; I've never seen a chipped or broken blade on one of these knives. They come sharp from the factory and are easy to keep sharp. A quick touch up on a Spyderco Tri-Angle will do it, five minutes maximum, and that's after some hard use.

Over the years, I have gone though four Military knives, not because any of them wore out or broke. I've gone through so many of these slim, tough folders because I have a weakness for active duty service people and have sent my personal Military to guys in the field on three occasions, and have had no reservations about doing so. In correspondence I am often asked for a recommendation for a folding knife suitable for a solider in the field. I frequently recommend the Military. Then the guy will say that as an enlisted man that knife is out of his price range and ask me for another suggestion. The next day my Military is on its way to an APO address.

In some ways, I think of the Military as today's Black Cat. Although the Military has a level of quality and strength I never dreamed of with the Black Cat, it has a similar slim profile and is a four-ounce featherweight, lending itself to effortless carry in boot tops and certain unlikely places. It's also black.

▲ Spyderco Military drilling holes for a fireboard.

▲ Spyderco triangle sharpener—a handy tool and easy to use.

I'm one of those guys who always have at least one knife at hand. Always. Due to its featherweight and slim configuration, its reliability, its known strengths and limits, and its rust protection, the Military is the folder I clip inside my running shorts when I drag myself away from the keyboard and hit the streets for a long, mind-calming run. For the same reasons, I clip it inside my swimming trucks at the beach. Hey, you never know. People get tangled in kelp. And sharks . . .

Well, never mind about the sharks. Is the Military perfect? Is anything? I would prefer a straight feed rather than the dropped handle of the Military, but that's just personal taste. I would like it better if the handle were shorter than its five-and-a-half inches, but for all I know that long handle may be required for the knife to have the level of strength it does. I travel six to nine months a year, and I usually have a Military in my bag when I check it at the airport. What else can I tell you?

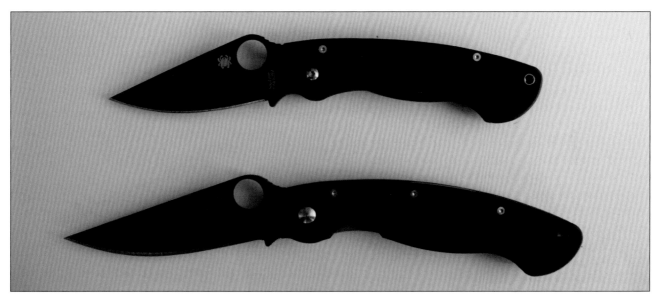

▲ Spyderco Para-Military and Military with black blades.

◀ Spyderco Para-Military with a digi-cam handle.

With its 3.3-inch blade, the **Para-Military** is a smaller brother to the Military. Its compression lock is as strong or stronger than the Military's nested liner. The overall proportions are about the same with a 4.75 inch handle. It has a straighter feed from point to heel (which I prefer) than the Military. It's just as tough as its big brother. I would recommend the Para-Military to anyone who wants a shorter blade than the Military.

Spyderco has updated the Para-Military, now the **Para-Military2**, with some subtle changes that make this model more refined and smoother.

I've been working with two models of the **Sage**, one with carbon fiber scales and a liner lock, the other a titanium framelock. The carbon fiber is a little lighter, and the framelock may be a little stronger. They're both terrific, sophisticated folders, in appearance gentlemen's pocket knives, in function, as tactical as you could ask for. The Sage blade design is deceptive; it appears relatively innocuous but performs better and cuts more efficiently than many larger, much more fierce-looking blades. With smooth lines and rounded corners, both are comfortable in hand and in the pocket. I like these folders very much.

The **Ulize** is a thin, strong lockback with a four-inch recurved blade that Shawn, the professional butcher who helps me with field reviews, said cut chicken and beef as well as his professional knives. It cut everything else well, too; the recurve makes a draw cut especially effective. Using little force, this blade slashed a twenty-seven-inch gash in double thick cardboard—out-cutting six other tactical folders. This unique folder handles and balances well, and feels good in hand. In fact, I like it so much that I'm considering replacing my Military with it. Well, not really. But that will give you an idea of how good this knife is.

Spyderco has quite a few fixed blades that fit into the tactical category; all of them are good knives, especially the old Morans. But one of my favorites is the **Fred Perrin Street Beat**, a small knife designed by the well-known French designer, martial artist, and veteran of Special Operations. The Street Beat has a good, smooth, functional flat grind, clean design, excellent quality, and a reserve of strength that is not immediately apparent.

The Street Beat is almost the perfect clandestine agent's fixed blade: functional and efficient for every-day use and strong enough to punch through a plaster wall with no damage. I tried it. I'm not talking just Sheetrock, I'm talking plaster and lath wall on an old school building—meant to last. It's light enough to carry anywhere—tucked in a sock, up a sleeve, or on a chain around the neck with a ball chain.

You can even carry this little knife in a pocket. Spyderco definitely knows how to handle VG-10, which is the blade steel for the Street Beat. It takes and holds an edge that will cut through denim like gauze. As a significant feature, the Street Beat has a nicely contoured handle, which makes it comfortable for extended work periods, even when cutting seasoned oak.

▲ Spyderco Fred Perrin lighting a fire using a ferrocerium fire starter.

▲ Spyderco Fred Perrin Street Beat is as good in the kitchen as it is on the street.

Also of critical importance, it is not black, which is a major plus. It is disarmingly pretty, which is a good thing. A fierce-looking black knife with teeth and barbs will not get a cutting job done any better than a nicely finished knife, such as the Street Beat, and those teeth will likely hang up on clothing. What your black knife will do is attract the alarmed attention of anyone who sees it: passersby, customs officials, cops, dog walkers, and bad guys.

The Perrin Street Beat looks like a polite picnic knife and will slice your baguette and spread your Brie without anyone raising an eyebrow. It will also do whatever needs to be done to help you escape those bad guys or otherwise deal with them according to your mission and disposition. I used to keep a Street Beat somewhere about my person, but I don't any longer. ML, my esteemed wife, got a look at it. ML is a pretty tough gal. She snatched it so fast I didn't see her hand move, and she won't let go of it. I'm not up for a fight, so I guess it's hers now. She always packs her Street Beat when we hit the road.

Spyderco recently rereleased an old favorite, the **Fred Perrin Street Bowie**, which for me ties with the Street Beat for first place in Spyderco's fixed blades. In the new version, the five-inch blade is black coated, which I can live with even though I'd prefer an uncoated blade. The extra blade length puts the Street Bowie solidly in the survival/utility/tactical category, and the cushioned handle makes working with it painless. Judging from it's name, the Street Bowie isn't designed primarily as an outdoorsman's knife, but it's as useful in the woods as it is anywhere and works a heck of a lot better as an outdoor utility knife than many that are designed for that purpose. One of these will be in my luggage when I next hit the road.

The **Endura** and **Delica** are modern icons and need no introduction to any knife user who hasn't been asleep for the past decade or two. Everyone knows these knives, and they buy and use them. How could they be bad? They're not. So, instead of writing about knives everyone knows about or owns, I'll mention a category of knives that, as far as I can tell, Spyderco invented. The little bitty folders I call tiny tacticals. (More about those can be found in Chapter 20.)

The **Jumpmaster** fits only one definition of a tactical knife: special purpose. But it's a knife that is needed. Paratroopers can get hung up while exiting an aircraft and then a knife is needed quickly. I recall one training jump during which the number three trooper out the door got hung up when his static line fouled.

▲ Two of ML's favorite knives, the Spyderco Fred Perrin Street Beat and Spyderco Cricket.

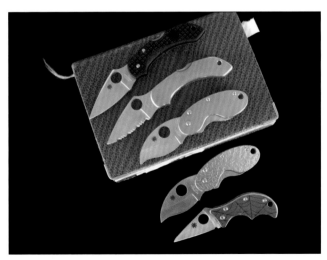

▲ A collection of Spyderco tiny tacticals.

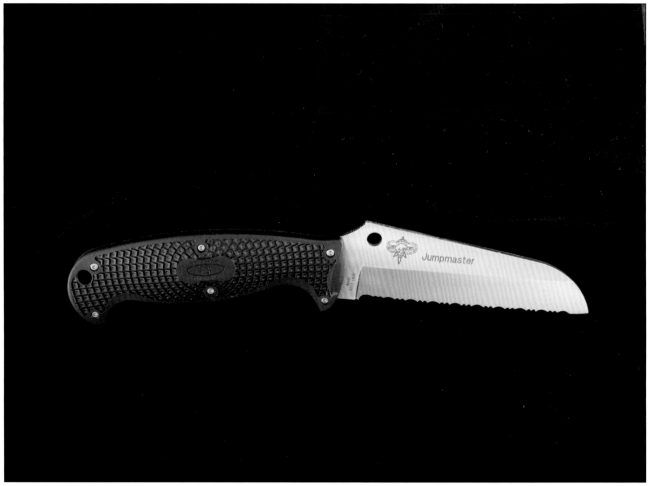

▲ Spyderco Jumpmaster, designed for 82nd Airborne Division, with a serrated blade.

Corrective procedure is for the jumpmaster to look out the door and make sure the trooper is conscious, which the trooper signals by putting one hand on top of his helmet. If the trooper is conscious, the jumpmaster cuts him free and the trooper can then deploy his reserve. If the reserve doesn't work . . . Well, you can always return your parachute for a new one.

In this instance, the jumpmaster determined the guy was awake and aware and decided to cut him free with his issue Schrade switchblade. But the Schrade was too dull to cut the nylon webbing of the static line. The jumpmaster sawed away. Time passed. No go. We still had a paratrooper behind the aircraft. This procedure needs to be done quickly, as hitting the tail of the plane can injure the trooper or he can pass out if his harness compresses his chest too much. As you might imagine, there was no shortage of knives in the stick. The hung up trooper was soon cut free with a KA-BAR. He got his reserve out and rode it in okay.

The Jumpmaster's 4.5-inch serrated blade will go through nylon webbing like a chainsaw. The blade is a sheepsfoot design with no point, which is a good thing. This application not only doesn't need a point, a point could cause injury. The sheath will hold it securely where the jumpmaster can get to it quickly. The non-slip handle is, in fact, nonslip, even in sweaty hands. I'd like to see this as an issue item for jumpmasters and for all paratroopers. It's not uncommon for a paratrooper to get fouled in lines and need to cut himself free. In the story above, the need for a better knife was glaringly obvious. The Spyderco Jumpmaster is that better knife. Every Spyderco knife I have reviewed is good to go.

Strider Knives

120 N. Pacific St. Unit L-7
San Marcos, CA 92069
(760) 471-8275
www.striderknives.com

Strider Knives was founded by Mick Strider, and the company is operated by Strider and Wayne Dwyer, both veterans who have been places, done things, and know from experience what tactical knives need to be in today's world. Strider Knives are built like main battle tanks based on the Strider and Dwyer's understanding of today's conflict zones and the changed nature of warfare today. Every Strider knife I have examined, both folders and fixed blades, has been built with the highest level of craftsmanship and from premium materials. These knives are muscular and tough and come from the factory as sharp as Einstein's brain, and they stay that way for a long time, even after cutting through walls and steel doors.

Strider's fixed blades are the fifty calibers of tactical knives, able to blast through barriers to reach their target. Their folders take a giant step toward redefining the genre. The folders are not just tactical or only suitable for daily chores and as emergency weapons; they are war knives. The refined thought in every detail, from the textured scales to the subtle blade grinds, reveals a level of sophistication regarding the rigors of combat that can only come from experience and careful consideration over time.

◀ Strider Model RC-C making a hobo stove from a coffee can.

◀ Strider Model RC-C being batoned with a limb.

In addition to experience, there has been important input from such distinguished knifemakers as Bob Terzuola, Bill Moran, Ernest Emerson, and Kit Carson, as well as a good deal of science behind the development of Strider Knives. During an interview with Wayne Dwyer, I realized I was talking to a man who was not only passionate about knives, but one who brought a background in science to bear on tactical knives. Dwyer uses instruments, such as an ultrasound radiograph, to analyze blade steel and other materials. In addition to the industry standard Rockwell testing, he also uses a Brunnell-Vicors oscilloscope to do sheer wave analysis. Dwyer tests his knives and the materials that go into them according to ISO (International Organization for Standardization) and ASTM (American Society for Testing and Materials) guidelines for material standards testing.

All of this background work led Dwyer to the conclusion that particle metallurgy is the biggest leap forward in blade science during the past century. According to Dwyer, they can now dial in the exact properties desired in a blade, and the uniformity of CPMS30V allows quality and consistency otherwise unobtainable.

I lack a background in science and can't evaluate Dwyer's position from a collegial position, but I think his position is important. What matters to me are two things: first, Dwyer has done his homework and he believes in his research; second, the knives actually work in rugged field tests. I wouldn't know an oscilloscope from a Geiger counter if they were on a bench in front of me. But I can for sure tell you if a knife does what it's supposed to do. Strider's knives perform as advertised.

▲ Strider making a fireboard.

While visiting family in the Midwest, I took along a **Strider RC-C** for evaluation. We managed to get in some dirt time, primitive camping, fishing, and foraging for wild foods. During this time, I used the Strider RC-C to cut and strip limbs for field expedient fishing rods and to clean the fish we caught. I made a hobo stove to cook the fish, and cut a bow stave to show my young nephew how to make a quickie bow.

The outing was fun and the RC-C worked fine for everything. But I realized that to evaluate this knife, I had to take it on its own terms. Using the Strider folder to clean fish was like using a Barrett .50 to hunt whitetail. You can do it, but it's just a little bit of overkill. One of my family members works for a company that owns a large plant facility with many buildings, some of which were long since out of use. With permission, I went through the abandoned factory building as if I were a POW trying to escape. I cut through sliding steel doors, ripped out walls, and pried steel frames for industrial windows from their mounting. The only damage to the RC-C was a few scratches on the finish.

Back at home, we were having some friends over for a barbeque. I gave the RC-C to the chef, my oldest son,

to cut up a few racks of ribs, some chickens, and three large tri-tips. The knife had not been sharpened since its previous use. At first he balked, thinking the knife was too thick for such work. Then he tried it. Then he got a smile on his face. When he was finished cutting all the meat, he washed the Strider folder and slipped it in his pocket. Took a good bit of persuasion to get it back.

SVORD

Smith Road
RD2
Waiuku
New Zealand
Phone: +64 9 2358846
www.svord.com

We don't see much of Svord knives here in the United States, and that's a shame. Although not marketed as tactical knives, I include them here because the ones I have tried are terrific knives regardless of their classification as sporting knives. They perform at the top level in terms of cutting ability and have prices

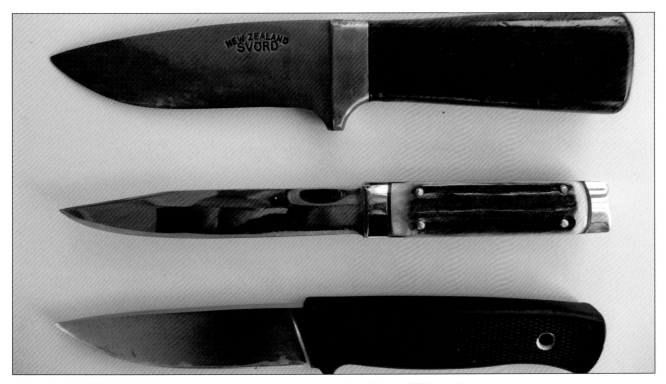

▲ Svord Model 320BB with a burl wood handle and carbon steel blade, Puma Boot Knife, and Fållkniven F1.

that are a bargain. They are certainly useful as tactical knives.

Svord was founded by Bryan Baker in 1983. His company history includes a Czech knifemaker who passed on to Baker a good bit of knifemaking know how, including a tempering process that Baker says gives his knives superior cutting ability and strength. All I know is that Svord knives look like old-school knives and perform well indeed.

In an era of thick blades, Svord blades are thin. In a time when stainless steel rules in terms of popularity, Svord uses carbon steel, except for their chef's knives. This is a novelty in the United States, where only a few factories produce carbon steel knives, leaving carbon mostly to custom makers.

I have used and loaned to students Svord's 3.75-inch **Drop Point**, 4-inch **Utility** (both of which come with synthetic handles), and their 4-inch **Tramper**, which has a nice burl wood handle.

The blades come with a convex grind, and they cut and cut and cut. They cut for a long time before needing a touch up and more importantly, as an old Army buddy used to say, they cut "sharply, harshly, deep, and to the bone." The thin blades offer less resistance to any given material. The convex grind helps, as discussed in the chapter on design. So, the geometry promotes efficient cutting. It would seem that the steel choice and the heat treat make up the rest of the qualities that produce good results.

▲ Svord 1990NZ beginning to cut hemp rope.

▲ Results of Svord 1990NZ hemp rope cut test.

I wouldn't try to suspend my two-hundred-twenty pounds from one of these thin-bladed knives, but I have bent the blade on the Tramper, with considerable effort, to about 35 degrees. The blade snapped back to true when I released it.

I haven't been able to locate a US distributor, but I would guess that if you sent Svord an email, they could fix you up with a good old-school knife that puts cutting ability first.

▲ Svord 320BB starting the cut on hemp rope.

TOPS Knives

Tactical Operational Products
P.O. Box 2544
Idaho Falls, ID 83403
(208) 542-0113
www.topsknives.com

Mike Fuller founded TOPS in 1998 with the idea of making high quality knives, not pretty ones, but highly functional and dependable knives. Mike told me he first saw this need back in the day, as my young friends describe the sixties, "when a solider had to spend a month's pay to buy what we believed was the best knife available, a Randall."

Although we never met, Mike was at Smoke Bomb Hill about the same time I was there. Our ideas about knives were formed in the same crucible. As a Special Forces soldier, Mike went on to years of globe-spanning service with SF and OGAs (other government agencies). From Southeast Asia to Africa, he served his country, expanded his experience, and refined his ideas about knives and what works and doesn't work in the harsh realities of real world combat. When Mike sits down to design a knife, he doesn't have to imagine what a combat knife should be; he knows.

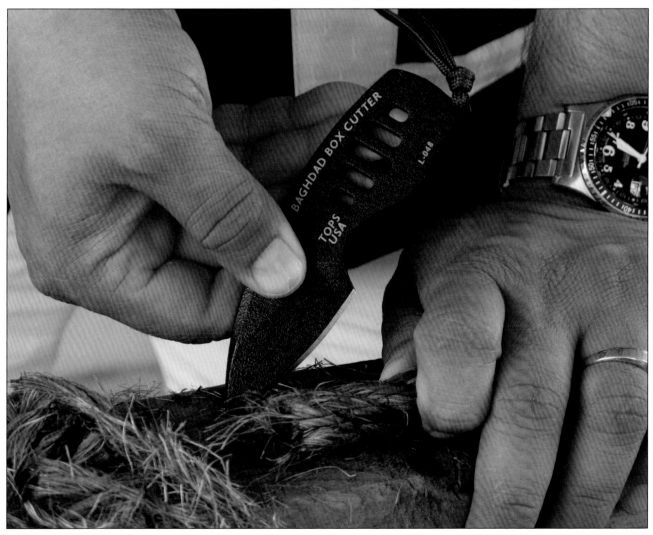

▲ TOPS Baghdad Box Cutter in the hemp rope test.

However, in spite of his extensive background, there's no trace of the know-it-all in Mike's manner. He's willing to listen to others' ideas and to act on them. Thus TOPS produces designs that come from people who have their own experience and their own take on what they need in a knife. These designers include Tom Brown "The Tracker" and Kelly Worden, well-known martial artist and specialist in the combat blade arts.

TOPS is the classic American success story. The company was founded at Mike's family kitchen table. The factory was in the garage. In the first couple of years, Mike and his wife Helene did everything in the business. TOPS' first knife was the **Steel Eagle**, which went out to old contacts—ninety-three people who knew knives and what they needed to do. From that beginning the company grew; there were two employees the second year, and today TOPS is a company that produces more than one-hundred-fifty different blades and ships them to Special Forces soldiers, covert operators, and active military in dozens of countries and conflict zones. And that first knife, the Steel Eagle, still sells very well.

You can see a Steel Eagle in the accompanying photo. That's it sticking in the side of a car door. There's also a photo of one of TOPS newer models, the **Mil-Spie 5**, sticking through the roof of another car. We had a busy day at the salvage yard. I recruited a young fellow with lots of energy and a desire to try out some knives and handed him a couple of TOPS knives. If we had completely turned him loose, I have no doubt he would have reduced a few auto bodies to their component parts and ribbons of steel. Unfortunately, we had agreed to pay for damaged auto bodies, broken windows, and so on. We did, however, do enough damage to a few cars to determine that in any encounter between a TOPS knife and a car, the car will come out second. There was no damage to any TOPS knife during this expedition—not even to the edges.

Don't get the idea that TOPS knives are only useful as destruction tools. Back at home we did the Attack of the Killer Tomatoes test and both TOPS knives passed with ease. We've also done all the cutting tests: rope, wood, cardboard, etc. TOPS knives are sharp and cut well. Over the years, we've had a good amount of

▲ TOPS Steel Eagle cutting into a car door panel.

▲ TOPS Mil-Spie 5 ripping open a car door.

experience with TOPS knives in the wilderness and as everyday tools.

A few years ago, we visited some relatives who live deep in the wilds of Arkansas. One summer evening, after the fish and ribs had been cleaned and cut up with a TOPS **Fire Hawke**, we were into the third bottle from a case of Beaujolais that I had trucked along when someone suggested we try and climb a tree using the Fire Hawke as a climbing aid. (Well, maybe it was the fourth bottle or fifth. Who counts?)

I pounded the Fire Hawke into the side of a tall pine tree about seven feet from the ground; I wanted to see the little guy jump. We started out with the little guy. Austin runs about a hundred and ninety pounds at five

▲ TOPS Fire Hawke being batoned through a tree limb.

▲ TOPS Fire Hawke ready for action.

feet eight inches. He jumped a couple of times and then caught ahold of the Fire Hawke and did some pull ups, just to show us he could. Then he dropped off, and I grabbed ahold and started walking up the side of the tree. As I was doing so, Joe, who weighs about two hundred, ran up and jumped on my back. I hung on. For a short time, the Fire Hawke was supporting more than four hundred pounds. Then I let go, and we dropped to the ground. Yeah, the knife bent. What do you think? But it only bent about 15 degrees and then went back to true. I call that good performance.

It's performance typical of all TOPS knives. TOPS knives are made from reliable 1095 carbon steel and heat treated by craftsmen who know what they're doing. There's an ancient Asian parable about the oak tree and bamboo. The strong oak, which resists all efforts to bend or break it, will break in a typhoon.

The bamboo will bend before extreme force, but will spring back and survive.

The **Travelin Man 2** fits perfectly into the traveler's knife category. Like other TOPS knives, it's tough, sharp and dependable. I have no doubt I could have pried open the door at the archaeological excavation that I wrote about in the traveler's knife chapter with this deceptively little but extremely tough one-piece blade. It comes with a clip-on Kydex sheath and an emergency whistle, and the overall package is one that I would recommend to any traveler.

TOPS knives cut well. They're tough. They work. As a former SF solider who has spent more time in combat than the average politician has spent begging for money, Mike knows what he's doing and is dedicated to completing his mission. Here's the thing: Mike won't let you down. Neither will his knives. They are good to go.

▲ TOPS Travelin Man 2 making a fireboard.

Victorinox Swiss Army Inc.

7 Victoria Drive
Monroe, CT 06468
www.swissarmy.com

Victorinox, the world famous maker of Swiss Army Knives, now makes a number of models with locking blades, some of them with one-handed openers, thereby qualifying them as tactical. While they initially appear to be built too lightly for extreme use, their newer models are in the pockets of almost every survival instructor I know. I use them too. I have for years carried the **Rucksack** model with a locking main blade, a wood saw—which actually saws—the usual assortment of screwdrivers, and the most important tool of all—the corkscrew.

The relatively new **One-Hand Trekker German Army** has been specially designed for and issued to German soldiers. The scales are a suitable army green, and on the side is embossed a handsome German Federal Eagle. The main blade opens with one hand—a most important feature and one that would persuade me to substitute my old knife for one of these robust-looking army models. Except for one thing. Somehow an egregious oversight has occurred. The army model lacks the essential tool; sadly, there is no corkscrew. In the location where corkscrews live on all righteous SAKs, there is a miserable Phillips screwdriver.

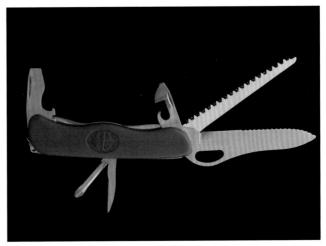
▲ SAK One-Hand Trekker German Army.

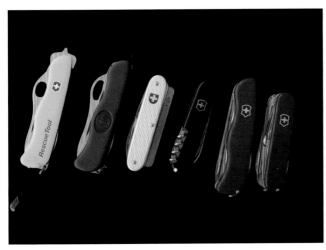
▲ SAK collection, closed view.

▲ Karin Drechsel with Victorinox and flint at Rabbit Stick gathering.

▲ Sometimes your best friend wears red.

I have read that Victorinox uses Sandvik 12C steel in their knives, but I have not been able to confirm this. The wizards of Switzerland appear to consider steel choice classified information. Whatever steel and heat treat they use, it works. Aside from the one thousand and one daily chores that about a hundred million people use their SAKs for, these red-handled icons of Swiss ingenuity are also tough enough to stand up to extreme use in some circumstances.

A few years ago while visiting friends in Washington, D.C., I met a fellow, let's call him Fred, who had recently returned from a harrowing experience in Africa. He had been working for an NGO (non-governmental organization) providing much needed relief to impoverished refugees from a war zone. While he was there, the war zone expanded and overran the station where he worked. He was taken prisoner by a ragtag group of teenagers with AK-47s. This group was known to everyone in the area and had the reputation of indulging in atrocities.

My new friend Fred told me he had been dragged into the tumbledown, shell-shot ruins of a former office building and locked alone in a small room the size of a closet; probably it even had been a closet. Late at night, after most of his captors were asleep, he went to work on the wall of his room with his only tool, a SAK. Little by little over the course of some hours, he managed to work his way through the plaster wall, which he said was lined with chicken wire or something like it, and into a room with a window. He escaped out the window. After three days of ducking and dodging, he made it to a secure area.

He showed me his SAK, which was in his pants pocket. (My guess is it will always remain in his pants pocket.) It was one of the ordinary, homely models we are all familiar with. The teeth of the saw blade were chewed up. The main blade was dull and the point broken off. The scales were scratched. Even the screwdriver blade was worn at the edge. Do you think Fred abused his knife, as some might say? I don't think so. I think it was used appropriately. This everyday pocket tool not only did its job, it performed with distinction.

Victorinox's new **Rescue Tool** is complete with a glass breaker and seat belt cutter. A young friend volunteered

▲ SAK—back in the day, you could add this to your key chain.

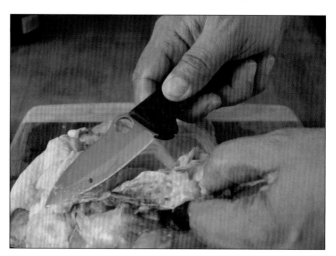

▲ This Victorinox Hunter Pro lockblade folder made light work of deboning the chicken.

to go to a nearby auto salvage yard to try out the rescue tools. It worked, unsurprisingly, like it was designed to enable someone to break out of a crashed car. The seat belt cutting blade cut through the seat belt webbing like thread. It cut so quickly and easily that we had trouble catching it and had to shoot it with our camera a couple of times. We didn't catch the window breaking. We were setting up the shot when young blood tapped the window in preparation for breaking free. The window exploded outward, showering everyone in window fragments. We had only paid for one window, so the experiment was over. Besides, the results were in: amazing performance from what amounts to a pocketknife. Now Fred doesn't have the only SAK rescue knife.

▲ SAK Rescue, a must for your car survival kit.

▲ Shattered car window from the Victorinox Rescue Tool.

▲ Driver cutting a seat belt with the Victorinox Rescue Tool.

Wayne Goddard Master Bladesmith

(541) 689-8098
www.goddardknives.com

At first glance, Wayne Goddard's knife designs are rather plain-looking fixed blades with wooden handles. In appearance, they're nothing to cause any heavy breathing among the tactical knife crowd. The truth comes out in the performance. I've seen more than one tactical knife aficionado jump up and shout, "No way!" And then, after seeing the way, try to get this knife away from me. Never happened.

Wayne Goddard, master bladesmith, made this knife. He calls it a **Camp Knife**. The basic design is a variation on an old long knife. The steel is L6, which is used for industrial saw blades and is known among knifemakers as being especially well-suited for knives that need toughness combined with cutting ability.

Wayne forged and tempered the steel and formed the blade so that there is a full convex grind from spine to edge and a slight curve to the edge from hilt to tip. This blade configuration has a good deal to do with this blade's extraordinary cutting ability. Everyone in my family, and all our friends who have worked with us doing survival skills, call it Wayne's Knife. As in, "Can I use Wayne's Knife?" After trying it once, everyone wants to use Wayne's Knife.

I hesitate to tell you how good this knife performs. I've seen looks of disbelief from semi-knowledgeable knife people when I've talked about it in the past. In cutting tests and fieldwork, including knife-on-knife impact testing, this deceptively simple-looking knife has out-performed every blade that has been measured against it since I first got it in 1992. We're talking more than twenty years and hundreds of knives. It weighs next to nothing, less than many four-inch survival knives.

▲ Three by Wayne Goddard (top to bottom): Scagel-style Bowie with an eleven-inch forged blade of 5160, mustard finish, bronze guard, and desert ironwood and deer antler handle; Customized Trailmaster Bowie with a commercially-blackened blade, stainless guard and skull crusher, and G10 and stag handle; TCK knife with a six-inch forged blade, antique finish, and brown canvas Micarta handle © Wayne Goddard.

▲ Wayne Goddard's magic Camp Knife.

▲ Wayne Goddard Camp Knife—one stroke to cut through a sapling.

The blade is only seven inches long, yet it has outperformed nine- and ten-inch choppers.

With proper technique, Wayne's Knife will slash though a three-inch standing sapling in one or two strokes. It slices meat like the best butcher knife and cuts through denim and heavy leather like tissue paper. It will cut rope without dulling until your hand gets tired, which is a fairly long time since little effort is required. When the edge is tuned up, it will cut a falling silk scarf, a test that comes down to us from ancient times. It stays sharp for a long time and is easy to sharpen when the time comes. I've placed the blade in a vise and, with difficulty, bent it to 30 degrees; it sprang back to true with no deformation.

At one time, I thought that this particular knife had to be a once in a lifetime kind of thing. You know, when everything comes together just right: steel, heat treat, geometry, and the moon is in the right place. Then at my request Wayne made two more for me to give to my sons. My sons' knives are slightly beefier than mine. They have a little more belly. But basically they're the same knife. Guess what? The moon must have still been in the right place. Their knives work as well as mine. You won't have any better luck getting them away from their owners than you would with mine. Wayne kids me about my enthusiasm for his magic Camp Knives. He says there's nothing magic in them, just knowledge and craftsmanship—

▲ Wayne Goddard LBK with a stacked laminate handle.

the right materials handled the right way. I'm sure he's right. The genius is in the execution of the entire package—heat treat, convex grind, the subtlety of the curved blade. But at times, it sure seems like a magic knife.

It's not really fair to compare this kind of knife to a factory knife. This is a custom knife made by one of the most respected and accomplished master bladesmiths in the country today. I've talked to some very knowledgeable knifemakers who run factories producing the best factory knives made today who agree with that statement. One man whose dedication and skill I respect told me that there's simply no way a factory can mass-produce this kind of knife. They can come close in performance, but they can't match it. So, fair is fair.

However, if you are looking for absolute performance without respect to price, and if you don't mind waiting months to get a knife, you should give Wayne a call. These days, Wayne is concentrating on Bowies, Camp Knives, and some tacticals. I'm pretty sure there are other bladesmiths of the ABS capable of making knives that perform in the same range, but I haven't used their blades, so I cannot comment on them. I have used Wayne's Knife, and will continue to do so.

If I were heading for a combat zone, I'd order a new one with a slightly thicker blade, a nonslip handle, and a small lower guard. I'd also like to have one with a

▲ Wayne Goddard forged L6 saw steel Camp Knife with a differential temper slicing a tomato.

▲ Wayne Goddard Custom slicing a lemon wafer thin.

nine-inch blade, and a four-incher, and one with a nice stag handle and . . .

Zero Tolerance Knives

KAI USA Ltd.
18600 SW Teton Avenue
Tualatin, Oregon 97062
(800) 325-2891
www.zt.kaiusaltd.com

Zero Tolerance Knives is a team effort between Strider Knives, Ken Onion, and Kai USA, the goal being to produce professional level knives for military, law enforcement, and others whose work depends on quality knives. ZT donates a portion of the proceeds from their sales to the Paralyzed Veterans of America.

The **Zero Tolerance 0301** is not the knife with which to spread your Camembert at a wine tasting unless shock and awe is your goal. The 0301 has all the subtlety of an Abrams tank crashing through your wall and it has the strength of a tank compared to folding knives. The other day I was at a film production company office and thought I'd have some fun. I took out the monster folder and said, "Hey guys check this out." As I did so, I flicked the opener and the blade flashed open with an audible SNAP.

One of the editors leaped out of her chair and shouted, "What the f*** is that?" You have to love a knife that will produce that reaction in a seen-everything twenty-something blonde. The ZT also works. You could field dress a Honda with it. Having field dressed more than one Honda—and Subaru—in the pursuit of knife knowledge, I know. ZT has fielded a range of folders and fixed blades all with the same consciousness and high degree of utility.

Zero Tolerance fixed blades are solid, sophisticated designs, well-made of high-tech steel. The **ZT 0100**

▲ ZT 0301 folder cutting cardboard, another sturdy bulldog.

◀ ZT 0121.

▲ ZT 0100 fixed blade in a wood cutting test.

is quite swoopy in appearance. Its reverse curved blade cuts soft materials quite well, but the thick bevels tend to hang up in wood. Still, it will do the job. The **ZT 0121** is a sturdy bulldog of a fixed blade, with a well-shaped handle and the ability to pry open a locked steel gate—I couldn't resist trying it, and it worked fine, no damage to the knife. There's a cord cutter designed to rip through 550 cord or wire insulation at the choil. I like the handle design very much. Many knife designers seem to have the notion that longer is always is better in handles. But not so. If ZT ever decides to smooth out the design a little, they will have a terrific covert knife—one handy enough for the civilian operative and strong enough to punch through walls, car doors, and so fourth. As is, it's a great little knife for the guys in uniform or civilians with similar needs.

Conclusion

he creative explosion in the development of tactical knives than began in the seventies continues today. Now there is a virtual river of steel made up of good quality knives to choose from. This book provides you with the knowledge you need to pick the right knife for your purposes, but you should also pick the knife that's right for you. To do that, when you've narrowed your choice down to just a few knives, direct all your attention to them and really see each knife; pick them up, heft them. Is there one that seems to attract you more than the others? Ask yourself if the attraction you feel for a particular knife is due to its flashy appearance. If so, and if you're looking for a working knife rather than one to add to your collection, put that one down and continue searching. As you pick up each knife, focus your attention on how it feels in your hand. Imagine using the knife for your purpose. Does it feel balanced, comfortable, right? When you find the knife that feels right, you've found your knife.

I don't have a crystal ball and cannot predict what the future will bring. I don't know if a new material is about to emerge from the laboratories that will render all knife steel obsolete or if the practitioners of the ancient art and craft of forging by hand and fire will continue to make amazing knives. My guess is that whatever the future of knife making, it will be interesting.